Foucault, Sport and Exercise

Michel Foucault is one of the most influential thinkers of the modern age. His work profoundly influences the way we think about society, in particular how we understand social power, the self, and the body. *Foucault, Sport and Exercise* explores how Foucauldian theory can inform our understanding of the body, domination, identity and freedom as experienced through sport and exercise.

- **Part I: Power, Knowledge and the Self** introduces Foucault and his ideas, highlighting key debates for sociologists of sport and exercise.
- **Part II: Foucauldian Interpretations of the Body and Lived Experiences in Sport and Exercise** uses Foucault's theories to explore power relations, the body, identity and the construction of social practices in sport and exercise.
- **Part III: Aesthetics of Ethical Self-Stylisation** examines the ways in which individuals make sense of the social forces surrounding them, considering physical activity, fitness and sport practices as expressions of freedom and sites for social change.

Accessible and clear, *Foucault, Sport and Exercise* considers cultures and experiences in sports, exercise and fitness, coaching and health promotion. In addition to presenting established Foucauldian perspectives and debates, the text also provides innovative discussion of how Foucault's later work can inform the study and understanding of sport and the physically active body.

Pirkko Markula is Senior Lecturer in the Department of Education at the University of Bath. **Richard Pringle** is Senior Lecturer in the Department of Sport and Leisure Studies at the University of Waikato.

Foucault, Sport and Exercise

Power, knowledge and transforming the self

Pirkko Markula and Richard Pringle

Routledge
Taylor & Francis Group

LONDON AND NEW YORK

First published 2006
by Routledge
2 Park Square, Milton Park, Abingdon Oxon OX14 4RN

Simultaneously published in the USA and Canada
by Routledge
270 Madison Avenue, New York, NY 10016

*Rouledge is an imprint of the Taylor & Francis Group, an informa
business*

© 2006 Pirkko Markula and Richard Pringle

Typeset in Sabon by Laserwords Private Limited, Chennai, India
Printed and bound in Great Britain by TJ International Ltd,
Padstow, Cornwall

British Library Cataloguing in Publication Data
A catalogue record for this book is available
from the British Library

Library of Congress Cataloging-in-Publication Data
Markula, Pirkko, 1961–
 Foucault, sport and exercise : power, knowledge and transforming the
self / Pirkko Markula and Richard Pringle.
    p. cm.
 Includes bibliographical references and index.
 1. Body, Human—Social aspects. 2. Physical fitness—Social aspects.
3. Body image—Social aspects. 4. Mind and body. 5. Power (Social sciences)
6. Foucault, Michel—Influence. I. Pringle, Richard, 1964– II. Title.
HM636.M34 2006
306.4'83—dc22
                                                                2006011572

ISBN 10: 0–415–35862–0 (hbk)
ISBN 10: 0–415–35863–9 (pbk)
ISBN 10: 0–203–00650–X (ebk)

ISBN 13: 978–0–415–35862–0 (hbk)
ISBN 13: 978–0–415–35863–7 (pbk)
ISBN 13: 978–0–203–00650–4 (ebk)

Contents

Acknowledgements

We would like to thank all of our colleagues who contributed to the completion of this book. In addition, we would each like to offer a word of personal thanks.

Pirkko Markula: I would like to acknowledge the Department of Education at the University of Bath for providing the academic and intellectual environment that allowed my part of this book to materialise. In addition, I would like to thank the British Academy for providing funding that made writing Chapter 9 in this book possible. Finally, I would like to extend special thanks to Jim Denison whose personal and intellectual generosity was invaluable in the process of writing this book.

Richard Pringle: I planned and wrote most of my contribution to this book while on study leave from teaching duties at the University of Waikato, New Zealand. I thank the Department of Sport and Leisure Studies for generously allowing time for this endeavour. Most importantly, I thank my family – especially Dixie, Zachary and Luke – for their love and support in creating the 'perfect' environment for writing and living.

Portions of this book have appeared partially and/or in earlier drafts in:

Markula, P. (2004) 'Fitness and Exercise: Embodied Knowledge?', in L. Bresler (ed.) *Knowing Bodies, Moving Minds: Toward Embodied Teaching and Learning*, Netherlands: Kluwer Academic.

Markula, P. (2004) '"Tuning into One's Self:" Foucault's Technologies of the Self and Mindful Fitness', *Sociology of Sport Journal*, 21, 190–210.

Markula, P. (2003) 'The Technologies of the Self: Feminism, Foucault and Sport', *Sociology of Sport Journal*, 20, 87–107.

Pringle, R. and Markula, P. (2005) 'No Pain is Sane After All: A Foucauldian Analysis of Masculinities and Men's Experiences in Rugby', *Sociology of Sport Journal*, 22, 472–497.

Introduction

Michel Foucault was one of the most influential scholars of his time. Even following his death in 1984 his work concerning the power/knowledge/self nexus remains at the centre of heated debates. There are numerous interpretations of his theoretical stance from several different social sciences' disciplines including our field of sport studies. There is, however, no comprehensive text on Foucault and sport although numerous, yet often contradictory citations to his work appear across sport studies. To examine his possible contribution to sport research, our idea to write a book devoted entirely to Foucault and sport started to evolve.

Foucault was a productive scholar whose published works included numerous books, interviews, papers and lectures. It is impossible to do justice to all of his work in one book. Regardless, in this book we aim to introduce Foucault's conceptual framework in an in-depth manner and we have, therefore, drawn from Foucault's own works as closely as possible rather than relying heavily on other scholars' Foucauldian interpretations. This does not mean that we entirely ignored all such works. On the contrary, there are many excellent and also often critical texts of Foucault's theory. Our main goal in this book, however, is to explain what Foucault wrote or said instead of defending him against his numerous critics – Foucault was quite capable of doing that himself.

Foucault did not explicitly address sport or physical activity in his work, although his emphasis on the body as a site for force relations resonates closely with our field of study. Therefore, while we aim to provide a reading of Foucault's theory based as closely as possible on his own writings, we also provide accounts from existing Foucauldian sport and exercise research. Our intention is to introduce readers to a range of examples on how Foucault's works can serve sport studies. Readers are then invited to form their own critical interpretations based on the variety of readings that Foucault's work offers. We also use our own work in sport and exercise to illustrate Foucault's conceptual framework throughout the book.

While we discovered Foucault's work through our own personal scholarly journeys, we both were originally interested in issues related to gender, power and resistance in sport. However, our research foci differed significantly. Richard was interested in issues of masculinity in rugby that in many ways epitomises the 'traditional' masculine values. Pirkko was interested in the construction of the feminine body in fitness, an environment that some would consider perpetuating 'traditional' femininity. While our research interests are quite different, they provide a wide base for a variety of examples of how Foucault's work can be used to interpret sport, fitness and physical activity in contemporary society. In addition, our international backgrounds – Richard is a New Zealander while Pirkko is a Finn currently living in England – could further highlight the possibilities of using Foucault's theory in different cultural contexts. Despite our current geographical distance, we were previously colleagues at the University of Waikato, New Zealand and, therefore, have collaborated on many of the research projects that we introduce in this book. The idea to write a book on Foucault also evolved from this collaboration. Although our data collection activities may have been carried out individually, to provide coherence to our book, we have chosen to use the pronoun 'we' throughout to further illustrate our collective effort to understand sporting experiences through Foucault's theory.

Foucault, as a historian of thought, focused on examining mainly historical documents. However, he continually urged his readers to get close to people's experiences to trace fully how power relations operate in the contemporary world. In this book, therefore, we aim to provide examples of Foucauldian readings of sporting and exercising women's and men's experiences to illustrate the operation of Foucault's three axes: power relations, knowledge and the self. To contextualise these experiences, we use both scholarly texts and popular media texts. We have divided this book into three sections to discuss Foucault's theory and to illustrate its appropriateness to global sporting and exercise contexts.

The first section, *Power, Knowledge and the Self*, introduces the theoretical tools of Michel Foucault. Foucault, who published extensively throughout the 1960s, 1970s and 1980s, recognised that his writings should not be considered as a global systematic theory, and therefore we aim to use his framework of ideas to provide conceptual tools for sport research. This section centres around the power/knowledge/self nexus that was at the heart of Foucault's theory. Chapter 1 provides a biographical sketch of Foucault to trace his theoretical lineage and the context within which his innovative ideas developed. In Chapter 2 we detail Foucault's prime research objective: how humans construct knowledge about themselves and how this knowledge subsequently shapes the experience of being human. Our focus within this chapter is on Foucault's concerns with 'technologies of dominance' and concepts such as discourse, disciplinary power, panopticism, biopower and governmentality.

In the second section, *Foucauldian Interpretations of the Body and Lived Experiences in Sport and Exercise*, we demonstrate how Foucault's theoretical concepts can be used to examine sport and exercise. These chapters draw from the existing literature on the construction of the sporting and exercising bodies but, in addition, they [will examine how the discursive power relations have been lived into existence through men's and women's sporting experiences.] This section, therefore, highlights the discursive construction of physically active bodies. Combining Foucault's archaeological and genealogical analyses, Chapter 3 highlights how the healthy body is discursively constructed through scientific research that emphasises the role of exercise as an important public health practice. Chapter 4 examines the connections between health, fitness and the ideal body. We analyse how individual exercisers are drawn into the quest for the ideal body through self-surveillance but also highlight their attempts to resist such a disciplinary, panoptic arrangement. In Chapters 5 and 6 we discuss how bodies are trained and subsequently disciplined in sport. We draw particularly from interview data that examined how rugby men participated in the discursive construction of gendered sporting identities.

[While Foucault is much criticised for favouring the analyses of power relations in society, he maintained that fundamental to his project was to understand the role of the individual within changing power relations.] Consequently, in his later years Foucault concentrated on the relationship of the self to power and truth: how human beings turn themselves into subjects through the technologies of the self. In the final section, *Aesthetics of Ethical Self-Stylisation*, we use Foucault's technologies of the self to examine how identities formed by current discursive power relations might be freed by sport and exercise practices. This section, then, aims to highlight Foucault's theory as a political strategy and to explore pragmatic possibilities for sport and exercise to enhance ethical social transformation. Chapter 7 details how Foucault developed his concept of the technologies of the self and second, how these technologies can become practices of freedom for the contemporary individual. Chapter 8 highlights possibilities for fitness practices to act as practices of freedom, drawing from ethnographic data that focused on mindful fitness instructors. Chapter 9 traces the technologies of the self for an academic self. In this chapter, Foucault's suggestion for writing 'hypomnemata' provides the pragmatics for 'academic' technologies of the self. Finally, in Chapter 10 we examine how academic teaching practices can act as the technologies of the self and how it might be possible to educate critically informed 'specific intellectuals' for the field of sport and exercise. In our conclusion, we summarise our understanding of Foucault's work and consider where to go from here. In this way, we hope to provide readers with an idea of how Foucault's concepts can serve as a vehicle for carrying out critically informed, ethical sport research.

Pirkko Markula
Bath, England

Richard Pringle
Hamilton, New Zealand

Part I

Power, knowledge and the self

Introduction to Foucauldian theorising

Chapter 1

An introduction to Michel Foucault

His work, life and effect

> People who read me, even those who appreciate what I do, often say
> to me, laughing: 'but in the end you realize that the things you say are
> nothing but fictions!' I always reply: who ever thought he [sic] was writing
> anything but fiction?
>
> (Foucault, 1991a: 33)

The social significance of sport and exercise has long been recognised,
particularly by educators, politicians and entrepreneurs, and, of course, the
many participants and spectators. Since the 1950s and 1960s a small but
growing number of sociologists have also acknowledged this importance
(e.g. Beisser, 1967; Loy, 1968; McIntosh, 1963; Sapora and Mitchell, 1961;
Stone, 1955). To help understand this social significance, these pioneering
researchers drew on social theories such as structural-functionalism, symbolic interactionism, liberal feminism and Marxism. From their formative
studies it became clear, to some, that sport and exercise were not social practices that were fundamentally meritocratic and democratising (e.g. Brohm,
1981; Felshin, 1974; Gruneau, 1976; Guttman, 1978; Hart, 1981; Loy and
McElvogue, 1970). In contrast, these researchers argued that these human
movement practices shaped and modified social meanings in a manner that
helped produce advantages and disadvantages for particular individuals and
social groups. Since the late 1980s this critical view has grown in prominence and sport sociologists have drawn on a wider range of theorists to
help examine the workings of power associated with sport and exercise.
Within this context, the ideas of Michel Foucault (1926–1984) have been
increasingly drawn upon.

Foucault (1988a: 17–18) suggested that his prime research objective had
'been to sketch out a history of the different ways in our culture that humans
develop knowledge about themselves'. To achieve this prime objective he
undertook a range of specific historical studies. He sketched, for example,
the development of understandings about madness, rationality, language,

economics, sexuality, punishment and ethics. In undertaking these studies Foucault paid attention to the relationships between particular social practices and the human sciences, such as economics, medicine, criminology, psychology and sociology. He was interested in these sciences, as he believed that they exemplified unique but influential ways that humans have attempted to understand and act upon themselves. In the process of undertaking these studies, Foucault developed an 'arsenal of subsidiary concepts' (Rabinow, 1984: 12) for understanding the constitution of individuals' subjectivities, social relations and the workings of power. Foucault somewhat modestly suggested that these concepts could be used like tools for research and that his books could be treated as toolboxes. In a more illustrious manner, Dreyfus and Rabinow (1983: xiii) stated that Foucault's writings 'represent the most important contemporary effort both to develop a method for the study of human beings and to diagnose the current situation of our society'. Foucault's tools have subsequently shaped the social sciences.

Nine years after the death of Michel Foucault, David Andrews (1993) lamented that the majority of critical sport sociologists had neglected to examine Foucault's ideas to any substantial depth. Andrews asserted that Foucault's radical approach to examining the socio-historic relationships between power, knowledge and the human body offered 'considerable relevance for the theoretical and substantive development of critical sport-oriented scholarship' (149). Andrews was writing at a time when the social significance of the 'body' was being rediscovered (e.g. Loy, 1991; Loy *et al.*, 1993; Rail and Harvey, 1995) and Foucault's theoretical focus on the body was of appeal. Yet Andrews' prime aspiration was to encourage greater critical examination of a social theorist he considered significant and unique.

Following Andrews' (1993) plea, the work of other influential sport sociologists (e.g. Cole, 1994; Hargreaves, 1986; Rail and Harvey, 1995; Theberge, 1991; Whitson, 1989) and the growing recognition of Foucault across the spectrum of the social sciences, Foucault's ideas have gained increased prominence within sport sociology. His theory, that was once considered revolutionary and potentially even dangerous, at least to some traditional liberals, is now frequently cited and discussed within sociological studies of sport and exercise. Accordingly, and with a tinge of irony, some of his ideas now appear orthodox. Yet at the same time his earlier archaeological studies are often ignored, while his influential genealogical research concerning power and the body can still cause controversy, puzzlement and misinterpretation. Furthermore, his later works remain largely under-examined. Sport sociologists are only now, for example, beginning to examine his ideas on the technologies of self (e.g. Chapman, 1997; Johns and Johns, 2000; Markula, 2003b, 2004), governmentality (Maguire, 2002), racism (Cole *et al.*, 2004) and ethics (Shogan, 1999; Shogan and

Ford, 2000). We do not accept, therefore, that it is timely to *forget* Foucault, as his compatriot, Jean Baudrillard (1987), once suggested, but believe that his ideas deserve close attention and have much to offer the sociological study of sport and exercise.

In this chapter, to help introduce the ideas of Michel Foucault, we discuss the influence that Foucault's work has generated within the social sciences. We then provide a 'still shaky profile of his *oeuvre*' (Foucault, 1972: 222) by discussing attempts to categorise his work. We conclude with a biographical sketch of Michel Foucault to help illustrate the context within which some of his prime ideas developed.

The Foucault effect

Foucault is regarded by many as one of the most influential thinkers of contemporary times (Miller, 1993; Mills, 2003; Olssen, 1999). Jürgen Habermas, a staunch critic who charged Foucault with being an irrationalist, nevertheless, acknowledged his significance by stating: 'Within the circle of the philosophers of my generation who diagnose our times, Foucault has most lastingly influenced the *Zeitgeist*' (1986: 107). Accordingly and regardless of one's views towards the fictions of Foucault, his status as a social theorist of significance ensures that 'serious scholars of sport cannot avoid Foucault's formulations' (Cole *et al.*, 2004: 207). Yet the widespread influence of Foucauldian theorising has not been without confusion or controversy.

In the early 1980s, Foucault was 'probably the most vilified and criticised of all the so-called "postmodern theorists" – figures such as Baudrillard, Derrida, and Deleuze' (Danahar *et al.*, 2000: 1–2). His ideas were seen as directly challenging the prime ontological and epistemological tenets that legitimated the human sciences. These were the disciplines that Foucault referred to with disdain as the 'immature sciences' and were often his target of academic and political concern. Alongside his scepticism of the truths produced in these disciplines, he critiqued the grand theorising of Karl Marx, the essentialist thinking of Sigmund Freud, Saussure's structuralist quest for a science of language, and the 'terroristic' existentialism of Jean-Paul Sartre. At the same time that Foucault critiqued these influential theorists, he drew on their work, extended some of their arguments and posed new ways of thinking about humans and the workings of power, truth and the governance of individuals/populations. Dennis Smith (1999: 90) summarised that Foucault worked 'against the grain of society, trying to disrupt our habitual assumptions ... [to] encourage us to question and re-evaluate the way we conduct ourselves'. Given Foucault's iconoclastic approach, it is not surprising that he sparked controversy and debate. Gilles Deleuze revealed aspects of this controversy:

Certain malevolent people say that he is the new representative of a
structural technology or technocracy. Others, mistaking their insults for
wit, claim that he is a supporter of Hitler, or at least that he offends
the rights of man (they will not forgive him for having proclaimed
the 'death of man'). Some say that he is a shammer who cannot back
himself up with reference to the sacred texts, and who seldom quotes
the great philosophers. Others, though, claim that something radically
new has appeared in philosophy, and that his work is as beautiful as
those it challenges. It celebrates the dawn of a new age.

(Deleuze, 1988: 1)

Deleuze's talk of the 'dawn of a new age' is more typically referred to
as the linguistic, narrative or postmodern turn within the social sciences.
An epistemological turn that Foucault helped initiate. Indeed, the influence
of Foucault 'is clear in a great deal of post-structuralist, post-modernist,
feminist, post-Marxist and post-colonial theorising' (Mills, 2003: 1). His
books and theories, more generally, have had considerable impact across
a diverse field of academic disciplines, from counselling and public health
to media studies and philosophy. His work, more specifically, has influenced the fields of anthropology, history, sociology, English studies, gender
studies, politics, queer studies, indigenous studies, management, economics,
pedagogy, psychology, cultural studies and sociological studies of sport.
The following four quotes from diverse fields of study help demonstrate
Foucault's remarkable influence:

there can be little doubt that his approach and his subject matter were,
and will continue to be of fundamental significance to sociology. . . . It is
arguable that his work has also been one of a number of key influences
on the widening of sociological interests, to the point where Foucauldian
concerns with the nature of 'discourse' have been internalized within
sociological debate.

(Hamilton, 2002: vii–ix)

Foucault's work on *Madness and Civilisation* (1967), on the way that
madness is constructed by society and its institutions has been profoundly influential, his work appearing at a time when the alternative
psychiatric movement in Britain and America, which tried to challenge
the medicalisation of mental illness, was beginning to develop.

(Mills, 2003: 98)

Foucauldian work has been remarkably successful in re-writing our
understanding of organizations ... some Foucauldians have entirely
re-written areas of organizational analysis such as human resource
management. ... Work influenced by Foucault is commonly found

in organizational journals, and Foucault now routinely features in introductory textbooks in the area. ... In sum, Foucauldian work has moved increasingly towards the centre stage of organizational studies.

(Newton, 1998: 416)

Foucault's work and life, achievements and demonisation, have made him a powerful model for many gay, lesbian and other intellectuals, and his analysis of the interrelationships of knowledge, power and sexuality was the most important intellectual catalyst of queer theory.

(Spargo, 1999: 8)

Foucault's work has also spawned specific research methods, such as discourse analysis and genealogical approaches. His considerable influence is undoubtedly a reflection of his prolific writings on diverse topics that spanned across the arts and sciences, and from ancient to contemporary times. Yet it is also related to the efficacy and creativity of his ideas. Ultimately, as Jana Sawicki (1991: 176) suggests 'the radical nature of Foucault's discourse, like any other, must be judged on the basis of the effects that it produces'. In this respect we suggest, regardless of whether one accepts or rejects Foucault's arguments, that the *Foucault effect* has been phenomenal.

The popularisation of Foucault has also been a cause of concern as some of his ideas, such as 'power is everywhere' or 'power is knowledge' have been misinterpreted and used in problematic ways (Danahar *et al.*, 2000; Halperin, 1995; Maguire, 2002). Foucault did not intend, as some interpretations of his ideas suggest, that contemporary forms of power are so complete that individuals are dominated by totalising forces without possibilities for resistance or change. Nevertheless, a dark version of Foucault's politics, somewhat akin to George Orwell's notion of big brother, has unwittingly continued to circulate to the detriment of the possibilities that Foucauldian theorising offers. Foucault was also critical that his theorising on power had degenerated into the crude slogan 'power is knowledge'. In response to this dumbing-down of his work he stated:

when I read – and I know it was being attributed to me – the thesis 'Knowledge is power' or 'Power is knowledge,' I begin to laugh, since studying their *relation* is precisely my problem. If they were identical, I would not have to study them and I would be spared a lot of fatigue as a result. The very fact that I pose the question of their relation proves clearly that I do not *identify* them.

(Foucault, 1994: 455, italics in original)

The recognition of Foucault's significance within the social sciences and the continued controversy, debate and, at times, misreading of his work, make it all the more important for sport sociologists to examine his once-radical ideas and his particular oeuvre or approach to knowing.

Foucault is Foucauldian

Our introduction to Foucault's life, theoretical lineages and writings is modest in relation to the breadth of his influence and the diversity of his work. For those whose social imaginations about Foucault are piqued, there is a veritable industry of books, journal articles, websites and even a specific journal (*Foucault Studies*) that can be drawn upon to gain further understanding. Despite the diversity of these sources and the different slants they take, many of these resources discuss the difficulty of attempting to define Foucault in relation to the multifaceted, original and changing focus of his work. Paul Bové, for example, reported that Foucault's politics have been categorised 'to the left, right, and center or sometimes off the political spectrum altogether' (1988: viii). Clifford Geertz even suggested that Foucault was better defined by what he was not, a 'non-historical historian, an anti-humanist human scientist, a counter-structuralist structuralist' (cited in Dreyfus and Rabinow, 1983: iii). The complexities associated with attempting to define Foucault have not escaped sport sociologists. He has been variously referred to as a 'prominent European philosopher' (Harvey and Sparkes, 1991: 167), a 'critical' researcher (Duncan, 1994: 52), a 'poststructuralist' (Heikkala, 1993: 398), a 'theorist of modernity' (Shogan, 1999: 8), 'an antidisciplinary scholar' (Andrews, 1993: 150) and as 'one of the leading poststructuralist/postmodernist thinkers' (Rail, 1998: xi). These descriptors all help reveal multiple truths about Foucault.

Part of the difficulty of attempting to put Foucault in a 'box', relates to Foucault's endeavours to avoid academic categorisation. He strongly rejected that he was a 'structuralist' (Foucault, 1970: xiv), stated that he did not consider himself a philosopher or historian (Foucault, 1991a), and that he did not even know what was meant by the terms postmodern or poststructuralist (Foucault, 1994: 448).[1] More typically, Foucault (1973: 17) refused to state how he viewed himself: 'Do not ask who I am and do not ask me to remain the same: leave it to our bureaucrats and our police to see that our papers are in order. At least spare us their morality when we write'. For some, such advice is likely to be frustrating yet we suggest it resonates with his concerns about processes of *subjectivation*, or the multiple ways in which humans get tied to particular identities. He was troubled with how being 'known' or categorised can act to constrain and *subject* people to certain ends, identities and modes of behaviour. Much of his concern with the human sciences was with regard to how the knowledge produced in these fields of study acts to construct humans as particular objects – such as Caucasians, asthmatics, homosexuals or morons (a scientific category of intelligence based on an IQ score between 50 and 69) – and how humans subsequently become subject to those scientific truths. We suggest, accordingly, that his concerns about processes of subjectivation are possibly what underpinned Foucault's desire not to be 'subject' to certain academic definitions. Yet Foucault was also aware that his ideas changed over time and that his work should not be considered as a coherent whole.

In recent years, despite Foucault's attempts to remain uncategorised, an increasing number of sport sociologists refer to his unique approach as simply 'Foucauldian'. So what does Foucauldian theorising mean? Moreover, in what context and under what influences did Foucault develop his ideas and political interests? To help answer these questions, we provide a biographical sketch. We do this understanding that Foucault was critical about biographies. He was concerned that these texts can overemphasise the roles of individuals in the discontinuous and complex play of history and social thought. Foucault, nevertheless, reflected: 'Each of my works is a part of my own biography. For one or another reason I had the occasion to feel and live those things' (Foucault, 1988a: 11). More specifically, he revealed that the process of writing allowed him to transform his own thinking with respect to his own life experiences:

> the books I write constitute an experience for me that I'd like to be as rich as possible. An experience is something you come out of changed. If I had to write a book to communicate what I have already thought, I'd never have the courage to begin it. . . . When I write, I do it above all to change myself and not to think the same as before.
>
> (Foucault, 1991b: 27)

To help understand Foucault's ideas it is helpful to know a little about the context of his life and times. In representing this biographical sketch we draw closely from Foucault's reflections and utterances. In the chapter following we then discuss in greater detail Foucault's prime theorisations.

A biographical sketch

Foucault was born in 1926 in Poitiers, an old Roman town to the southwest of Paris and was christened Paul-Michel: named after his father Dr Paul Foucault, a surgeon of some local renown. He was raised in '*haute bourgeoise* comfort' (Miller, 1993: 39) with a nurse and cook helping care for him, his older sister and younger brother. Due to his father's concerns with his son's academic progress at the local state school, Paul-Michel was transferred in 1940 to a highly orthodox Catholic secondary school. His father had strong expectations that he too would become a medical doctor, like both of his grandparents. Within this regimented and disciplined school, Paul-Michel began to excel academically, showing particular ability in philosophy, history and literature. Despite Foucault's academic success, his school years were reportedly unhappy (Miller, 1993). The German occupation of France during the war years contributed to his malaise and left an indelible mark on Foucault. In 1981, talking of his fears during the war he reminisced:

> I have very early memories of an absolutely threatening world, which could crush us. ... To have lived as an adolescent in a situation that had to end, that had to lead to another world, for better or worse, was to have the impression of spending one's entire childhood in the night, waiting for dawn. That prospect of another world marked the people of my generation, and we have carried with us, perhaps to excess, a dream of Apocalypse.
>
> (cited in Miller, 1993: 39)

The prospect of creating 'another world' became a guiding idea that influenced Foucault's future writings. He asserted that this new society needed to be radically different 'from the one in which we had lived; a society that had accepted Nazism, had prostituted itself before it, and then had come out of it *en masse* with De Gaulle' (Foucault, 1991b: 47). Foucault, however, was concerned that the existing political options 'between the America of Truman or the USSR of Stalin ... or between the old French SFIO and the Christian Democrats' (47) did not offer sufficient alternatives for the prospects of creating a radically new society. In years to come, as Foucault's ideas matured, he came to the conclusion that to change society, the focus should not be on attempting to change social structures, such as systems of politics, but on promoting new ways of knowing ourselves, and ways of being.[2]

Foucault, in 1945, unaware of the formative influence that his war experiences would have on his later writings, but no doubt troubled and puzzled by the war, rejected his father's plea to study medicine and opted to study philosophy in a quest, according to Alan Sheridan (1980), to help unravel the meanings or secrets of life. To help fulfil this aim he gained entry to the esteemed *École Normale Supérieure*, by coming fourth in an open and highly competitive examination. The *École Normale Supérieure* was an elite school, described by Miller (1993: 45) as a 'kind of monastery for boy geniuses' where 'day and night the chosen few pore over the canonic works of western civilisation, from Plato to Kant' (42). The chosen few amounted to a total of 36 students in Foucault's year. The school itself not only demanded study of the canonic works but it also helped produce them. Jean-Paul Sartre was a student at *École Normale Supérieure* in 1924, and Louis Althusser, Jean Hyppolite and Maurice Merleau-Ponty were all lecturers while Foucault undertook his studies. It was in this hothouse of philosophical thinking that Foucault was schooled in the ideas of Heidegger, Kant, Hegel, Marx, Descartes and Husserl and emerged in 1948 with a university *licence* or degree.

His philosophical desire to know the secrets of life, however, remained un-satisfied and, according to Sheridan (1980: 4–5), 'the prospect of spending the rest of his life teaching philosophy appalled him'. Foucault's pessimistic outlook deepened during his philosophical studies and he attempted suicide more than once. James Miller (1993) surmised that these attempts were perhaps due to anxiety about his homosexual activities or his heavy drug use.[3] Foucault's distressed father in response arranged for psychiatric treat-ment (Simons, 1995). Miller reported, however, that one act of 'nominal self-mutilation' (1993: 63) that Paul-Michel successfully completed, was that he 'chopped off his *nom du pére*, becoming simply Michel Foucault' (63). An act of self-assertion designed by Foucault to hurt his father. Al-though tensions existed between Foucault and his father, he remained close to his siblings and mother (Marshall, 1996).

Foucault, interested in a different academic direction and perhaps swayed by his own experiences of depression, completed a degree in psychology in 1950 and was awarded a Diploma in Psycho-Pathology in 1952. During these studies he gained intimate experience of the workings of positivism and experimental science. He also gained work experience in a psychiatric asylum as both a technician and intern. Foucault (1988b: 11) reported that: 'After having studied philosophy, I wanted to see what madness was: I had been mad enough to study reason; I was reasonable enough to study mad-ness'. Yet Sheridan (1980: 6) suggested that Foucault's 'search for scientific understanding proved as illusory as the philosophical quest'. After three years of moving between patients and hospital attendants in a somewhat ambiguous position and witnessing the growth of neurosurgery and psy-chopharmacology, Foucault questioned the necessity of these treatments. It was at this time that he also discovered and was subsequently rocked by the iconoclastic work of Nietzsche: the so-called 'spiritual grandfather of postmodernism' (Peters, 1996: 34).

Foucault (1988a: 13) reported that reading Nietzsche was a revelation that allowed him to escape intellectual and personal entrapments: 'I felt that there was someone quite different from what I had been taught. I read him with a great passion and broke with my life'. Foucault (1988b: 11) quit his job at the asylum and 'went to Sweden in great personal discomfort and started to write a history of these (psychiatric) practices'. The subsequent book, *Madness and Civilisation: A History of Insanity in the Age of Reason* was published in France in 1961 (English translation, 1965). Under the sponsorship of Georges Canguilhem it served as Foucault's Doctoral thesis.

Madness and Civilisation traced the development of understandings about madness and sanity, providing an exploration of the changing social context that allowed for the development of psychiatry. In following Canguilhem's work on the history of science, Foucault wanted to explore how groups of ideas develop, change and mutate over time within complex fields of relations.[4] Foucault (1991b: 64) examined madness and sanity, in part, because he considered psychiatry and psychology as 'less consolidated disciplines whose constitution was relatively more recent. ... And whose scientific character was least certain'. He was critical of how the truths developed within these 'immature' sciences produced the 'reciprocal genesis of the subject and object' (Foucault, 1991b: 63). Foucault was particularly interested to examine how 'madness' became an object of analysis but also how, at the same time, there was the corresponding construction of the 'rational subject who "knew" about madness' (Foucault, 1991b: 65) and attempted to control it.

From Nietzsche, Foucault gained an understanding that history was not progressive or continuous but the result of accidents, violence, disputes and clashes of will. Foucault also resonated with Nietzsche's anti-humanist stance and his de-centring of the human subject. Foucault (1980d: 132–133) further acknowledged that Nietzsche encouraged his recognition that truth is not discovered but invented; and that power struggles are continually fought 'around truth': 'The political question, to sum up, is not error, illusion, alienated consciousness or ideology; it is truth itself'. This line of reasoning undoubtedly contributed to Foucault's concerns about Marxism.

After the Second World War the theoretical and political influence of Marxism was strong and many French academics, including Foucault, became members of the communist party. Foucault (1991b: 51) reported that in 1950 'without knowing Marx very well, refusing Hegelianism, and feeling dissatisfied with the limitations of existentialism, I decided to join the French Communist Party'. Yet many French academics did not accept Marxism *carte blanche* and there were valuable attempts to wed the existentialist thinking of Jean-Paul Sartre and/or Husserlian phenomenology with Marxism.[5] From 1945 to 1955, Foucault (1994: 436) reflected: 'the entire French university – the young university, as opposed to what had been the traditional university – was very much preoccupied, even occupied, with the task of building ... the phenomenology–Marxism relation'. Throughout the late 1950s and early 1960s, with growing recognition of the social significance of language, Foucault (1994: 436) reported that 'we saw structuralism replace phenomenology and become coupled with Marxism'. Against this theoretical backdrop Foucault (1991b: 51), nevertheless, became aware that a 'Nietzschean Communist ... (was) something a bit ridiculous' and he left the party in 1951.

Foucault was critical of Marxism due to its totalising account of history, its reliance on the assumption that history was following a progressive path towards a socialist utopia, its economic reductionism, and the assumptions inherent within the concept of ideology. Foucault (1980d: 118) was concerned that the notion of ideology 'always stands in virtual opposition to something else which is supposed to count as truth'. He was particularly critical that the concept of ideology presupposed that there were true and false ways of viewing reality. Foucault, in contrast, was interested in 'seeing historically how effects of truth are produced within discourses which themselves are neither true or false' (118). 'Truth', in this respect, refers to what individuals *believe* to be true.[6]

After one-year stints in Warsaw (1958) as the Director of the French Institute, and a similar position in Hamburg in 1959, Foucault returned to France in 1960 to become head of the philosophy department at the University of Clermont-Ferrand (Sheridan, 1980). In 1961 Foucault published an analysis of the avant-garde French poet Raymond Roussel, followed in 1963 (English translation, 1973), by his second major work *The Birth of the Clinic: An Archaeology of Medical Perception*. Here Foucault extended themes he had explored in *Madness and Civilisation* and traced how humans constitute themselves as objects of scientific study. Foucault illustrated how changes in the way of viewing patients (e.g. the medical gaze), talking about the human body (e.g. clinical discourses), and in the architecture of the hospital, corresponded to changes in the practice of medicine. Such changes, Foucault (1973: 197) argued, heralded the widespread growth of the human sciences: 'Western man [sic] could constitute himself in his own eyes as an object of science, he grasped himself within his language and gave himself, in himself and by himself, a discursive existence'. Foucault illustrated that the growth of the human sciences, around 1800, significantly shaped how humans understood themselves and the knowledge of normal and abnormal behaviours.

Foucault's next book, *The Order of Things*, published in 1966 (English translation, 1970) built on his earlier work by illustrating how the scientific analysis of economics helped *objectify* the labouring subject, philology the speaking subject, and biology the living subject. Foucault (1970: x), however, moved on from his previous works by providing a comparative study of the development of these three modes of inquiry (economics, philology and biology) as related 'to the philosophical discourse that was contemporary with them during a period extending from the seventeenth to the nineteenth centuries'. He was interested in 'the suddenness and thoroughness with which certain sciences were sometimes reorganized; and the fact that at the same time similar changes occurred in apparently very different disciplines' (xii). Yet rather than focusing on the role of groundbreaking scientists and 'the expression of genius and freedom' (Foucault, 1972: 210), Foucault examined the discourses, or sets of rules, that shaped and modified the generalised conditions of scientific thought. Foucault called his attempt to historically excavate and reveal the rules of formation that underpinned the changes in scientific knowledge, *archaeological*. His texts from this period have subsequently been referred to as his archaeological studies (e.g. Foucault, 1965, 1970, 1972, 1973).

The publication of *The Order of Things* helped consolidate Foucault's growing academic reputation in France. The first edition of 3,000 copies sold out within a week. A second edition of 5,000 copies was sold out within six weeks and the book topped the non-fiction best-seller list (Mills, 2003). By 1979 50,000 copies of the French edition had been sold (Sheridan, 1980). Mills (2003) reported that philosophy has long been an integral part of the school curriculum in France and during the 1960s and 1970s, in contrast to England, French culture warmly received philosophical texts. Books by Barthes, Lacan, Levi-Strauss, Deleuze and others were also commercially successful in this period despite the issue, as reported by Sheridan (1980), that some of these texts were impenetrable.

In 1969, three years after *The Order of Things*, Foucault published *The Archaeology of Knowledge* (English translation, 1972) to similar commercial and critical acclaim. Within this text Foucault (1972: 15) lamented that the methods that he employed in his earlier books 'were outlined in a rather disordered way, and their general articulation was never clearly defined'. *The Archaeology of Knowledge* was, accordingly, his attempt to give 'greater coherence' (15) to his archaeological method and to provide detail of his theory of discourse. In contrast to his earlier works, he shifted his focus away from the analysis of social institutions, such as mental asylums and hospitals, to focus on a more abstract analysis of the workings of discourse. His subsequent arguments were complex, somewhat circular and have been the subject of several critiques (e.g. see Dreyfus and Rabinow, 1983). Nevertheless, Foucault's concept of discourse and the notion of the dispersed (fragmented) self have been influential.

In 1970, at the age of 44, Foucault accepted a chair at France's most prestigious institution, the *Collège de France*. The title he created for himself was 'Professor of History of Systems of Thought'. This appointment occurred when Foucault was shifting his methodological preference from archaeology to genealogy and from a tentatively structural analysis of discourse to what has been typically termed as post-structural. At the heart of these discontinuities, despite his continuing interests in the human sciences, was Foucault's awakening to the significance of the workings of power in relation to the human body. He did not relinquish his concept of discourse but reformulated it to theorise about the linkages between discourse, knowledge and power. In this manner he politicised the workings of discourse to fundamentally ask 'whom does discourse serve?' This innovative conjoining of discourse and power within a materialist realm has subsequently proven fruitful as a tool of critical interpretation.[7] Although Foucault denied being the first to link knowledge with power he commented on the difficulty he had in formulating this connection:

> When I think back now, I ask myself what else it was that I was talking about, in *Madness and Civilisation* or *The Birth of the Clinic*, but power? Yet I'm perfectly aware that I scarcely ever used the word and never had such a field of analyses at my disposal. I can say that this was

an incapacity linked undoubtedly with the political situation we found ourselves in. It is hard to see where, either on the Right or the Left, this problem of power could then have been posed.

(Foucault, 1980d: 115)

With reference to the constraints of the political context of the 1960s, Foucault suggested that the Right tended to link power to the constitution, laws and sovereignty, whereas the Left correlated power with the workings of the State and economic modes of production. Foucault (1980d: 115–116) was concerned that these circumscribed conceptualisations of power, limited acknowledgement of the 'way power was exercised – concretely and in detail – with its specificity, its techniques and tactics'. Moreover, he lamented that existing accounts of power could not provide critical readings of diverse yet socially significant aspects of human life. Foucault (1980b: 98) was particularly interested in how 'certain bodies, certain gestures, certain discourses, certain desires, come to be identified and constituted as individuals' and the mechanisms of power that underpin these complex processes. Foucault's (1980d) theoretical project, that subsequently shaped his work throughout the 1970s, was to re-conceptualise the notion of power to help understand the daily lives and experiences of humans and broaden the field of political analysis.

Foucault's interest in examining the workings of power had been prompted by the May rebellion of 1968 in Paris. Although Foucault (1980d) was living in Tunisia at the time (1966–68), the protests in France helped him recognise that the issues he had been raising in his earlier works were important but without a direct link to the workings of power they were 'timid and hesitant' (111). He stated that the May rebellion encouraged a change of focus in his work: 'Without the political opening created during those years, I would surely never had ... pursued my research in the direction of penal theory, prisons and disciplines' (111). Yet, he also recognised that the protests helped create greater interest in his own writings:

> at this time in France studying psychiatry or the history of medicine had no real status in the field. Nobody was interested in that. The first thing that happened after '68 was that Marxism as a dogmatic framework declined and new political, new cultural interests concerning personal life appeared. That's why I think my work had nearly no echo, with the exception of a very small circle, before '68.
>
> (Foucault, 1997a: 125)

The global activism of the late 1960s and early 1970s captured Foucault's imagination and provided the impetus for *Discipline and Punish: The Birth of the Prison* (1975, English translation, 1977). He was interested in knowing why dissatisfaction was being felt in countries as diverse as

Tunisia, Poland, France and the United States of America. He surmised that the material conditions in these countries 'were no worse than at other times' (Foucault, 1991b: 144). In an attempt to explain this widespread display of dissatisfaction, Foucault theorised that it was a 'rebellion against an entire network of forms of power that made their mark on youth culture and on certain strata of society' (145). Foucault assumed, more generally, that these protests signalled 'it was no longer acceptable to be "governed" in an extended sense' (144). These speculations encouraged his focus on forms of power that insidiously control and shape social life and subjectivities. Foucault's seminal idea was that a *disciplinary power* is exercised over all citizens in contemporary societies, and although individuals find it difficult to discern the workings of this form of power it, nevertheless, contributes to a general discomfort that pervades life. In a press conference, Foucault commented: 'They tell us that the prisons are over-populated. But what if it were the population that were being over-imprisoned?' (cited in Macey, 1994: 258). In this manner, he wanted to examine the forms of power or technologies of domination that work to control social relations and shape individuals.

With the publication of *Discipline and Punish* Foucault had reached, what David Andrews (1993: 153) respectfully called 'a disheartened and cynical intellectual maturity'. The enhanced sophistication of his conceptual tools for analysing human experience and understanding resulted in greater attention to his work. Foucault's broadened conceptualisation of power, for example, allowed understanding of the political significance of popular cultural activities, such as sport, fitness and leisure practices. In addition it provided a framework for interrogating the workings of power in specific locations and in a manner that did not reductively focus on laws, class, gender, the economic base or state apparatus. Given these abilities it is perhaps not surprising that Foucault's genealogical examinations have increasingly influenced the sociology of sport (Rail and Harvey, 1995).

Foucault's concerns about the workings of power were not confined to his theoretical projects. Although he was now a renowned Professor, he was also politically active and, at times, in a militant manner. In 1971, he was involved in establishing the *Group d'information sur les prisons,* which aimed to raise concerns about the conditions within jails and the treatment of prisoners. The *Group* organised demonstrations, conducted surveys of prisoners and disseminated results and information leaflets. Foucault eschewed typical liberal reform techniques that involved the paternalistic stance of talking 'on behalf' of others and provided prisoners the opportunity to voice, in their own words, concerns about their inhumane treatment. Foucault was arrested in a protest while distributing leaflets outside La Santé prison in 1971. In 1975 his protests against the execution of Basque separatists in Spain resulted in his expulsion back to France. By 1976, however, his political actions were starting to influence policy and Foucault was invited to serve on a French Government commission investigating strategies for penal reform. Foucault's political actions have subsequently been recognised as playing a leading role that led to the 1981 abolishment of the death penalty and subsequent reforms in government systems of punishment. Foucault stated that although these changes encouraged rejoicing it was not a time for self-congratulation, as there was more work to be done in attempting to reduce governmental violence:

> Giving up the habit of lopping off a few heads because blood spurts, because it is something no longer done among civilized people, and because there is sometimes a risk of decapitating an innocent person is relatively easy. But giving up the death penalty while citing the principle that no public authority has the right to take anyone's life (any more than any individual does) is to engage an important and difficult debate. The question of war, the army, compulsory military service, and so on, immediately takes shape.
>
> (Foucault, 2000: 459–460)

Throughout the 1970s Foucault was also involved in protests against racism, the war in Vietnam, the treatment of Soviet dissidents, and was politically supportive of the solidarity movement in Poland and, in the early stages, the Islamic revolution in Iran. Yet as soon as the 'spiritual revolution' in Iran was tainted by abuses of human rights, Foucault sent an open letter to the Iranian prime minister condemning the violent revolutionary tactics. Later in the 1970s and early 1980s he was modestly active in the gay rights movement (Mills, 2003) and contributed several interviews to this political cause (e.g. Foucault, 1997b, 1997c, 1997d). During this time period, Foucault's political activism and writings helped to promote the perspective that one could aspire to so-called Left values while also being staunchly anticommunist and anti-revolutionary (Gordon, 2000).

Despite Foucault's overt political actions and critical works, he has been variously critiqued for being apolitical; with the prime criticism being that his 'histories of the present' graphically point out a range of social problems, yet they do not provide clear or coherent guidelines to help challenge or overcome these problems (Smart, 1986). Jürgen Habermas (1982) for example, labelled Foucault as a neo-conservative because he failed to provide a strategy for political intervention. Foucault, in response, stated:

> I am sure I am not able to provide these people with what they expect. (Laughs) I never behave like a prophet – my books don't tell people what to do. And they often reproach me for not doing so (and maybe they are right), and at the same time they reproach me for behaving like a prophet.
>
> (Foucault, 1997a: 131)

In more general terms, Foucault did not believe that it was his role to tell others what to do. Indeed, he was highly critical of all the 'prophecies, promises, injunctions, and programs that the intellectuals have managed to formulate in the course of the last two centuries' (Foucault, 1991b: 11). In contrast, he thought it more appropriate to perform critical analyses that reveal the strengths and weaknesses in the workings of power associated with specific social practices, such as punishment or sexuality, so that individuals who were directly involved in political action could be better informed in their design of strategies and actions.

Foucault has also been critiqued for not being *more* overt about his sexual preferences. In defence of Foucault, Eribon (1991) pointed out that Foucault loathed the act of *confession* and was critical of the gay-rights strategy of 'coming out'. Foucault was concerned that this political strategy of identifying one's subjectivity solely in relation to his/her sexual preferences acted to categorise one restrictively. He explained:

> if identity becomes the problem of sexual existence, and if people think that they have to 'uncover' their 'own identity', and that their own identity has to become the law, the principle, the code of their existence; if the perennial question they ask is 'does this thing conform to my identity?' then, I think ... it limits us, and I think we have – and can have – a right to be free.
>
> (Foucault, 1997d: 166)

On a more general level, concerned with the distinctions between his private and academic life, Foucault reported:

> Anyway, my personal life is not at all interesting. If somebody thinks that my work cannot be understood without reference to such and such a part of my life, I accept to consider the question. (Laughs) I am ready to answer if I agree. As far as my personal life is uninteresting, it is not worthwhile making a secret of it. (Laughs) By the same token, it may not be worthwhile publicizing it.
>
> (Foucault, 1997a: 133)

With the 1976 publication of *The History of Sexuality, Volume 1: An Introduction* (English translation, 1978), Foucault extended his theorisations concerning power and techniques of domination to produce a genealogy of the way in which 'sex is put into discourse' (Foucault, 1978: 11). In undertaking this project, Foucault rejected the idea that sexuality was a historical constant and aimed to provide a history of the experiences of sexuality. Foucault's prime concern was to 'define the regime of power–knowledge–pleasure that sustains the discourse on human sexuality' (11). Although not a manifesto for sexual reform, *The History of Sexuality, Volume 1* has been cited by David Halperin (1995: 15) as the 'single most important intellectual source of political inspiration for contemporary AIDS activists' due, in part, to its innovative conceptualisations of the links between power, sexuality and subjectivity.

Foucault's tools of analysis concerned with discourse and power, as elaborated on in a small section in the middle of *The History of Sexuality* (92–102) have, more generally, played a pivotal role in the development of gender studies, queer studies and feminist post-structuralism. In discussing the complementary links between feminism and Foucauldian theorising, Diamond and Quinby (1988: x) suggested that they both locate the body as the site of power, focus on the personal and local rather than the macro-workings of power, are concerned with revealing marginalised discourses, and critique how 'humanism has privileged the experience of the Western masculine elite as it proclaims universals about truth, freedom and human nature'. Yet Diamond and Quinby also stated that the possibility of a convergence between Foucault and feminists 'is not without tensions' (ix), given that Foucault's work has an 'almost exclusive focus on works by men' (xvi). They argued that his androcentric focus could indirectly act to marginalise women's political activities. Irrespective of these tensions, the critical appropriation of Foucault's work 'by post-structuralist feminists has generated some of the most vibrant and incisive work related to the cultural politics of gender and sex' (Andrews, 2000: 125).[8] Moreover, it has been the Foucauldian influenced form of feminist post-structuralism that has dominated sociological studies of sport and exercise (e.g. Chapman, 1997; Cole, 1994; Duncan, 1994; Markula, 1995; Theberge, 1991).

On the back cover of the first edition of *Volume 1* Foucault announced, ambitiously, that he would publish an additional five volumes concerning sexuality. The proposed titles were: Volume 2, *The Flesh and the Body*; Volume 3, *The Children's Crusade*; Volume 4, *Woman, Mother, Hysteric*; Volume 5, *Perverts*; and Volume 6, *Population and Races*. His planned studies were to have followed the same theoretical approach used in his earlier genealogical studies. Foucault became aware, however, that the arguments he would have developed would have been similar to his earlier work and this did not inspire his creativity. In fact, he stated that he now found the topic of sex 'boring' (Foucault, 1997g: 253) and acknowledged: 'I found myself confronted with a choice that was a long time in unravelling: a choice between fidelity to the chronological outline I had originally imagined, and a different line of inquiry' (Foucault, 1997f: 204). The 'long time in unravelling' amounted to eight years. It was not until 1984 that Foucault published his second and third volumes on sexuality, *The Use of Pleasure* (English translation, 1985) and *The Care of the Self* (English translation, 1986). Foucault (1985: 3) subsequently noted: 'This series of studies is being published later than I had anticipated, and in a form that is altogether different'. To help explain this delay and change in form, he stated:

> There are times in life when the question of knowing if one can think differently than one thinks, and perceive differently than one sees, is absolutely necessary if one is to go on looking and reflecting at all. . . . But, then, what is philosophy today – philosophical activity, I mean – if it is not the critical work that thought brings to bear on itself? In what does it consist, if not in the endeavour to know how and to what extent it might be possible to think differently, instead of legitimating what is already known? . . . The 'essay' – which should be understood as the assay or test by which, in the game of truth, one undergoes changes, and not as the simplistic appropriation of others for the purpose of communication – is the living substance of philosophy, at least if we assume that philosophy is still what it was in times past, i.e. an 'ascesis,' askêsis, an exercise of one self in the activity of thought.
>
> (Foucault, 1985: 8–9)

In this manner, Foucault not only explained his detour but also helped to introduce the different themes of inquiry that he was now pursuing; which revolved less around sexuality and focused more on humans as *subjects* of desire and the various *techniques of self-formation* or, in his words: 'the games of truth in the relationship of self with self and the forming of oneself as a subject' (Foucault, 1985: 6). Foucault's new interest in examining the 'techniques of the self' was assumed by Colin Gordon (1991) to have developed in relation to critiques of Foucault's genealogies of punishment and sexuality. These critiques typically argued that Foucault's focus on specific techniques of domination directed little attention to the relations between the State and society, the potential for social transformation and the recognition of individual freedom.

In the late 1970s and early 1980s, Foucault refined, rather than re-worked, his core conceptual tools as related to subjectivity and power. In his lectures (e.g. Foucault, 1991c) and writings (e.g. Foucault, 1983a) on the art of governing or what he termed governmentality, he also extended his discussion about the influence of the State over populations to talk in more detail of the links between micro- and macro-workings of power. He illustrated how his theorisations concerning the workings of power at local levels could similarly be used to understand the broader workings of power associated with State governments. Foucault's writings on subjectivity also changed in emphasis, away from his focus on the constitution of subjectivity via the workings of discourse, to constitution via lived practices. He accordingly emphasised how the 'self' emerged through relations with others and through one's negotiations with self and ethical dilemmas.

Foucault's (1988a, 1988b, 1987) interests in subjectivity, freedom and the workings of power encouraged his focus on ethical modes of existence. He still argued against the humanist idea that a work of self upon self can be thought of as a mode of liberation; such a notion could suggest the existence of a real human foundation. Yet he illustrated that if individuals exist in relations of power and have degrees of liberty within these relations, that an ethical issue arises: 'How can one practice freedom?' (Foucault, 1987: 4). Foucault's academic trajectory, accordingly, culminated with his interest to examine the 'problems' of how to live an ethical life.

To help examine this issue Foucault (1985) produced a genealogy of Ancient Greek ethics in relation to technologies of self and sexual practices (*The Use of Pleasure*) and of Roman ethics (*The Care of the Self*) in the 'first centuries of our era' (Foucault, 1986: 235). His interest in the Ancient Greeks and Romans did not stem from an admiration of these historical cultures. In fact, Foucault was clearly critical of the treatment of slaves and females in Greece. He bemoaned, for example, that 'women were underdogs whose pleasures had no importance, whose sexual life had only to be oriented toward, determined by, their status as wives' (Foucault, 1997g: 256–257). Yet he believed there were similarities associated with how the 'free men' of these ancient cultures and contemporary individuals in Western societies negotiate ethical issues. Foucault explained this similarity by stating that Greek ethics were 'not related to any social – or at least to any legal – institutional system' (1997e: 255) and that in contemporary society many 'no longer believe that ethics is founded in religion, nor do we want a legal system to intervene in our moral, personal, private life' (255). Foucault further stated:

> Recent liberation movements suffer from the fact that they cannot find any principle on which to base the elaboration of a new ethics. They need an ethics, but they cannot find any other ethics than an ethics founded on so-called scientific knowledge of what the self is, what desire is, what the unconscious is, and so on.
>
> (Foucault, 1997g: 255–256)

In relation to this current dilemma on how one should conduct and practice an ethical life without recourse to a universal set of ethical guidelines, Foucault assumed that there could be advantages in studying pre-Christian or pagan cultures. Yet he was not looking to find a solution to the current ethical dilemma: 'You can't find the solution of a problem in the solution of another problem raised at another moment by other people' (Foucault, 1997g: 254). Foucault believed, nevertheless, that valuable lessons could still be learnt from such an examination. Within his genealogical examinations Foucault studied ancient texts that were:

> written for the purpose of offering rules, opinions, and advice on how to behave as one should: 'practical' texts, which are themselves objects of a "practice" in that they were designed to be read, learned, reflected upon, and tested out, and they were intended to constitute the eventual framework of everyday conduct.
>
> (Foucault, 1985: 12–13)

These texts described the 'arts of existence' (Foucault, 1985: 10); which Foucault defined as 'those intentional and voluntary actions by which men not only set themselves rules of conduct, but also seek to transform themselves ... and to make their life into an oeuvre that carries certain aesthetic values and meets certain stylistic criteria' (10–11). Through examining these texts Foucault emphasised that it is possible and, more specifically, important to reflect and experiment upon one's relation to one's self to help create new modes of ethical and aesthetic existence. His underpinning aim was to 'show people that they are much freer than they feel, that people accept as truth, as evidence, some themes which have been built up at a certain moment during history, and that this so-called evidence can be criticized and destroyed' (Foucault, 1988a: 10). In this respect, he hoped to 'change something in the minds of people' (10), as he believed that the possibilities of social transformation stem initially from such personal changes.

Paul Rabinow (1997: xxiv), commenting on Foucault's personal life during the time that Foucault was planning, researching and writing his sexual/ethical genealogies, stated: 'it seems fair to say that Foucault was experimenting in his own life with the twin imperatives to "know thyself" and to "care for thyself"'. During this time Foucault made frequent visits to New York and California and held teaching and research appointments at the University of Berkeley and the University of Vermont. While in San Francisco, Rabinow stated that Foucault's 'explorations and reflections on gay life ... are well known; less has been made of the fact that ... he spent his days ... working in the libraries, talking with colleagues, holding seminars, and meeting students' (1997: xxiv). Indeed, his passion for writing, researching and teaching remained strong until his untimely death, at the age of 57, from an AIDS related illness in June 1984. Foucault, for example, had nearly completed *Confessions of the Flesh* – a text that due to conditions in Foucault's will is unlikely to be published – and had completed 'more than a draft of a book about sexual ethics in the sixteenth century' (Foucault, 1997g: 255).

Despite the breadth of Foucault's academic and political interests, Rabinow (1997) predicted that: 'Ultimately ... Foucault may well be remembered as one of the major ethical thinkers of modernity' (xxvi). Yet, at this stage, his work on ethics remains less well known in comparison to his examinations of discipline, normalisation, madness, medicine and sexuality. Although Foucault's interests and approaches changed markedly throughout his academic career, Foucault (1988a: 15) reflected: 'I sometimes appear to myself much too systematic and rigid'. To help support this self-critique he offered this overview of his life's work:

> What I have studied are the three traditional problems: (1) What are the relations we have to truth through scientific knowledge, to these 'truth games' which are so important in civilization and in which we are both subject and object? (2) What are the relationships we have to others through those strange strategies and power relationships? And (3) what are the relationships between truth, power and self? I would like to finish all this with a question: What could be more classic than these questions and more systematic than the evolution through questions one, two, and three and back to the first? I am just at this point?
> (Foucault, 1988a: 15)

Our sketch of Michel Foucault's life, in an attempt to help understand how his ideas and theories developed, leads into the next chapter in which we discuss in more detail his theoretical 'tools'.

Chapter 2

Technologies of dominance
Power, discourses and the disciplined bodies

In this chapter we illustrate how Foucauldian theorising can be valuable for understanding the social influence of sport and exercise practices. Underpinning Foucault's seemingly divergent projects was his desire to understand how people, throughout history, have created knowledge about humans and how such knowledge has shaped the experience of being 'human'. Foucault (1983a: 208) researched this broad area of social importance by focusing on what he called the 'three modes of objectification': scientific classification, dividing practices and subjectivation. These three modes relate to processes associated with the social construction and modification of humans, so that humans acquire 'certain attitudes' (Foucault, 1988b: 18) about themselves and others. We draw on his schema of the modes of objectification to introduce his theoretical ideas.

More specifically, we focus on the first two modes: scientific classification and dividing practices (Chapter 7 focuses on the third). The first two modes are primarily concerned with how people are classified, disciplined and normalised by social processes that they have little direct control over. Foucault (1988b: 18) referred to these social processes as 'technologies of power', which he defined as specific social practices that 'determine the conduct of individuals and submit them to certain ends or domination' (18). Foucault primarily studied these technologies of power within his archaeological examinations of the human sciences and genealogical studies of punishment and sexuality. In relation to this research we first provide an overview of Foucault's concerns with the human sciences, elaborate on his archaeological method and then focus on his influential concept of discourse. This is followed by an introduction to his approach for undertaking genealogical research and a discussion concerning Foucault's understandings of power. The section on power provides us with a context for discussing many of Foucault's concepts that have received attention from sport scholars – such as discipline, panopticism and surveillance – and to elaborate on other concepts (e.g. biopower and governmentality) that have received scant attention.

Scientific classification and dividing practices

Foucault was concerned that many social problems primarily stem from the imposition of particular ways of knowing one's self and others. The 'knowledge' of men as leaders and women as subservient, for example, helps to produce the problem of sexism. In this manner, Foucault defined (1983a: 212) 'knowledge of humans' as a form of power that 'categorizes the individual, marks him [sic] by his own individuality, attaches him to his own identity, imposes a law of truth on him which he must recognise and which others have to recognise in him'. This form of power, Foucault continued, constitutes individuals as 'subjects' in the dual sense that one becomes 'subject to someone else by control and dependence, and tied to his [sic] own identity by a conscience or self-knowledge' (212). His political concern, accordingly, was not to look for the 'chief enemy' or to 'attack ... an institution of power, or group, or elite, or class' (212) but to analyse the various forms and techniques of power.

Foucault's concerns with specific techniques of power and the social construction of subjectivities underpinned his interest in the human sciences, such as 'economics, biology, psychiatry, medicine and penology' (Foucault, 1988b: 18). He argued that contemporary understandings of humans were developed in the shift between Classical knowledge and modernity: 'It was upon this threshold that the strange figure of knowledge called man first appeared and revealed a space proper to the human sciences' (Foucault, 1970: xxiv). Yet rather than celebrating this accumulation of knowledge, Foucault viewed the human sciences as a form of power that categorised and controlled individuals.

His first mode of objectification, namely scientific classification, was concerned with how the human sciences construct particular ways of knowing so that people come to recognise themselves as objects and subjects of scientific knowledge. In the human sciences, subjects are measured via a variety of procedures, such as intelligence tests or skin-fold callipers, and the results are statistically analysed so that the subjects can be classified, via norms and standard deviations, into select groups. Foucault (1970) argued, accordingly, that the human sciences help to construct universal classifications of people, and in the process people become objectified. The body under the clinical gaze of doctors, for example, becomes an anatomical machine, that is, subjects become objects under the regime of medical truth. The power effect of this objectification process results, for example, in the production of 'asthmatics', 'diabetics' and 'epileptics'.

A number of scholars have drawn on Foucault's concerns to reflect on the power effect of the sport sciences (e.g. Duquin, 1994; Harvey and Sparks, 1991; Pronger, 1995; Whitson and MacIntosh, 1990). Brian Pronger (1995), for example, drew on Foucault in arguing that 'gross anatomy' classes encourage physical education and sport students to view the body as an object or machine. This reductive view of the body, he argued, tends to ignore the social and emotional aspects of human movement and infiltrates the practice of sport and exercise professionals in an oppressive manner. Within this book we continue to examine how individuals become objects under sport science but also subject to this knowledge. Chapter 3, for example, examines how scientific discourse shapes discursive understandings of the healthy body and, accordingly, influences movement practices.

Foucault (1983a: 208) called his second mode of objectification 'dividing practices'. He explained that primarily through the workings of science and the related development of institutions such as mental asylums, jails, schools and hospitals, subjects get divided into categories such as: 'the mad and the sane, the sick and the healthy, the criminals and the "good boys"' (208): or more broadly speaking, the socially constructed division between the abnormal and normal. The knowledge that helps create the divisions simultaneously justifies the confinement, isolation and control of certain groups of people. Foucault (1965) illustrated, for example, how the growth of the human sciences during the Classical Age corresponded with the objectification of certain individuals as 'mad' or 'debauched' and the subsequent isolation of these individuals in the institutions vacated by the lepers. Dividing practices are, therefore, concerned with social and spatial divisions and the control of individuals and, more broadly, populations. Foucault was concerned that these divisions produced, and were reflective of, particular sets of oppressive power relations, such as between doctors–patients, scientists–subjects and heterosexuals–homosexuals. Yet he was also concerned with how the diverse workings of science and related institutions help to produce subjects that are internally divided or dispersed. These internal divisions can explain the inner tensions and contradictions that many people may experience.

To help examine the workings of science and its associated dividing practices, Foucault developed various theoretical tools to understand the complex linkages between the development and dissemination of knowledge, the construction of subjectivities and the workings of power. He began developing and using these 'tools' within his archaeological studies.

The archaeological approach for examining humans

Within his archaeological studies Foucault (1965, 1970, 1972, 1973) examined how the knowledge that produced the scientific classifications and dividing practices was created, legitimated and mutated. His aim in undertaking these studies was *not* to suggest that the knowledge produced in the human sciences was false or in need of replacement by a more superior form of knowledge. Foucault (1973: xix) stated bluntly, for example, in his examination of the development of medical practices: 'I should like to make it plain ... that this book has not been written in favour of one kind of medicine as against another kind of medicine, or against medicine and in favour of an absence of medicine'. His academic objective was, nevertheless, critical as he wanted to reveal how 'ideas could appear, sciences be established, experience be reflected in philosophies, rationalities be formed, only, perhaps, to dissolve and vanish soon afterwards' (Foucault, 1970: xxii). In this manner, he argued that the human sciences should not necessarily be treated reverentially but could be considered as specific *games* of truth that, at times, undergo abrupt *rule* changes.

Underpinning Foucault's archaeological approach and indeed all of his work, was a 'systematic skepticism toward all anthropological universals' (Florence, 1998: 461). To reveal particular anthropological 'universals' as historical constructs, Foucault (1970) examined different systems of thought in three broad epochs: the Renaissance, the Classical Age, and Modernity. In discussing these three historical periods he introduced his notion of the *episteme*, which Foucault (1970: xxii) referred to as the 'epistemological field' of a particular time:

> This episteme may be suspected of being something like a world-view, a slice of history common to all branches of knowledge, which imposes on each one the same norms and postulates, a general stage of reason, a certain structure of thought that the men [sic] of a particular period cannot escape – a great body of legislation written once and for all by some anonymous hand.
>
> (Foucault, 1972: 191)

Foucault argued that within different *epistemes*, different sets of understandings or discursive conditions shape what can be known but simultaneously obscure other forms of knowledge.[1] He further suggested that knowledge generated in different *epistemes*, including modernity, was not necessarily superior or inferior to previous knowledge but was simply subject to the discursive conditions of a different epistemological field. In this manner, Foucault called into question the modernist notion that scientific knowledge accumulates in a unilinear fashion and contributes to human advancement. Moreover, he rejected the positivistic belief that knowledge could be constructed objectively. In contrast, he argued that knowledge was always subject to certain epistemic conditions and that truth, accordingly, was always a 'partial, localised version of reality' (Rail, 2002: 183–184). Genevieve Rail (2002) suggests that Foucault's scepticism of grand narratives and modernist ideals of human progress resonates with aspects of postmodernist thinking.

The archaeological examinations that Foucault undertook were largely driven by his anti-humanism and anti-essentialism. Foucault was critical of how humanism acted to position the 'individual' at the centre of research focus and as free, authentic, rational, unitary and fully coherent. In contrast he regarded the individual as the *effect* of the workings of power. He was concerned, accordingly, with humanism's promotion of the idea of an inner or essential human condition that, irrespective of social context, could seemingly be relied upon for developing further understandings about humans. Yet his greatest concern related to the manner in which humanism had not necessarily acted to free or liberate humans, but had served as a conceptual tool of domination that resulted in more constrained modes of human behaviour:

> These sciences, which have so delighted our 'humanity' for over a century, have their technical matrix in the petty, malicious minutiae of the disciplines and their investigations. These investigations are perhaps to psychology, psychiatry, pedagogy, criminology, and so many other strange sciences, what the terrible power of investigation was to the calm knowledge of the animals, the plants or the earth.
>
> (Foucault, 1991a: 226)

With these concerns in mind, Foucault (1972) argued that historians have typically focused on extended periods of time in a manner that propagates images of relative stability and continuity; images that help support the centrality and rationality of human consciousness and the doctrine of humanism:

> If the history of thought could remain the locus of uninterrupted continuities, if it could endlessly forge connections that no analysis could undo without abstraction, if it could weave, around everything that men [sic] say and do, obscure synthesis that anticipate for him, prepare him, and lead him endlessly towards his future, it would provide a privileged shelter for the sovereignty of consciousness.
>
> (Foucault, 1972: 12)

Foucault's anti-humanist desires encouraged his focus on the discontinuities, ruptures and transformations in the history of ideas to de-centre the human subject and de-emphasise the role of human consciousness. Within *The Archaeology of Knowledge* Foucault (1972) attempted to show how the human sciences developed in relative autonomy and how they could be conceptualised as having their own systems of self-regulation: systems that worked in relation to the concept he termed *discourse*. In contrast to his earlier works, he shifted his focus away from the analysis of social institutions, such as mental asylums and hospitals, to focus on a more abstract analysis of the workings of discourse. Archaeology can, therefore, be considered as a method of historical analysis concerning discourse or systems of thought: or more precisely, as the analysis of the unconscious 'rules of formation' (Foucault, 1972: 38) which shape the workings and emergence of discourse in the human sciences. So what is a discourse?

Foucault's archaeological understandings of discourse

Discourse was important to examine, Foucault contended, as the workings of discourse help provide the appearance of stability and continuity amongst the human sciences. Foucault, however, illustrated that when one examines a scientific book or the works of an author or an academic discipline or even his own works, that there are contradictions, gaps, confusions and oppositions. This recognition encouraged Foucault to argue that the totality of statements within a given science or book only appear to have continuity due to the workings of 'discourse'. Within *The Archaeology of Knowledge* Foucault (1972) attempted to clarify his concept of discourse. He began by discussing the relevance of written or spoken *statements* within scientific works. He focused narrowly on 'statements' as he believed that they were the building blocks of discourses or 'the atom of a discourse' (Foucault, 1972: 80). Statements in this respect were not conceived as the expression of a *secret structure* but as real practices in certain locations at a certain time. He stated, accordingly, that the analysis of discourse was the analysis of the 'punctuality in which it appears, and in that temporal dispersion that enables it to be repeated, known, forgotten, transformed, utterly erased, and hidden, far from all view, in the dust of books' (Foucault, 1972: 25). Foucault, accordingly, treated discourse as actual occurrences or events.

Foucault (1972) used the word 'discourse' in multiple ways and suggested that this 'fluctuating meaning' (80) was not a fault of imprecision but a strength that added to the complexity and usage of the concept. He suggested, nevertheless, that he used the term in three prime ways: 'treating it sometimes as the general domain of all statements, sometimes as an individualizable group of statements, and sometimes as a regulated practice that accounts for a certain number of statements' (Foucault, 1972: 80). Let us examine each of these meanings in turn with respect to sporting examples.

The first meaning suggests that discourse, as a reference to the *general domain of statements*, is concerned with statements that coalesce within specific social contexts and have some particular meaning or effect. The *effect* refers to a momentary production of a phenomenon, such as the production of objects, subjects or conceptual understandings. The discursive effect could accordingly produce, for example, a soccer ball, a soccer player, a passion for soccer or the official and unofficial rules that shape participation in soccer. This does not mean, however, that an object such as a soccer ball does not exist in material terms before the discourse of a soccer ball is enunciated, but that one would simply not recognise the spherical object as a soccer ball. Foucault (1972) stressed that the objects of discourse (e.g. soccer) and the discourses that constitute those objects (e.g. discourses of soccer) emerge at the same time. The related task of the archaeologist is to expose this emergence and examine the workings of discourse as related to social change and transformation.

Foucault argued that the complex workings of discourse were influential in the construction of 'subjects' or, more specifically, disunited or fragmented subjects. The discourse of soccer, for example, does not simply objectify the participant in soccer as *a* 'soccer player'. The participant in soccer is also subject to the workings of various discourses that shape their identities as soccer players. Given that individuals are subject to multiple discourses, Foucault (1972: 55) argued that discourse analysis can illustrate the 'dispersion ... and ... discontinuity' of the subject. Foucault's theory of discourse, therefore, acts to decentre the significance of individual humans and consciousness: 'Thus conceived, discourse is not the majestically unfolding manifestation of a thinking, knowing, speaking subject, but, on the contrary, a totality, in which the dispersion of the subject and his discontinuity with himself may be determined' (55). Foucault, accordingly, rejected the liberal-humanist notion of the self that presupposes the subject as 'stable, unified and whole' (Andrews, 2000: 115). Provocatively, Foucault (1970: xxiii) even suggested: 'it is comforting ... to think that man is a recent invention, a figure not two centuries old, a new wrinkle in our knowledge, and that he will disappear again as soon as that knowledge has discovered a new form'. Jon Simons (1995: 25) summarised that Foucault positions humanism as a 'failed philosophical project because it takes Man to be its foundation for knowledge, whereas he is one of its effects'. Foucault's deeply anti-humanist position shaped his later discussion of the technologies of the self: how individuals begin to understand themselves as human beings within discursive power relations (see Chapter 7).

Foucault's (1972) second usage of the term discourse referred to an *individualisable group of statements* or to statements that refer to the same phenomenon, such as discourses of rugby union or discourses of health. Although some discourses appear to refer to the same phenomenon, these discourses should not be viewed as necessarily unified or consistent. Discourses of rugby, for example, can be linked to sets of statements that are concerned with rugby but nevertheless construct the sport in a divergent manner, such as a sport suitable for gentlemen or barbarians (e.g. Dunning and Sheard, 1979). Despite these seemingly contradictory understandings, the multiple discourses of rugby help identify the sport as different from other competitive movement activities, such as soccer or boxing. Yet rugby is not simply spoken or written into existence. Foucault (1972: 44) explained: 'the conditions necessary for the appearance of an object of discourse ... are many and imposing. Which means that one cannot speak of anything at any time'. Indeed, he suggested that the objectification processes were the complex result of various social practices, historical conditions and social relations. In this respect, the concept of a discourse is related to more than the workings of linguistics, yet he stated: 'Of course, discourses are composed of signs; but what they do is more than use these signs to designate things. It is this *more* that renders them irreducible to the language (*langue*) and to speech' (Foucault, 1972: 49, italics in original). Foucault, more specifically, emphasised that discourses should not be treated as 'groups of signs (signifying elements referring to contents or representations) but as practices that systematically form the objects of which they speak' (1972: 49). Discourse should, therefore, *not* be considered as a simple translation between reality and language but as *practices* that shape perceptions of reality.

This leads to Foucault's (1972: 80) third usage of the term discourse, as a 'regulated practice that accounts for a certain number of statements'. By this usage he is referring to the unwritten 'rules' that guide social practices and help to produce and regulate the production of statements that, correspondingly, control what can be understood and perceived but at the same time, act to obscure. Let us provide an example to help clarify how discourse, in specific locations, can shape but also obscure perception and social practices. Within some countries such as Iran, Argentina or England, soccer may typically be thought of as a male sport. This particular discourse of soccer, or way of knowing soccer encourages male participation but acts to limit recognition that females may enjoy or even participate in the sport. In New Zealand, in contrast, multiple discourses circulate that act to position soccer as a sport for foreigners, gentle males, or as a girl's sport. These discourses undervalue soccer in 'the order' of male participation sport and help to prevent recognition of the skill and physicality needed to play the sport, while indirectly supporting a version of masculinity that centres on male aggression and physicality. This discourse, nevertheless, encourages greater participation in soccer by females, although in a manner that marginalises recognition of their accomplishments. These sporting discourses can, therefore, be regarded as rules that shape particular social practices and gender relations in specific contexts.

Foucault (1972: 129–130) used the term *archive,* not to refer to a dusty collection of historical documents, but to the unwritten discursive rules connected to the '*system of enunciability* ... that causes a multiplicity of statements to emerge as so many regular events, as so many things to be dealt with and manipulated'. Archaeological analysis is, accordingly, concerned with excavating the *archive* to reveal the interplay between discourses and the associated sets of rules that shape/constrain reality, and guide social practices. Foucault, in summary, was interested in examining the various procedures that regulated the production, prohibition and related workings of discourse in different social contexts and time periods.

Although Foucault's understandings of the rules of formation of discourse have been influential within social science research, we are unaware of any sport and exercise researchers who have drawn *directly* from Foucault's *archaeological* method.[2] In Chapter 3, given this recognition, we provide an example of how to employ his archaeological tools to help to understand the discursive construction of the fit body. This chapter, more specifically, introduces and provides details of how to analyse the discursive objects and formations, enunciations (statements), concepts and theories that define contemporary knowledge about how to practise 'fitness'.

Foucault (1972: 208) acknowledged that his theory of discourse and historical change was 'still (at the) rudimentary stage of mapping'.[3] He further recognised that what he had obscured and de-emphasised within his theory of discourse, to its detriment, was the workings of power. This came to fruition in his subsequent books (e.g. *Discipline and Punish* and *The History of Sexuality, Volume 1*) with their explicit focus on the conjoint workings of power and knowledge on the body. Foucault's shift to a focus on the body and material workings of power corresponded to his shift away from archaeology to genealogy, and with the sophistication of his critical approach for investigating the social lives of humans. Yet it should not be thought that Foucault abandoned archaeology. In contrast, Foucault (1980e: 85) stated that archaeology is the 'appropriate methodology of analysis of local discursivities, and "genealogy" would be the tactics whereby, on the basis of the descriptions of these local discursivities, the subjected knowledges which were thus released would be brought into play'. In this manner, he envisaged that archaeology and genealogy complemented each other. So what is genealogy?

Foucault's genealogical approach

Genealogy is an important analytical tool that Foucault (1977c) adapted from Nietzsche. In short, genealogy is an examination of the relations between history, discourse, bodies and power in an attempt to help to understand social practices or objects of knowledge that 'continue to exist and have value for us' (Foucault 1977c: 146). Genealogy, accordingly, provides a 'history of the present' (Foucault, 1991a: 31) and reflects, what sport historian Richard Holt (1989) believes is the necessary interdependence between the disciplines of history and sociology, to help identify and understand contemporary social practices and issues. A prime outcome of genealogical research 'is to discover that truth or being do not lie at the root of what we know and what we are, but the exteriority of accidents' (Foucault, 1977c: 146). Foucault believed, accordingly, that history is discontinuous, and origins are historical/social constructions.

Foucault's approach to genealogical examination revolved around analyses of descent (*Herkunft*) and emergence (*Entstehung*). The analysis of descent is concerned with 'bodies' and their articulations with discourse throughout history, but not in a manner aimed at constructing concrete and absolute accounts of bodily practices. The analysis of descent, more specifically, aimed 'to expose a body totally imprinted by history and the process of history's destruction of the body' (Foucault, 1977c: 148). Foucault asserted that discourses constitute a coherency of self – through bodily practices, thoughts and beliefs – to the extent that people are unaware of their sense of self being socially constructed over time through disparity. The goal of an analysis of descent is, therefore, to show how the illusion of 'bodily' (i.e. self)coherency and naturality has been constituted, not through a tidy and rational historical process, but through contingency, chance, accidents, and even mistakes. Subjects are, therefore, not the living evidence of destiny or design or even modernist beliefs of rationality, control and progress.

Foucault asserted that the recognition of contingency in the play of life could be liberating; it helps to remind us that we do not have to perform, think or believe in set or rigid ways. Hence, ethics, modes of existence and bodily practices, including sport and exercise activities, are potentially open for negotiation. This negotiation process occurs, however, in social realms where all voices do not have the same opportunities to be heard. This concern with social voices of domination and subjection becomes the analysis task of *emergence*. The analysis of emergence aims to reveal the productive influence of the workings of power over time. However, this analysis does not aim to single out particular individuals as solely responsible for systems of domination or oppression. The analysis of emergence, in contrast, is concerned with examining the historical workings, shifts and junctures of relations of power between people. In this sense, Foucault (1977c) asserted that current power relations are not secure but are subject to change; therefore, people can be active in attempting to change the workings of power. He accepted, however, that this political task is fraught with problems due to the incredible complexity of attempting to understand the workings of discourse/power in conjunction with the workings of contingency. Thus, it is possible that individuals or groups with specific political intentions can enact social change in a way that acts *against* their desires. Foucault was accordingly reluctant to offer 'universal' strategies for political problems.

Although Foucault was pessimistic about controlling the workings of power he was not resigned to accepting social practices or beliefs that *he* believed were unjust or unsound. His genealogy of discipline and punishment, for example, can be read as a protest against the dominant beliefs that inform penal practices (Foucault, 1991a). His genealogy of sexuality similarly aimed to promote subjugated knowledge and marginalised voices as acts of resistance against oppressive social practices. Foucault, more generally, stated that his genealogies aimed to provide a history of the development of dominant and marginalised knowledge that has influenced individuals' understandings of themselves, to help make people aware of how these truth games still exert contemporary influence. Foucault's genealogical approach, therefore, aimed to raise critical consciousness of the workings of discourse and power. We examine next how Foucault conceptualised the working of 'power'.

Power relations

Foucault (1978) recognised that he needed to clarify what he meant by 'power' given that the term, although commonly used, was 'apt to lead to a number of misunderstandings ... with respect to its nature, its form, and its unity' (92). In somewhat typical fashion, Foucault defined his understanding of power with reference to what he did not mean it to be. Power, he suggested, was not a possession that could be 'acquired, seized, or shared' (Foucault, 1978: 94). Nor should it be thought of as a 'group of institutions ... that ensure the subservience of the citizens of a given state' (92), or a manner of subjugation that operated via laws or a 'system of domination exerted by one group over another' (92). Thus, although governments, social institutions, laws and dominant groups are commonly assumed to *hold* power, Foucault emphasised that they represent 'only the terminal forms power takes' (92).

Foucault (1978) argued that it would be negligent to begin an analysis of the workings of power by assuming 'that the sovereignty of the state, the form of the law, or the over-all unity of domination are given at the outset' (92). Foucault was not undermining the social importance of governments, dominant groups or laws, nor neglecting the massive social inequalities that exist yet he thought it more important to understand how power was exercised with respect to the formation and legitimation of these influential social phenomena. He asserted that dominant individuals, groups, corporations and states do not arrive at their position because they have power, but they become influential due to the contingent workings and, at times, tactical usages of 'discourses'. This, according to Foucault (1983a: 223), 'makes all the more politically necessary the analysis of power relations in a given society, their historical formation, the source of their strength or fragility' in order to understand possibilities and tactics for transforming the workings of power.

Foucault's analysis of the relations of power extended beyond a focus of the State or business elites because, as he explained, the 'State, for all the omnipotence of its apparatuses, is far from being able to occupy the whole field of actual power relations, and further because the State can only operate on the basis of other, already existing power relations' (Foucault, 1980d: 122). In similar fashion, he was critical of analyses of power that reductively focused on the economy or juridical structures. Under juridical theory, for example, 'power is taken to be a right, which one is able to possess like a commodity, and which one can in consequence transfer or alienate ... through a legal act or through some act that establishes a right ...' (Foucault, 1980e: 88). Yet Foucault was critical of conceptualising power as a possession because he believed it encourages one to question: 'Who then has power and what has he [sic] in mind? What is the aim of someone who possesses power?' (Foucault, 1980e: 97). Moreover, he suggested that attempts to answer these questions typically lead, in circular fashion, back to a focus on the law and the economy. Foucault (1980e), however, was adamant that power was not in a 'subordinate position relative to the economy' (89) nor was it 'ultimately answerable to, the economy' (89). Also, he thought that the law was a somewhat crude and coercive method of attempting to control people: a method that was often ineffectual in its attempts. He relatedly thought it problematic to conceive of power in a juridical or economical manner.

Foucault's (1983a: 217) political focus turned away from attempting to answer 'What is power? and Where does power come from?', to an examination of *how* is power exercised and what, as a result, actually occurs? He suggested that this focus avoids treating power as an ontological substance in favour of a 'flat and empirical' (217) examination: a matter-of-fact examination that recognises power as fundamentally concerned with 'relations between individuals (or between groups)' (217). 'Power' from a Foucauldian perspective refers to relations between people. In fact, Foucault (1987: 11) reflected: 'I hardly ever use the word "power" and if I do sometimes, it is always a short cut to the expression ... the relationships of power'. Foucault (1983a: 221) defined a relationship of power as an action by one person to help guide another's *conduct* or direct 'the possible field of action of others'. This implies that an individual's action, within a relationship of power, does not determine or physically force the actions of others. A coach and an athlete, for example, exist within a specific power relation, in that the coach typically attempts to guide the athlete's conduct or performance. Although the coach can develop strategies to direct the actions of the athlete, such as by keeping an athlete on the bench, the athlete is still relatively 'free' to decide his/her response and ultimately whether he/she will continue to be coached. The actions of the athlete can also reciprocally influence the actions of the coach. If the athlete, for example, were to tell the coach that he/she is thinking of quitting this might induce a change in the coach's future actions. Thus, although the coach and athlete's relationship of power may be unbalanced, they can still be thought of as existing within a specific power relation.

This sporting example helps to reveal an important aspect of Foucault's (1983a: 221) understanding of power relations: 'that power is exercised only over free subjects, and only insofar as they are free'. In contrast to traditional assumptions about power, Foucault did not view power and freedom as mutually exclusive but accepted that freedom (not an *essential* freedom) is a precondition for a relationship of power. This means that within a relation of power 'there is necessarily the possibility of resistance, for if there were no possibility of resistance – of violent resistance, of escape, of ruse, of strategies that reverse the situation – there would be no relations of power' (Foucault, 1987: 12). Without the possibility of recalcitrance the relationship would be one of violence or physical determination.

Let us provide another sporting example to help differentiate a power relation from a relationship of violence or physical constraint. In this example, we imagine a young boy whose poor family was paid by a deceiving entrepreneur so that the boy could live and race camels in a foreign country. After time spent abroad the boy has become desperately homesick but is unable to return home as his 'owners' do not pay him money or allow him to keep his passport. The young camel jockey is, in fact, a slave in a relationship of physical restraint. A relation of power, in contrast, even if unbalanced, is *not* a 'system of domination which controls everything' (Foucault, 1987: 13) but is one that allows opportunity for freedom.

Foucault's seemingly simplistic view of power as a relationship between 'free' people in which one tries to govern the actions of others, provided him with a platform for the development of his radical but influential ideas concerning the workings of power: ideas that stood in noticeable contrast to Marxist, hegemony theory and juridical interpretations of power (Pringle, 2005). Indeed, rather than conceiving of power as being located in a central source from which 'secondary and descendant forms would emanate' (Foucault, 1978: 93), Foucault conceptualised power as *omnipresent* as it was 'produced from one moment to the next, at every point, or rather in every relation from one point to another' (93). In this manner he conceptualised power as a *capillary-like network* that 'ends by forming a dense web that passes through apparatuses and institutions, without being exactly localized in them' (96). He further conceived that embedded within this power network was a multiplicity of 'points of resistance' (95) or struggle, each of which was a special case that should not be simply viewed as reactions or passive rebounds against the workings of power.

The workings of power, accordingly, were deemed to stem 'from below' and not from some fundamental opposition between 'rulers and ruled' (Foucault, 1978: 94) or the State and its citizens. Foucault (1980e: 99) therefore advocated an '*ascending* analysis of power', which he suggested should be conducted initially through an examination of the:

> infinitesimal mechanisms, which have their own history, their own trajectory, their own techniques and tactics, and then see how these mechanisms of power have been – and continue to be – invested, colonised, utilised, involuted, transformed, displaced, extended etc., by ever more general mechanisms and by forms of global domination.
>
> (Foucault, 1980e: 99)

In this manner, Foucault did not deny that global forms of domination might exist, such as sexism or racism, but suggested that to examine how such problematic forms of power operate one should not 'attempt some kind of deduction of power starting from its centre and aimed at the discovery of the extent to which it reproduces itself down to and including the most molecular elements of society' (Foucault, 1980e: 99). In contrast, he encouraged researchers to begin an analysis of power at the micro-levels of society. For example, one could initially examine relations of power between males and females in the family or in sporting contexts, and if such an examination revealed practices of disharmonious dominance then, he suggested, 'what must be shown is the manner in which they [i.e. the power relations] are invested and annexed by more global phenomena' (Foucault, 1980e: 99). In other words, one could undertake an ascending analysis of power to understand how gender relations at the micro-levels of society articulate with sexist practices in global sporting competitions, such as the Olympics.

Foucault (1978: 95) further theorised that 'there is no power that is exercised without a series of aims and objectives'. Yet he stressed that these aims and objectives should not be thought of as the independent 'choice or decision of an individual subject' (95) but were related to the somewhat anonymous workings of *discourse* or the rules of formation that shape and obscure perceptions of social reality. In this manner, Foucault (1978: 100) linked and adapted his theory of discourse to the material workings of power and argued: 'it is in discourse that power and knowledge are joined together'. Accordingly, he suggested that the rationality that underpins the exercising of power often appears:

> perfectly clear, the aims decipherable, and yet it is often the case that no one is there to have invented them, and few who can be said to have formulated them: an implicit characteristic of the great anonymous, almost unspoken strategies which coordinate the loquacious tactics whose 'inventors' or decisionmakers are often without hypocrisy.
>
> (Foucault, 1978: 95)

Rugby union within New Zealand, for example, is typically known as the country's national sport, yet the 'power' source of this nationalistic discourse is somewhat unidentifiable; it is everywhere and no-where in particular, circulating in a dispersed fashion through multiple networks of social relations in a manner that simultaneously helps produce rugby's social dominance.

A consequence of Foucault's ideas concerning 'power' is that relationships of power can be perceived as *productive* rather than prohibitive or repressive. In other words, it is the daily and ceaseless relations that occur between all people in all locations that ultimately *produce* subjectivities, economic systems, laws and, more generally, social realities and transformations. The 'major dominations' (Foucault, 1978: 94), such as racism and sexism, are also the effects or products that are generated by the tangled web of power relations. Yet, at the same time, so are the many projects aimed at social transformation, such as the civil rights and feminist movements. In this manner, Foucault did not conceptualise relations of power as essentially positive or negative. Indeed, he asserted that the idea of a society without relations of power was a utopian fantasy. Yet Foucault (1983a: 212) was concerned with forms of domination, such as 'ethnic, social, and religious' dominations, that stem from specific relationships of power and act to limit the field of possible actions for some individuals or groups of people. He accordingly suggested:

> The problem is not of trying to dissolve them [i.e. relations of power] in the utopia of a perfectly transparent communication, but to give one's self the rules of law, the techniques of management, and also the ethics, the *ethos*, the practice of self, which would allow these games of power to be played with a minimum of domination.
>
> (Foucault, 1987: 18)

Foucault's ideas on how to make the social world a more harmonious place focused on the ability of people to cultivate new senses of self and more ethical modes of existence. He acknowledged that the ability to develop new ways of understanding one's self was a difficult challenge and it was this challenge that intrigued Foucault (1985, 1986, 1987, 1988d, 1988e) with his subsequent examinations of ethics and 'technologies of self' (as discussed in Chapter 7). However, before Foucault focused on technologies of self he was interested in examining 'technologies of domination' or the forms of power that limit the field of possible actions.

Technologies of domination: disciplinary power

Foucault's concept of power as relational, presupposed that there are multiple forms of power. In a lecture in 1976 Foucault stated that the form of power he was primarily interested in examining was one that was: 'susceptible of producing discourses of truth that in a society such as ours are endowed with such potent effects' (Foucault, 1980e: 93). The 'potent effects' he was particularly concerned about referred to the control, judgement and normalisation of subjects in such a way that they were 'destined to a certain mode of living or dying' (94). Foucault (1991a) called this type of power 'disciplinary power' (105) and argued that the emergence of this power, during the seventeenth and eighteenth centuries, was intimately linked with the development of capitalist states and the 'man [sic] of modern humanism' (141). Foucault's writings on the topic gained early attention from sport sociologists. Jean-Marie Brohm (1981) suggested, for example, that sport is possibly the best exemplary context for conceptualising Foucault's understandings of the workings of disciplinary power and the political investment of the body. So what is disciplinary power and how did it emerge and proliferate?

Foucault (1991a) proposed, within his genealogy of punishment and the 'power to judge' (23), that during medieval times the rule of the King, or sovereign power, acted as a central form of social control. This form of control stemmed in a top-down manner and was focused on violent public spectacles involving executions and torture. These public displays were a 'policy of terror: to make everyone aware, through the body of the criminal, of the unrestrained presence of the sovereign' (49). Yet by the 'beginning of the nineteenth century ... the great spectacle of physical punishment disappeared; the tortured body was avoided; the theatrical representation of pain was excluded from punishment' (14). Foucault commented that many believe that this reduction in the severity of physical punishments was linked to an assumed growth in human civility. Foucault (1991a: 7), however, suggested that this reduction 'has been attributed too readily and too emphatically to a process of "humanization", thus dispensing with the need for further analysis'. In contrast, he suggested that the disappearance of the spectacle of punishment was linked to the emergence of disciplinary power: a form of power focused on the control and discipline of bodies and exercised fundamentally 'by means of surveillance' (104). Although he recognised that the techniques of disciplinary power – such as the use of hierarchical observation, timetables and systems of rank – had long been in existence in monasteries and armies, he argued that during the course of the seventeenth and eighteenth centuries these specific techniques dispersed and pervaded social life: 'First the hospital, then the school, then, later the workshop' (224) to help produce the disciplinary society.

These disciplinary techniques focused on the body as the 'object and target of power' (Foucault, 1991a: 136) in a manner that shaped and trained the body. Yet the techniques of discipline were different from those employed in slavery; they dispensed with the high cost of policing and the risks of violent retaliation, were relatively invisible and aimed to increase the mastery of each subject over his own body. Foucault further explained that disciplinary power:

> defined how one may have a hold over others' bodies, not only so that they may do what one wishes, but so that they may operate as one wishes, with the techniques, the speed and the efficiency that one determines. Thus discipline produces subjected and practised bodies, 'docile' bodies.
>
> (Foucault, 1991a: 137–138)

Docile or well-disciplined bodies were economically efficient but politically obedient: bodies that were ideal for employment within the capitalist workforce. Indeed, disciplinary power was considered by Foucault (1991a) to be 'one of the great inventions of bourgeois society' (105) and was integral to 'the constitution of industrial capitalism and of the type of society that is its accompaniment' (105). In this manner, Foucault argued, in an oft repeated quote, that the body is 'directly involved in a political field; power relations have an immediate hold upon it; they invest it; mark it, train it, torture it, force it to carry out tasks, to perform ceremonies, to emit signs' (25). Foucault's focus on the body as the target for the workings of power, rather than the individual, was significant as it reflected his anti-essentialism. The individual, according to Foucault, was already the *effect* of the workings of power and not some inner essence.

Foucault's focus on the politics of the body has been influential within sport research through stimulating theoretical debate (e.g. Andrews, 1993; Cole, 1994; Gruneau, 1993; Harvey and Sparkes, 1991; Maguire, 2002), a turn to poststructuralism within feminist analyses (e.g. Cole, 1994; Markula, 1995; Theberge, 1991), a greater recognition of the importance of the body and embodied representations (e.g. Hargreaves, 1986; Loy, 1991; Loy et al., 1993; Rail and Harvey, 1995), and analyses of the production of particular sporting bodies (e.g. Chapman, 1997; Duncan, 1994; Hargreaves, 1986; Heikkala, 1993; Kirk, 1996; Markula, 1995, 2000; Pringle and Markula, 2005). John Hargreaves (1986), more generally, provided an exemplary summary of the interplay between sport, disciplinary power and bodies:

> The primary focus of attention in sport . . . is the body and its attributes . . . this need not imply that the mind is not involved . . . but it is the body that constitutes the most striking symbol as well as the material core of the sporting activity. The primacy accorded to the mind in western civilization has ensured that . . . the body has been almost entirely eliminated from social-science discourse. . . . [Nevertheless] power is literally incorporated or invested in the body, most obviously perhaps through such practices as gymnastics exercises, muscle-building, nudism, practices glorifying the body beautiful, and insistent, meticulous work on the bodies of children, hospital patients, keep-fit enthusiasts and sport participants. Such work reproduces the social body: it exemplifies the materiality of power and culture in the sense that social relations are the outcome of material operations on the bodies of individuals carried out with the aid of a vast economy and technology of control. The body is not the object of consensus – it is the site of socials struggles.
>
> (Hargreaves, 1986: 13)

To understand how disciplinary power can have such a hold on bodies it is necessary to examine the actual 'techniques and tactics of domination' (Foucault, 1980e: 102) and the material operators of power.

Examining disciplinary techniques

Although Foucault (1991a: 139) did not aim to write the complete history of the different disciplinary institutions he did analyse 'some of the essential techniques' of discipline, which he classified into three broad groups: (1) the art of distributions, (2) the control of activity and (3) the organisation of geneses. These techniques are fundamentally concerned with controlling the location of individuals and the production of work – via manipulation of space or architecture, the organisation of time (e.g. rigid timetables) and the use of graduated, repetitive and systematised 'exercises' – to help produce docile but productive bodies. These techniques, as Debra Shogan (1999: 19) demonstrated, 'map very well onto sport, thus illustrating that the classificatory and controlling impulses of modern power are also central to high-performance sport'. In this book we also illustrate how these disciplinary techniques relate closely to aid in the production of docile but productive bodies within a fitness centre (see Chapter 4 for a detailed analysis of these techniques) and in sporting contexts (Chapter 6), and why sport can be considered a 'modern discipline' (Chapter 6).

The employment of disciplinary technologies helps constitute *different* individuals. Within a fitness centre, for example, disciplinary technologies help produce a multitude of bodies (e.g. overweight, underweight, fit, unfit, beautiful, masculine, feminine, muscular and emaciated). These broadly defined subject positions, however, do not reveal specific knowledge about the subject located in each of these positions. Yet such knowledge is also necessary for the smooth production of disciplined bodies. An exercise psychologist, for example, with knowledge of a client's psychological profile could design an appropriate mental skills training programme to aid in the production of the motivated exerciser. The collection of personal knowledge is, accordingly, an important disciplinary technology.

Foucault (1991a: 170) explained that personal knowledge is collected via the use of three 'instruments; hierarchical observation, normalizing judgment and their combination in a procedure that is specific to it, the examination'. These three instruments help transform athletes into 'objects of knowledge' (Heikkala, 1993: 401) so that they can be more efficiently controlled and shaped. Through hierarchical observation, for example, a coach can implement additional workouts for the unfit, skill sessions for the unskilled, and punishing drills for the tardy. Hierarchical observation, therefore, reflects the connection between visibility and power: a visible body is a knowable body that can subsequently become subject to the workings of power. However, it is very difficult for a single pair of disciplinary eyes to gaze on the actions of all workers or competitors, hence the need for a series of supporting eyes to contribute to the surveillance. Within professional rugby league, for example, the referee, touch 'judges', surveillance cameras, participants and even the spectators contribute to the hierarchical observation of the sporting event and act to help control the sporting bodies.

The processes of surveillance subject each individual to a gaze of normalising judgement: a judgement typically accompanied by a whole schema of punishments, 'from light physical punishments to minor deprivations and petty humiliations ... for the slightest departures from correct behaviour (Foucault, 1991a: 178). These punishments are designed to encourage subjects to desire, at the least, to be normal. Yet Foucault reported that acts of punishment are often best avoided in favour of rewards: 'The lazy are more encouraged by the desire to be rewarded in the same way as the diligent than by the fear of punishment' (180). Techniques of normalisation, therefore, revolve around a 'double system: gratification – punishment' (180).

Foucault (1991a: 184) asserted that normalisation is 'one of the great instruments of power'. Yet this does not mean that normalisation is akin to the production of clones or dupes. Indeed, the 'power of normalization', according to Foucault (1991a), 'imposes homogeneity; but it individualizes by making it possible to measure gaps, to determine levels, to fix specialties and to render the differences useful by fitting them one to another' (184). The most effective means of individualising occurs through use of 'the examination' (Foucault, 1991a: 184), as it measures, classifies, differentiates, punishes, rewards, records and qualifies subjects: 'this is why, in all the mechanisms of discipline, the examination is highly ritualised' (Foucault, 1991a: 184). Fitness tests and sporting competitions, as examples, can be considered as forms of examinations. Within the 100 metre sprint, for instance, the performance of different competitors is measured via time and place, accolades are given to the champions, records are kept, and differentiated subjectivities are constituted.

The widespread use of 'examinations' as a disciplinary technology and the associated collation of records and files contributes to our current audit culture and helps make each individual the effect and object power (see Chapter 4). More generally, the various disciplinary techniques help to produce what Foucault referred to as the disciplinary society or panopticism.

Panopticism

Foucault (1991a) summarised that 'the existence of a whole set of techniques and institutions for measuring, supervising and correcting the abnormal' (199) is architecturally representative of the '*Panopticon*' (200). The Panopticon, perhaps the most widely discussed Foucauldian concept within the sociological study of sport (e.g. Andrews, 2000; Chapman, 1997; Cole,

1993; Cole *et al.*, 2004; Duncan, 1994; Markula, 1995; Rail and Harvey, 1995; Rinehart, 1998; Shogan, 1999), refers to Jeremy Bentham's design for a building to maximise the efficient workings of power. It consisted of a tower at its centre with windows looking down on a peripheric building that was divided into separate rooms or cells. Within each cell an individual, such as a 'madman, a patient, a condemned man, a worker or a schoolboy' (Foucault, 1991a: 200), is located in a position to be observed by the supervisor in the tower, yet is unable to tell whether he/she is being observed. Each cell becomes a small theatre 'in which every actor is alone, perfectly individualized and constantly visible' (200). The prime effect of the panopticon was to induce for each 'actor' or inmate 'a state of consciousness and permanent visibility that assures the automatic functioning of power' (200). The omnipresent gaze of authority subsequently disciplines the subjects to survey their own behaviours in a manner that renders them docile: they become their own supervisors.

On a broader scale, panopticism refers to a 'political anatomy' where the mechanisms of surveillance and discipline are no longer locked within specific buildings or institutions but 'function in a diffused, multiple, polyvalent way throughout the whole social body' (Foucault, 1991a: 208–209). Foucault argued that this occurred throughout the eighteenth and nineteenth centuries with the growth of disciplinary institutions (e.g. schools, hospitals, jails, factories, gymnasiums), the de-institutionalisation of disciplinary methods (e.g. surveillance cameras in city streets), and the gradual state-control of disciplinary technologies (e.g. government control of the police force) so that we can now speak of existing within a disciplinary society.

Margaret Duncan's (1994) textual analysis of fitness magazines provides a feminist example of the workings of panopticism. She argued that these glossy magazines – replete with stories of dieting and exercise successes combined with pictures of slender and glamorous models – help expose women to a panoptic gaze: A gaze that encourages women to survey, with degrees of distress, their own bodies for signs of abnormality against an unrealistic body image. In an attempt to explain why women do not openly resist such seemingly oppressive practices she suggested:

> The disciplinarian is a disembodied authority. The invisibility and ambiguity of the source of that gaze encourage women to believe that the body standards they apply to their own bodies are personal and private standards. Thus women may blame themselves – instead of social institutions and public practices – for their anguished relationships with 'their own bodies'...
>
> (Duncan, 1994: 50)

This example helps reveal what we might call the 'problematic efficiency' of the workings of a panoptic power. Individuals who became their own disciplinarians, for example, are not physically coerced into policing their own bodies, so the workings of power do not require an institutionalised and expensive system of supervisors. In contrast, the individuals spontaneously respond to the panoptic gaze. Yet this response does not take place in a level playing field; the possible field of appropriate actions has been effectively constrained by the technologies of dominance. The individual's freedom, therefore, does not make the situation any easier for those struggling with what they believe to be a transgressive body.

Foucault's ideas on the workings of panoptic power, nevertheless, rest on the assumption that individuals are free and this relative freedom relates to the problematic efficiency of panopticism. Neo-liberal states, for example, '*require* citizens to be free, so that citizens can assume from the state the burden of some of its former regulatory functions and impose on themselves – of their own accord – rules of conduct and mechanisms of control' (Halperin, 1995: 18, italics in original). The increase in personal freedom that occurred within the shift from the brutality of sovereign power to the development of the disciplinary society has subsequently generated considerable costs for modern citizens. These costs are associated with the efforts required to achieve normality and the range of micro-penalties associated with deviations from the 'norm'. The costs for females who are subject to a panoptic bodily gaze, for example, include the anguish of not having a 'normal' body, the efforts required with dieting and training, and even the social isolation or ridicule that can target bodies deemed 'abnormal'. The ultimate penalty for the most deviant – the criminal, the sexual pervert, or the insane – is the removal of one's liberty through incarceration.

Foucault (1991a) argued that within the disciplinary society the 'judges of normality are present everywhere ... (and) it is on them that the universal reign of the normative is based' (304). His concern with power in modern society is, accordingly, not that people are not free, but that the workings of power have proliferated and infiltrated into all reaches of social life – schools, scientific research, the media, gymnasiums, sports fields and the like – so that disciplinary techniques exert an omnipresent influence: power relations are everywhere. David Halperin summarised Foucault's concerns by stating:

> Modern liberalism has eliminated certain modes of domination only to produce many others (which do not present themselves as modes of domination and are all the more difficult to challenge or oppose); it has championed an ethic and an ideal of personal freedom while making the exercise of that freedom conditional upon personal submission to new and insidious forms of authority, to ever more deeply internalised mechanisms of constraint.
>
> (Halperin, 1995: 19)

A complex challenge for contemporary researchers stemming from Foucault's concerns with panopticism is to identify the mechanisms of disciplinary power and the related modes of domination. Within the sociological study of sport and exercise a number of scholars (e.g. Cole, 1993: Halas and Hanson, 2001; Hargreaves, 1986; Heikkala, 1993; Markula, 1995, 2001) have undertaken this challenge by examining how sport and fitness practices act as technologies of domination that encourage individuals 'into a discursive web of normalizing practices' (Markula, 2003b: 88). These studies illustrate how sport and exercise programmes discipline and normalise participants to render their conforming but biomechanically or physiologically efficient bodies 'docile'. In this broad manner we can consider fitness instructors, physical education teachers, sport scientists and coaches as 'agents of normalization' (Halas and Hanson, 2001: 123). Relatedly, we can understand how the sport and fitness disciplines are an integral part of the workings of disciplinary power in contemporary societies. Yet, more importantly, it can be recognised that 'we are all active participants in numerous relationships of power with respect to sport and fitness practices, and that the combined total of these power relations produces the overall shape of sport and fitness practices. A responsibility stems from this recognition, a responsibility that invites us to negotiate our various power relations with a sense of ethics and a desire to minimise harmful modes of domination.

Bio-power, sexuality and governmentality

The focus and mechanism of disciplinary power, as a technology of domination, was the body. This mechanism of individualisation directs the dilemma of social problems onto individuals. The health of a state, as an example, rests, in part, on the discipline of individuals to maintain a normal body size, practice safe sex, avoid harmful drugs, maintain active lifestyles and the like. Within the *The History of Sexuality, Volume 1*, Foucault (1978: 137) revealed his interest in another technology of domination that also developed in the classical period but whose target of control was much grander: 'the level of life, the species, the race, and the large-scale phenomena of population'. He called this different form of power '*a biopolitics of the population*' (139), its concern being the fostering of biological existence for the citizens of a particular state: 'propagation, births and mortality, the level of health, life expectancy and longevity, with all the conditions that can cause these to vary' (139). The exercising of a form of power designed to promote, nurture and protect life sounds optimistic, and in many cases its outcome is likely to be positive, yet Foucault also pointed to the dark side of this technology of dominance:

> Wars are no longer waged in the name of a sovereign who must be defended; they are waged on behalf of the existence of everyone; entire

> populations are mobilized for the purpose of wholesale slaughter in the name of life necessity: massacres have become vital. It is as managers of life and survival, of bodies and the race, that so many regimes have been able to wage so many wars, causing so many men [sic] to be killed. . . . The atomic situation is now at the end point of this process: the power to expose a whole population to death is the underside of the power to guarantee an individual's continued existence.
>
> (Foucault, 1978: 137)

Foucault firmly linked diverse atrocities such as the holocaust, racism, war and, on a less grand scale, the death penalty, to the functioning of bio-politics and the governance of a population. He, therefore, provided tools of analysis for understanding these atrocities. Yet he more specifically used his analysis of bio-politics to provide a context to illustrate the 'importance assumed by sex as a political issue' (1978: 145). Sexuality, he argued was directly tied to the 'disciplines of the body' (145) but also the 'regulation of populations' (145). Sexuality, therefore, straddled the two prime technologies of dominance and through doing so it gave rise to 'infinitesimal surveillances, permanent controls, extremely meticulous orderings of space, indeterminate medical or psychological examinations, to an entire micro-power concerned with the body' (146). The power of sexuality produced new subjectivities such as 'homosexuals' and 'paedophiles', new laws of social control, programmes of economic intervention (e.g. programmes designed to curb or enhance the birth rate), moral campaigns, and grand scale surveys of populations. These surveys collected information about the health of bodies, birth rates, modes of family relations, sexual connections, patterns of disease and even the overall shape and size of bodies. The knowledge provided by these surveys was essential for the productive workings of bio-politics.

Jennifer Maguire (2002: 301) summarised the necessity of this power/ knowledge nexus by stating that 'the population, like the individual body, is rendered knowable (and thus subject to regulation via normalisation) through the production of knowledge'. Thus during the same time period as the development of bio-politics, the sciences of demography, eugenics, sociology, psychoanalysis, public health and epidemiology were developed. Sexuality, in the process, became an 'object and a target' (Foucault, 1978: 147) for the workings of power, and this sexual power produced different understandings of women, men and children and different social relations, but also a greater desire for sex: to talk about it, tell the truth about it, have it, discover it, liberate it, identify with it, control it, forbid it, and confess in relation to it. Foucault, accordingly, rejected the idea that sex was simply a natural phenomena that had been socially repressed, in favour of the inverse: that a veritable explosion of sexual discourse had occurred, particularly during the Victorian era.

Foucault argued that bio-power, as similar to disciplinary power, was intimately linked to the development of capitalism: the growth of capitalism 'would not have been possible without the machinery of production and the adjustment of the phenomena of population to economic processes' (1978: 141). Capitalism, more specifically, needed techniques of power that could control a population's aptitudes without making a population 'more difficult to govern' (141). Indeed, capitalism requires a healthy, skilled, educated but also docile population in order to have a productive workforce and an efficient economy. Thus, the education and health of a population becomes a concern within modern states. In essence, bodies need to be physically educated so that they can be productive. Given this requirement, it is perhaps not surprising, that physical education has long been a core curriculum subject within schools in most Western states (see also Chapter 3 with reference to bio-politics, bodies and public health). Yet the related analysis of physical education as a governmental technology that regulates and shapes bodies has only been informed by Foucauldian theorising in more recent years (e.g. Burrows, 2004; Hargreaves, 1986; Kirk, 1998, 2004a; Wright, 2004). In Chapter 10 we contribute to this analysis by drawing on Foucault's ideas of social transformation to examine how an academic can teach as an ethical and critical pedagogue to help disrupt processes of normalisation.

Technologies of dominance: final comments

Foucault's tools concerning the workings of discourse, knowledge and power in the production of disciplined and normalised subjectivities have received increased attention over the last 15 years from scholars of sport and exercise. This attention helps reflect the utility of Foucault's cache of concepts. However, it can also cause confusion. Some might question, for example, that if athletes are suitably disciplined by their training regimes, why are there so many infamous examples of ill-disciplined athletes both on and off the field? Athletes, for example, who are involved in serious cases of violence and rape, and other deviances associated with sex, drugs, gambling and cheating. Yet such a question misunderstands Foucault's concerns about the formation and functioning of disciplinary societies. Foucault did not suggest that the spread of disciplinary technologies actually resulted in the creation of a well-disciplined or orderly society. Likewise, we suggest that one should not assume that the employment of disciplinary technologies in sport would necessarily produce well-disciplined athletes. In contrast, a major argument developed by Foucault (1991a) was that disciplinary institutions do not always produce their intended 'outcome'. He illustrated, for example, that jails have typically failed to reduce crime and may actually help produce recidivists. Likewise, we suggest that the sporting disciplines not only produce winners and 'moral characters' but also losers and the debauched, but more often subjects that are respectfully fragmented.

Concern has also been expressed that research focus on 'technologies of dominance' might result in a pessimistic representation of sport and exercise practices. Richard Gruneau (1993), for example, stated that such a focus 'can too easily deflect attention from analysing the creative possibilities, freedoms, ambiguities, and contradictions also found in sport' (104). Yet, in defence of Foucault, he never suggested that 'disciplinary powers' were the only forms of power or even the most important form. Foucault (1997f), nevertheless, acknowledged with reference to his examinations of asylums, hospitals and prisons: 'I perhaps insisted too much on the techniques of domination. What we call "discipline" is something really important in this kind of institution; but it is only one aspect of the art of governing people in our societies' (177). He further clarified: 'If one wants to analyze the genealogy of the subject in western civilization, one must take into account not only techniques of domination but also techniques of the self. One must show the interaction between these types of technique' (177). His writings after *The History of Sexuality, Volume 1* were devoted to studying techniques of the self and how the techniques of self and domination interact to produce specific 'mentalities' that work to govern people and populations.

Despite Foucault's subsequent texts and writings on the 'technologies of self' and governmentality, Jennifer Maguire (2002: 294) lamented that the sociology of sport 'is only just beginning to take notice of his later work ... [consequently] Foucault remains an incomplete figure for the field, to its detriment'. In the last section of this book we introduce Foucault's later work on the technologies of the self and the construction of ethical modes of existence. Prior to discussing this later work, however, we aim to provide examples of how Foucault's 'tool kit' of technologies of dominance can inform examinations of sport and exercise. In the next chapter we return to Foucault's concept of discourse to discuss the construction of the fit and healthy body.

Part 2

Foucauldian interpretations of the body and lived experiences in sport and exercise

Chapter 3

Knowledge and truth

Discursive construction of the fit and healthy body

This chapter aims to tease out the discursive construction of the healthy body through an archaeological and genealogical examination of physical fitness. More specifically, we combine Foucault's archaeological method to make explicit the discursive field where fitness has developed, and Foucault's genealogy to recognise how the potent combination of knowledge and power, localised in the body, acts as a general mechanism of domination in western society. In addition, this chapter is based on a reading of a variety of media texts around the health benefits of physical activity. Therefore, a further purpose of this chapter is to provide an example of how to conduct a Foucauldian analysis of a mediated discourse. There are several Foucauldian inspired studies that have examined the mediated discourse surrounding sport from a cultural studies perspective (e.g. Cole, 1996; Dworkin and Wachs, 1998) and Debra Shogan (1999) has examined the discursive construction of sport ethics. In addition, Chapters 5 and 6 in this book focus on the discursive construction of sporting identities. Therefore, readers interested in further analysis of the sporting context are directed to these chapters.

All forms of physical activity are currently closely linked to improved health, particularly under the banner of the obesity epidemic and, therefore, locating the discursive 'knots' between the physically active body and health can be of interest to researchers of physical education, sport, coaching or fitness alike. To set up our analysis of the healthy, fit body, we first elaborate on Foucault's understanding of discourse that we introduced in Chapter 2. Second, we attempt an archaeology of concepts that build into theories of the healthy body. We then embark into a genealogy to trace the construction of the fit body as an 'illness-free body'. Finally, we conclude how building an illness-free body links with Foucault's concept of bio-power or what he later referred to as governmentality.

Foucault and discourse

In his analysis of discourses, Foucault was involved in an examination of a verbal performance. As we explained in Chapter 2, discourses as groups of statements define the practices that people engage in everyday life but discursive practice provides the conditions for the function or meaning of discourse. Furthermore, discursive formations accumulate meaning within a specific cultural and historical context. Therefore, to trace the discursive formations of fitness, one should examine the historical development of the way fitness has been understood in a particular culture rather than searching for a founding moment or a founding father/mother of fitness. To do this, according to Foucault, an archaeologist should identify what are the objects, enunciations, concepts and theories that inform a particular discursive practice. Our task, therefore, is to identify precisely those objects, enunciations, concepts and theories that define how we know to practise 'fitness' in the western cultural context.

First, what are the objects of fitness knowledge? In his work, Foucault (1972) started by identifying the objects for psychopathology. Psychopathology was concerned with madness, but also related issues like motor disturbances, speech disorders and hallucinations. These were the specific topics around which the knowledge of psychopathology accumulated in specific historical circumstances. Therefore, to analyse fitness discourses, the first task is to ask what are the specific topics for knowing about fitness. Broadly speaking these topics can be, for instance, the body, health and movement (e.g. the type of movement that improves one's physical health).

Second, what are the enunciations for knowledge on fitness? To identify enunciations, Foucault (1972) asked how the objects are talked about, where the statements are found, and what types of statements exist around a particular knowledge. Fitness knowledge can be found in a variety of locations in contemporary culture. These include exercise videotapes, professional literature for fitness industry professionals, fitness conferences, popular magazines, newspapers and television programmes that contain qualitative descriptions, interpretations, scientific research, biographies, personal experiences and practical advice on fitness-related topics.

Third, Foucault (1972) asked which concepts are developed in these enunciations and how are they organised? These concepts, then, form group relations that belong to a specific discourse defining the rules of their coexistence. What fitness-specific concepts emerge from the multiple enunciations of fitness in contemporary society? Having not yet engaged in an archaeology of discourses of fitness, we can only speculate on such concepts, but they can revolve around such notions as a healthy lifestyle, the fit body and movement prescribed specifically for the purposes of physical health.

Finally, an archaeologist needs to identify the theoretical formations that evolve from the concepts. For Foucault, such theories are always strategic choices to construct certain kinds of knowledges, the discourses:

> Such discourses as economics, medicine, grammar, the science of living beings give rise to certain organizations of concepts, certain regroups of objects, certain types of enunciation, which form, according to their degree of coherence, rigours, and stability, themes or theories.
>
> (Foucault, 1972: 64)

As theories 'are regulated ways of practising the possibilities of discourse' (Foucault, 1972: 70), certain theoretical knowledge regulates the possibilities for effective and safe fitness practices. For example, choices for the correct amount, intensity and frequency of effective fitness training are formulated through the scientific principles of exercise physiology that then provides the theoretical grounding for exercise prescription. Similarly, exercise psychology provides a theory for improving exercise adherence and the motivation to exercise. However, the purpose of Foucault's archaeological analysis was not to discover the 'true' (medical, psychoanalytical or economical) knowledge that would provide secure answers to the problems we face in society, nor debate the worth of individual viewpoints in the formation of these knowledges.

> And just as one must not relate the formation of objects either to words or to things, nor that of statements either to the pure form of knowledge or to the psychological subject, nor that of concepts either to the structure of ideality or to the succession of ideas, one must not relate the formation of theoretical choices either to a fundamental *project* or to the secondary play of *opinions*.
>
> (Foucault, 1972: 70, italics in original)

While discursive formations are not necessarily scientific disciplines, they do form coherent propositions, develop exact descriptions and help verify theories. For example, rather than a scientific discipline, fitness is a coherent discursive formation based on theories, concepts and descriptions from several disciplines such as exercise physiology, psychology, nutrition or medicine. Foucault summarised that groups of elements, like fitness, that are 'formed in a regular manner by a discursive practice, and which are indispensable to the constitution of a science, although they are not necessarily destined to give rise to one, can be called *knowledge*' (Foucault, 1972: 182, italics in original). Knowledge and discursive practice, therefore, are inextricably linked. Knowledge is discursive and discursive practices form knowledge: 'knowledge is defined by the possibilities of use and appropriation offered by discourse ... there is no knowledge without discursive practice; and any discursive practice may be defined by the knowledge that it forms' (Foucault, 1972: 182–183).

We can conclude that archaeology is the analysis of how knowledge and discourse are intertwined into societal practices as we know them in a particular historical moment and in a particular societal context. To engage in an archaeology of fitness one would need to examine the discursive practices employed in fitness behaviours and fitness representations: what is the group of objects that can be talked about (or that are forbidden to be talked about)? What is a field of possible fitness enunciations (whether in scientific or popular cultural language)? What is the group of concepts emerging from these fitness enunciations? What is the set of choices for practising fitness provided by these concepts? Such an archaeology would be successful, Foucault (1972: 193) asserted, if it showed 'how the prohibitions, exclusion, limitations, values, freedoms, and transgressions of [fitness], all its manifestations, verbal or otherwise, are linked to a particular discursive practice'. While archaeology provided Foucault with the tools to analyse the formation of knowledge(s) in society, his later genealogical method examined how knowledge became a vehicle of power.

As we explained earlier in Chapter 2, Foucault's genealogical analysis consists of three modalities. It is parodic in a sense that it opposes any type of analysis as the recognition of reality (an examination of how things 'really' happened). It is dissociated in a sense that it opposes research as a continuity or representation of a tradition. It is sacrificial in a sense that it is directed against excavating one truth but instead it assumes knowledge as a form of practising power:

> There are manifold relations of power which permeate, characterise and constitute the social body, and these relations of power cannot themselves be established, consolidated nor implemented without the production, accumulation, circulation and functioning of a discourse. There can be no possible exercise of power without a certain economy of discourses of truth which operates through and on the basis of this association. We are subjected to the production of truth through power and we cannot exercise power except through the production of truth.
> (Foucault, 1980e: 93)

The task of a genealogy is to tease out the relationship of a discursive production of truth and power. What does this, then, mean in terms of conducting a discursive analysis of fitness?

To attempt a genealogy of fitness, one must first acknowledge that what we know about fitness has evolved through disruptions rather than through a solidified, logical growth and therefore consists of heterogeneous layers of discourses. A genealogy of fitness is thus parodic. What we know about fitness is a perspective formed by stages of forces, not a truth reflecting 'real' fitness knowledge created in logical scientific succession. A genealogy of fitness is thus dissociated. Fitness knowledge also acts as a tool of power, a form of domination and can, thus, be dangerous to some. Finally, a genealogy of fitness is sacrificial. The intention, however, is not to identify powerful fitness industry figures who possess the power to dominate others. On the contrary, a genealogy aims to look at how those things nearest to us – the body, physical activity, a healthy lifestyle and diet – are enmeshed with relations of power and how they, weaved in discourses, provide a base for a certain type of knowledge construction. A fitness genealogy is, therefore, concerned with the relations of power in the production of discourses that assert the 'truth' about fitness.

However, to research the discourses surrounding fitness one cannot ignore the role of archaeology. It is important to first engage in an archaeology of statements, enunciations, and concepts that form fitness knowledge in the discursive field of fitness and then, through a genealogy, to examine how – through what relations of power – these particular ways of knowing have come to occupy the discursive space of fitness. After this archaeological excavation of the fitness field, we can conclude our genealogy to show how power is imprinted on our bodies and bodily practices through the knowledge production of fitness.

Excavating physical activity, fitness and health

To begin our archaeology of fitness we need to first identify its objects. We assume that it is mainly concerned with the physical condition of the body. However, to identify enunciations of fitness, we need to find sources in which the body's physical conditioning is talked about. As we stated earlier, there are several possible fields of fitness enunciations, but in this chapter we focus on the scientific enunciations of the fit body. In Chapter 4 we continue our discussion on how fitness is constructed within the field of popular cultural fitness enunciations.

A large part of fitness knowledge is based on medical, psychological and physiological research that then dominates the field of fitness. Fitness practices, subsequently, are developed based on this knowledge. This scientific knowledge composes a large discursive field where fitness practices and practitioners operate. Therefore, fitness is not different from any other discursive field in contemporary society, where as Foucault maintained, much of our knowledge stems from objective scientific research and where such knowledge dominates other ways of knowing. It is in this field of enunciations that we begin to identify possible concepts characterising the discourse of fitness.

From the scientific literature concerning fitness, we find that the concept linking the theoretical schemas of science and fitness is health. In other words, the most widely accepted justification for promoting fitness is its predicted health benefits. The efforts to formally conceptualise the link between fitness and improved predicted health began in 1966 (Bouchard *et al.*, 1990). However, it was the 1990 Conference on Exercise, Fitness, and Health that established formally the 'complex relationships between the levels of habitual physical activity, physical and physiological fitness, and health' (Bouchard *et al.*, 1990: 5). This relationship was expressed as positive, direct and logical: increased physical activity leads to improved fitness which then results in low risk of chronic disease and thus improved health.

Based on our reading, we deduct that the concepts physical activity, fitness and health appear to form a 'group relation' that allows for further theoretical formulations regarding what it means to have a physically fit body. The next step in our archaeology is to examine such theoretical formations in more detail.

Medical and physiological research has provided strong evidence to connect improved physical fitness to the prevention of coronary heart disease and related hypertension (high blood pressure), type II diabetes, some types of cancer, osteoporosis, depression and anxiety (e.g. ACSM, 2000; Blair *et al.*, 1994; Haskell, 1994; Paffenberger *et al.*, 1994; Pollock *et al.*, 1995; Shephard, 1995). As a result, this knowledge now shapes the way scientifically 'correct' fitness programmes are prescribed. This knowledge also dominates university degree programmes that offer exercise-related degrees. For example, the textbooks used by undergraduates studying health and exercise invariably refer to the association between an illness-free body and physical fitness. These textbooks generally open with a chapter regarding the health benefits of exercise by stating that physical activity reduces the risk of numerous chronic diseases (e.g. Corbin and Lindsay, 1994; Heyward, 2002; Howley and Franks, 2003; Sharkey, 2002). Vivian Heyward's (2002) book *Advanced Fitness Assessment and Exercise Prescription* is particularly illustrative of this genre. Her first chapter titled 'Physical Activity, Health, and Chronic Disease' explains how physical activity can prevent cardiovascular disease, musculoskeletal disorders, psychological disorders, pulmonary diseases, cancer and metabolic disorders. In general, scientific research postulates that the better our physical fitness, the better our predicted health will be. The theoretical position connected to this understanding of the fit body can be characterised by the term 'health related physical fitness' (e.g. Corbin and Lindsey, 1994).

One of the earliest researchers to popularise the notion of health-related fitness was Dr Kenneth Cooper in his 1968 book *Aerobics*. Cooper's text also provided one of the first practical fitness programmes designed to meet the gap between health and activity. Cooper, who was at the time a medical doctor for the United States Air Force, became concerned with men's lack of fitness: Americans had become sedentary and overweight. Consequently, Dr Cooper believed that this explained the prevalence of heart disease in American men. He set out to develop a scientifically based aerobic fitness programme that could be adjusted to an exerciser's gender, age and fitness level in order to improve the condition of the lungs, cardiovascular system and the heart. Cooper now heads his own research institute, the Cooper Institute in Texas, devoted to scientific research concerning the health benefits of physical fitness. Cooper's legacy is important for our archaeology of fitness as the current fitness practices are grounded on this positive correlation between the absence of illness and physical activity. Health-related fitness, thus, has emerged as a 'theory' that regulates the ways of practising fitness. As a theory, it is firmly grounded on the physiology of the diseased body. However, the notion of health related physical fitness has expanded beyond Cooper's focus on cardiovascular fitness. This means further groups of concepts now embed the theory of health-related fitness.

In today's scientific literature, health-related physical fitness encompasses features beyond improving cardiovascular conditioning. Health-related fitness is now divided into components that in addition to cardiovascular fitness include flexibility, muscle strength and endurance and body composition. Also, health-related fitness is carefully separated from the so-called skill-related fitness: health-related fitness has a direct relationship to health whereas skill-related fitness is specific to motor skills that are needed mostly in high performance sport. Therefore, health-related fitness is further distinguished as its own discursive formation separate from competitive sport training that has its own coherent and exact groups of concepts and theories. Such a conceptual separation also allows health-related fitness to become a concern for an 'average' or 'normal' individual who would not participate in high performance sports. Health-related fitness, thus, should reach the masses who are generally susceptible to the chronic illnesses preventable by engagement in physical activity. Dividing health-related fitness into distinct components clarifies the process of developing suitable exercise programmes that can then be prescribed to individuals. Consequently, there are detailed instructions on how to compile the most effective exercise programmes.

Our archaeology has demonstrated thus far that such concepts as health, fitness and physical activity join together to create a specific theoretical space for health-related fitness. This theory of fitness is supported by the scientific knowledge of human physiology that then dictates how fitness is actually practised. Fitness practices specific to health-related fitness have been recorded in a specific 'exercise prescription', a further concept introduced within the theory of health-related fitness that links together the scientific knowledge and practice into a discursive field. As discursive practice provides the conditions for the function or meaning of discourse, to continue our archaeology, we next examine what rules make up an actual exercise prescription. The American College of Sport Medicine (ACSM) provides scientifically tested, precise guidelines for prescribing exercise.

The ACSM was originally founded in 1954 during an annual meeting for the American Association for Health, Physical Education and Recreation (AAHPER) as the Federation of Sport Medicine, but changed its name to ACSM in 1955. In its mission statement, the ACSM 'advances and integrates scientific research to provide educational and practical applications of exercise science and sports medicine' (<www.acsm.org>). To fulfil this mission, the ACSM published the first edition of *Guidelines for Exercise Testing and Prescription* in 1975. These guidelines undergo regular revisions and are currently in their sixth edition. The ACSM guidelines are based on the division of physical fitness into the previously mentioned components, and specific exercises have been designed to improve each of these components of physical fitness. Exercise prescription for each component includes the mode of exercise, exercise intensity, exercise duration and exercise frequency. For example, to improve cardiovascular fitness and body composition, one has to engage in aerobic exercise such as running, walking, cycling or swimming (mode of exercise). For selecting the proper intensity the ACSM guidelines prescribe intensities between 55/60 per cent and 90 per cent of maximal heart rate or between 40/50 per cent and 85 per cent of the oxygen uptake reserve (VO_2R) or heart rate reserve (HRR) (ACSM, 2000). Exercise for cardiovascular fitness should be scheduled for three to five days a week (frequency) and include 20–60 minutes of continuous activity (duration). The ACSM exercise prescription for muscular fitness can be summarised in the following table:

Mode	Intensity	Repetitions	Sets	Frequency	No. of exercises
Resistance training (static or dynamic)	70–80% 1-RM	8–12	>1	2 days per week	8–10

To improve flexibility, the ACSM suggests stretching three days a week (frequency) to a position of mild discomfort (intensity), holding each stretch 10 to 30 seconds (duration) and doing three to five stretches in each session. The actual ACSM guidelines do not include prescriptions for improving body composition, but several textbooks have adapted these guidelines to include nutrition and weight management programmes aimed at improving body composition (e.g. Heyward, 2002).

To summarise our excavation of the fitness field, our archaeology first directed us to the scientific texts on fitness. In these texts we identified concepts of physical activity, fitness and health that evolved into a theoretical schema of health-related fitness. Health-related fitness, in turn, defined specific fitness practices labelled as exercise prescription. It is evident, as Foucault (1972) asserted, that fitness knowledge and its discursive practice are inexplicably linked together into a discursive field. Therefore, to engage in an archaeology means an analysis of knowledge that appropriates certain types of practices. To analyse whether this appropriation is limiting or enabling, we need to embark upon a genealogical analysis of fitness: how knowledge turns into a vehicle of power. Foucault (1984b) advised that a genealogist, to record the emergence of discourse, must look into those things nearest to us. In what follows, we will return to the actual bodily practices, the exercises, emerging from the theoretical concepts of health-related fitness.

Exercise prescription: 'The means of correct training'?

As we noted earlier, Foucault embarked in genealogical analysis to examine how knowledge turns into a form of practising power. He also demonstrated that 'theoretical, unitary, formal, scientific discourse' (Foucault, 1980e: 85) was particularly coercive and therefore, its functioning needed a closer scrutiny by a genealogist. We have demonstrated through our archaeology that health-related fitness practices derive directly from scientific knowledge of the diseased human body. We now plan to engage in a genealogy to examine if this knowledge operates as tactics that are used to subject individual fitness practitioners to 'the effects of the centralising powers which are linked to the institution and functioning of an organised scientific discourse' (Foucault, 1980e: 84). To analyse if power is imprinted on individual bodies through the effects of a scientific discourse we first make a couple of observations regarding the discursive practices, the exercise prescription, that define health-related fitness.

The exercise prescription guidelines provide very detailed and mostly clearly measurable quantifiers for exercise. To adhere to these descriptors and to improve one's health, it is obvious that the exerciser has to engage in constant surveillance of the appropriate intensity, frequency and duration of each physical activity component. For example, to exercise one's cardiovascular fitness at the proper level, one must constantly monitor the exercise intensity either by regular measurement of one's heart rate or by regular monitoring of a RPE scale (Rate of Perceived Exertion). As we discussed in Chapter 2, according to Foucault (1991a: 170), such self-surveillance can act as 'a means of correct training': it is an instrument of disciplinary power. The continuous, functional surveillance of one's exercise practice turns into a technique of discipline that, without physical force or material constraints, controls individuals. Such surveillance, according to Foucault (1980b: 155), is a rather 'superb formula': power is exercised continuously and with minimal cost because all that is needed is an inspecting gaze that each individual turns into him/herself. As Foucault stated: 'An inspecting gaze, a gaze which each individual under its weight will end up interiorising to the point that he is his own overseer, each individual thus exercising this surveillance over, and against himself' (Foucault, 1980b: 155). Therefore, the gaze of self-surveillance allows for a form of multiple, automatic and anonymous power that is everywhere and always alert; it is silent yet permanently present. Because exercise prescription enables an operation of such a gaze, we could conclude that it is part of the tactics to submit individuals to coercive, centralised power relations. But could monitoring one's fitness level necessarily mean that exercise is an instrument of disciplinary power? To verify such a position, we need to examine the exercise prescription more closely.

In addition to the surveillance of one's exercise intensity, an individual's exercise prescription includes a 'rate of progression': a gradual increase in the amount of exercise. ACSM guidelines recommend three stages of progression: initial conditioning stage, improvement stage (more rapid progression rate) and maintenance stage (maintaining the achieved fitness level). However, several texts on exercise prescription introduce the term 'overload': 'to increase the functional capacity of a tissue, it must be overloaded (i.e., subjected to a load to which it is not accustomed)' (Howley and Franks, 2002: 162). When following an exercise prescription, one's body gets used to the current exercise load, and one needs to increase the amount of exercise regularly to gain a training effect and the subsequent health benefits. For Foucault (1991a) such exercises 'that are intensified, multiple forms of training, several times repeated' (180) were further signs of bodily discipline: corrective effects on the unfit body are obtained through training the body at gradually increasing levels of effort. We conclude that as every exerciser is urged to obtain a training effect, exercise also normalises each body into a common working regime. Such normalisation, according to Foucault, further cements one's body into the surveillance of the invisible power relations. Foucault (1991a) however, asserted that to gain its full impact, one's level of normalisation needed to be regularly observed. We next analyse if health-related fitness subscribes to regular monitoring techniques through its exercise prescription.

When reading various guidebooks for exercise prescription one is struck by the amount of space devoted to the testing protocols. For example, ACSM guidelines contain an equal amount of text for testing to the actual exercise prescription. In addition, physical fitness textbooks include substantive descriptions of physical fitness testing. It is blatantly obvious that fitness testing procedures occupy an important role in any exercise prescription.

Furthermore, it appears that to obtain an impact, the testing has to be done by following strict, scientifically proven measurement techniques.

The testing is to begin prior to starting any exercise programme to allow for the appropriate level of prescription. The physical fitness textbooks detail several tests for each component of physical fitness. Cardiovascular fitness level should be determined through submaximal cycle ergonometer tests, treadmill tests, step tests or field tests. Muscle strength and endurance should be assessed with static isometric dynamometer or tensiometer tests or dynamic tests such as a one repetition maximum test or a push-up test. Tests for flexibility, similar to exercise prescription for this component of physical fitness, are much less elaborate, but include such tests as goniometer tests or indirect measurements such as sit-and-reach test. Contrary to the relatively unsophisticated tests to measure flexibility, body composition can be measured with very advanced techniques such as hydrostatic weighing, air displacement plethysmography, dual-energy X-ray absorptiometry, skinfold measures, bioelectric impedance method or body mass index (BMI) (e.g. Heyward, 2002). It is curious that, although there is no specific exercise prescription for body composition, multiple tests have been included in the fitness texts to accompany this aspect of fitness. We note, however, that body composition is the most visible of all the components of physical fitness (we can 'see' who is obese, overweight, normal or thin). Therefore, the body is the most open to the normalising gaze through its relative content of fat and lean body mass.

After these observations it seems obvious to suggest that from a Foucauldian perspective, exercise prescription operates as a tactic for increased bodily discipline by continually monitoring an individual's physical fitness level. In this sense, exercise science seems to operate as a vehicle of control by recommending regular bodily measurement as an integral aspect of an individual's exercise regime. Such monitoring, according to Foucault (1991a), was a method used to normalise individuals into docile bodies useful to the functioning of the social body. This normalisation process implied a certain sense of sameness: all the individuals adhered to the same norms and thus, turned out as a unitary mass of bodies. We note, however, that exercise prescription is adapted for an individual's needs and the tests are designed to detect individual differences in fitness levels. Foucault did not discount such diversity but saw an account for individual difference as an essential part of the normalisation process through the disciplinary techniques:

> the power of normalization imposes homogeneity; but it is individualized by making it possible to measure gaps, to determine levels, to fix specialities and to render the differences useful by fitting them one to

another ... the norm introduces, as a useful imperative and as a result
of measurement, all the shading of individual differences.

(Foucault, 1991a: 184)

Therefore, the detection of differences at the starting level only highlights
the quest for eventually reaching the same standard of physical fitness. Some
exercisers just require more discipline to obtain the required level and testing
will usefully render each individuals' current state of fitness more visible
and comparable to the norm. Foucault (1991a) further argued that such a
visible classification is required for an individual to realise his/her current
deviance from the accepted norm and consequently, the individual becomes
aware of his/her need to engage in practices that discipline the body back to
the 'normal'. Testing developed as a means to determine deviance from the
norm. Foucault explained that testing

> measures in quantitative terms and hierarchizes in terms of value the
> abilities, the level, the 'nature' of individuals. It introduces, through
> this 'value-giving' measure, the constraint of a conformity that must
> be achieved. Lastly, it traces the limit that will define difference in
> relation to all other differences, the external frontier of the abnormal.
> ... The perpetual penalty that ... compares, differentiates, hierarchizes,
> homogenizes, excludes. In short, it normalizes.
>
> (Foucault, 1991a: 182–183)

Based on our genealogy so far, we conclude that exercise prescription and
its auxiliary, fitness testing, allow the materiality of power to operate on the
very bodies of individuals (Foucault, 1980c). Fitness testing, Foucault would
argue (1991a), functions as a form of surveillance designed to quantify and
classify individual's level of abnormality. Based on testing, it is possible
then to determine the proper curative exercise. Fitness testing turns into a
part of disciplinary technique because it can make a previously undetected
deviance visible to the normalising gaze. An exerciser, through exposing
his/her insufficient physical fitness following a fitness test, becomes an object
of disciplinary power. According to Foucault, the detailed documentation
of results increases the body's visibility to the disciplinary gaze. Based on the
documented testing results, exercisers also receive an exercise programme
chart where they can carefully note the date, the type, duration, intensity and
frequency of their exercise routine. It is easy to follow one's progress from
such a log. Therefore, based on fitness testing and the designated exercise
prescription, an exerciser could be said to resemble a medical patient. As a
patient, the individual 'may be described, judged, measured, compared with
others, in his very individuality; and it is also the individual who has to be
trained or corrected, classified, normalized' (Foucault, 1991a: 191). Health
related physical fitness programmes, through numerical measurements and

recording charts, turn into 'norms' that regulate the individual as a part of the 'healthy' social body. We continue by further excavating how the concept of health shapes exercise practices.

Health-related physical fitness as discourse

In this part of our chapter we aim to further examine the construction of health-related fitness as discourse that, as embedded in science, might subject individual bodies to dominant power relations. To engage in such an analysis, Foucault suggested identifying

> the accidents, the minute deviations – or conversely, the complete re-versals – the errors, the false appraisals, and the faulty calculations that gave birth to these things that continue to exist and have value for us; it is to discover that truth or being does not lie at the root of what we know and what we are, but the exteriority of accidents.
>
> (1984b: 81)

Searching for minute contradictions might help determine whether self-evident truths about fitness are mere constructions, 'accidents' formed within discursive forces. We will begin with a closer analysis of the concept of health that provides the dominant justification for exercise prescriptions.

We first note that the texts for health-related fitness do not devote significant space to discussion of health *per se*. For example, many physical fitness texts do not include an explicit definition of health (Heyward, 2002). Others have included it only in their glossaries (e.g. Howley and Franks, 2002) or refer instead to 'health benefits' (ACSM, 2000; Hey-ward, 2002) or 'healthy behaviours' (Sharkey, 2002). As stated earlier, however, such benefits or behaviours are presented as reducing the risk of illness and are followed by a list of diseases that regular exercise can prevent. Therefore, without a closer scrutiny, the reader will get a general impression of health relating to the absence of illness. However, when attempting to find a definition of health in these texts, they appear somewhat broader. Howley and Franks (2002), for example, define health as 'being alive with no major health problem. Also called *apparently healthy*' (550, italics in original). Corbin and Lindsey have included a similarly broad definition:

> Health is optimal well-being that contributes to quality of life. It is more than freedom from disease and illness, though freedom from disease is important to good health. Optimal health includes high-level mental, social, emotional, spiritual, and physical fitness within the limits of one's heredity and personal disabilities.
>
> (Corbin and Lindsey, 1994: 3)

Health is defined more formally in the 1990 Consensus Statement on knowledge of exercise, fitness and health:

> Health is a human condition with physical, social, and psychological dimension, each characterized on a continuum with positive and negative poles. Positive health is associated with a capacity to enjoy life and to withstand challenges; it is not merely the absence of disease. Negative health is associated with morbidity and, in the extreme, with mortality.
>
> (6–7)

This definition draws from the World Health Organisation's official definition of health. Despite these broad characterisations, the discourse on health-related fitness is much more narrowly centred on the disease-free body. It seems that often, when referring to health benefits, scientific research is actually focusing on the ability of physical fitness to prevent illness. This message is also strongly communicated to the general audience. Information from the website of the prestigious and influential President's Council on Physical Fitness and Sport (<www.fitness.gov>) can serve as a case in point. In an informative fact sheet titled 'Physical Activity and Health', the authors emphasise how physical inactivity causes cardiovascular disease, obesity and diabetes both in adults and children and how physical activity can prevent these diseases. They also refer to a report by the US Department of Health and Human Services entitled 'Physical Activity Fundamental to Preventing Disease'. This report begins by stating that '[r]egular physical activity, fitness and exercise are critically important for the health and well being of people of all ages' (US Department of Health and Human Services, 2002: 1) and then continues to demonstrate how regular physical activity can reduce morbidity and mortality from many chronic diseases. In this report, general information regarding physical fitness and health, enjoyment or the social dimensions of health do not feature. In addition, the text emphasises that to gain health benefits an individual must obtain a scientifically described level of physical fitness. Therefore, it is important to observe a proper, regular exercise prescription, because mere participation in physical activity does not provide sufficient preventative effect.

Our genealogy demonstrates so far that the scientific discourse of fitness defines health rather narrowly. Therefore, health-related fitness is based on a limited definition of health as absence of illness rather than a more holistic healthy lifestyle or wellness. The narrow definition of health, in turn, manifests in the actual bodily practices. It limits the type of movement acceptable for exercise prescription: only exercise and regular training result in improved physical fitness that has been scientifically proven to prevent illness. Therefore, the desired health benefits can occur only through involvement in exercise regimes for physical fitness that are prescribed by fitness experts.

This implies that without a clearly defined programme, everyday physical activities, such as walking, are insufficient health practices. An exercise prescription is tightly defined to act as a means of preventing illness which, like any medicine if one abuses the proper dosage, provides no health benefits. Therefore, exercise prescription leads to tightly disciplined bodies that only move in certain, scientifically proven ways to avoid disease. The exercising body is normalised to adopt these particular practices as its preferred practices. It is also clear that the connection between health and physical fitness has been medicalised in this scientific discourse by underlining the definition of health as the absence of illness. In addition, exercise scientists align themselves strongly with medicine, for example, by labelling their organisation as sport medicine and grounding their recommended exercise prescription, another medical term, on the scientifically proven link between the absence of illness and physical fitness. While it is definitely appropriate to exercise in order not to become ill, a singular focus on this exercise benefit can mask other reasons to be physically active and other, multiple ways of maintaining one's health. To further embark on the genealogical excavation of this fitness discourse, we ask next: Why has illness prevention become the dominant fitness discourse? Why haven't researchers focused on a more holistic notion of health and well-being? This is where the notion of power re-enters into our Foucauldian analysis of knowledge production: an emergence of knowledge is always produced through a particular stage of forces. Genealogy, then, 'seeks to reestablish the various systems of subjection ... the hazardous play of dominations' (Foucault, 1984b: 83) by focusing on how various forces of power shape the formation of knowledge in society.

Politics of the fit, healthy bodies in the twentieth century: governed by disease control

When we search the President's Council on Physical Fitness and Sport web site we have an answer to our question regarding the focus on exercise as a means of disease control: taking care of ill people is expensive. On this website, the report by the US Department of Health and Human Services states: 'A physically inactive population is at both medical and financial risk for many chronic diseases and conditions' (US Department of Health and Human Services, 2002: 2). The financial risk is a combination of health-care costs and the costs associated with the value of lost wages and lost productivity by people unfit to work. For example, in 2000 heart disease cost the USA $183 billion, cancer $157 billion, diabetes $100 billion and arthritis $65 billion (US Department of Health and Human Services, 2002). Hardman and Stensel (2003) reported that the cost of medical care due to physical inactivity ranges from about 2.4 per cent in the Netherlands to about 6 per cent in Canada and 9.4 per cent in the USA of total health sector costs. In a similar vein, a governmental health campaign titled 'Push Play' in New Zealand uses predicted significant saving in public funding as its main justification:

> Active people enjoy a better quality of life, are healthier and generally live longer. Getting more people more active saves lives and money. A 10% increase in the number of adults who are active would prevent hundreds of premature deaths and return health cost savings of at least $55 million. Young people who are active are healthier and perform better at school. Society also benefits. Active communities are more united, more likely to share an identity, and experience less anti-social behaviour, especially among young people. Active lifestyles bring tangible benefits to the economy. The sport and leisure sector contributes over $1.7 billion to GDP and supports 31,000 jobs. It is one of the more dynamic sectors of our economy.
>
> (SPARC, 2005)

These are powerful statistics. Obviously preventing disease by exercising will result in substantial monetary savings and is, therefore, an entirely justifiable reason to promote physical fitness programmes. In addition, by placing the responsibility to undertake a sufficient level of exercise onto the individual, a healthy social body that is both docile and useful is achieved with the lowest possible cost (Foucault, 1991a). Samantha King's (2003) ethnographic study of the 'National Race for the Cure', a 5 km run to raise funds for breast cancer research, offers an example of how self-responsibility for health is promoted through a charity event. The Race for the Cure, King asserted, offers the US government a site for producing 'civically active, self-responsible citizens' (2003: 297) through the Race's festive, prideful, patriotic and consumerist environment. Such citizens are 'proper American citizens' who take pride in being self-responsible for preventing illness by taking part in this running event and at the same time embrace the preferred humanistic values for performing organised, charitable works. King concluded that such a commitment, in addition to promoting the economic privitisation of health care, is about the 'capacity to solidify the contemporary articulation of physical health to moral and civic fitness' (2003: 298). In this regard, today's health-related fitness practices are not too dissimilar to the politics of health that, Foucault argued, originated from the eighteenth century.

Foucault (1980a) observed that in the eighteenth century regulating the health of the population became one of the essential objectives of power. As a consequence, different apparatuses of power were called upon to take charge of bodies 'to help and if necessary constrain them to ensure their own good health' (Foucault, 1980a: 170). It is evident that such governmental organisations as the Presidents Council on Fitness and Sports (PCFS), the Centres for Disease Control and Prevention (DCD) in the USA, and other governmental departments of health together with the ACSM are essential parts of such an apparatus. This apparatus together with the scientific knowledge, Foucault added, turns health into an imperative for all: 'at once the duty of each and objective of all' (Foucault, 1980a: 170). As physical fitness now appears as an essential variable of a healthy body, it is each individual's responsibility to become fitter as that contributes to the general good of the social body as a whole: we all could pay less for health care, if only we were to start exercising. Foucault identified the individualisation of health care as part of the 'biopolitics of population': the attempts to control the health of the population as a whole by disciplining individual bodies.

It is clear that, like in the eighteenth century, we now have multiple apparatuses governing individual's health behaviours, and the fitness-related discourse is only one part of the general discourse of illness prevention in society. As such, physical fitness continues the eighteenth-century legacy of 'the disposition of society as a milieu of physical well-being, health and optimum longevity' (Foucault, 1980a: 170). Foucault also argued that, as a result of this legacy, there is now a constant need to survey and analyse the population's health behaviours, because a successful implementation of governmental health programmes depends initially on the collection of statistical data. Indeed, there are numerous statistics on longevity and exercise, general physical activity levels of the population and particularly the obesity levels of the population in western societies. These statistics allow for increased scrutiny of the individual's usefulness for society because the population, once known, can then be categorised and acted upon in order to control it. In recent years, a plethora of these data collection studies have occurred within the exercise sciences. These studies reveal which particular categories of people are inactive, overweight, lack appropriate motivation and maintain unhealthy diets and, therefore, pose a health risk and potential economic cost to a society. Within New Zealand, for example, teenage girls, Pacific Island and Asian people have all been identified as (problem) groups that need to become more active or change their dietary habits (SPARC, 2005). Once such 'health' knowledge has been gained, specific campaigns or strategies, such as the Canadian ParticipACTION or the New Zealand 'Push Play' programme, can be designed and enacted. These campaigns and exercise strategies are then typically justified in relation to the economic and social benefits deemed important for the cohesive maintenance of a modern state. This justification mirrors what Foucault (1978) discussed as the links between bio-power and capitalism as related to the production of an educated, productive, efficient, responsible and docile population or workforce. For example, from a Foucauldian perspective one might argue that one's fitness level (e.g. BMI or VO_2 max) now serves as a new variable for economic management: it functions as a marker for individual's utilisability for profitable investment. Because high BMI level or poor cardiovascular condition now predicts an increased risk of cardiovascular disease and thus, a shorter lifespan, it is a better investment to employ a thinner or fitter person. Foucault noted: 'The biological traits of a population become relevant factors for economic management, and it becomes necessary to organise around them an apparatus which will ensure not only their subjection but the constant increase of their utility' (Foucault, 1980a: 72).

Foucault (1980a: 176) further observed that with the need to raise the general level of health, medicine as a general technique of health and medical doctors as its practitioners won 'footing within the different instances of social power'. Medical doctors were bestowed with surplus of power: they observed, corrected and improved the social body by monitoring its permanent state of health. When reading texts on physical fitness, the connection to medicine is striking: the names of scientific organisations, the constant references to scientific literature, the qualifications of the scientific experts on physical fitness, the requirement for medically supervised fitness testing, the demand for reaching an appropriate physical fitness level to prevent illness all speak the language of medicine. It is clear that the medicalisation of the fitness discourse allows for governmentality of the fit body.

Foucault (1984b) also observed that discourses evolve through an interrupted, disjunctural process and therefore, are never finalities, but rather continually changing manifestations of emerging themes. Accordingly, the medicalised discourse of fitness with its carefully detailed exercise prescription has not gone without challenges. Foucault characterised the need to implement modifications as 'strategic elaboration' by the discursive apparatus.

'Strategic elaboration'

Foucault (1980h) asserted that once an apparatus is constituted, its effects – whether positive or negative, intentional or unintentional – enter 'into resonance or contradiction' with other, already existing effects. Therefore, there needs to be a continual re-adjustment of various elements within the apparatus. This translates into a 'perpetual process of strategic elaboration' of the different effects (Foucault, 1980h: 195).

The discourse surrounding the illness-free body is also in a continual process of elaboration based on what effects it has managed to implement. At the moment, this discourse has not entirely fulfilled the intention by the governing apparatus. No doubt, it is important to stay illness free, and improved physical fitness has an important role to play in the battle for a 'healthier' nation. But the body is disciplined through a carefully designed, scientific exercise plan and constantly monitored for continually improved fitness and remaining illness free, therefore, requires an exercise regime designed to become gradually more demanding. This necessitates hard work and despite the multifaceted health apparatus in today's society many people fail to maintain regular exercise schedules or do not exercise at all. Indeed, the disciplinary requirements of physical fitness prescription have failed to increase people's physical activity levels and, thus, the general health of the social body. In 1998, for example, almost 40 per cent of American adults (US Department of Health and Human Services, 2002), 30 per cent of Germans, 35 per cent of French and 60 per cent of the Portuguese remained inactive (Hardman and Stensel, 2003). In the UK, where only 24 per cent of population was classed as sedentary, 63 per cent of men and 75 per cent of women did not exercise enough to gain health benefits (Hardman and Stensel, 2003). As we noted in Chapter 2, Foucault pointed out that disciplinary techniques do not always succeed in producing the desired outcome. However, as Foucault continued, this does not mean that 'power weakens' but rather that it 're-organises its force' (Foucault, 1980c: 56) elsewhere. Therefore, a strategic elaboration of exercise practices might be needed for the health apparatus to complete its function of building healthier nations of physically fit bodies. Indeed, the level of failure to increase the physical fitness of the population has not gone unobserved by organisations like the ACSM, DCD and PCPFS who have issued a new position statement to supplement the earlier ACSM exercise prescription guidelines.

While the level of exercise recommended by the ACSM guidelines continues to focus on disease prevention, the new position statement includes objectives for both exercise and more moderate physical activity on the premise that a nation's health can be improved if the sedentary population begins *any* type of physical activity. This 'public health' approach promotes moderate, daily physical activity as opposed to medically supervised exercise prescription (ACSM, 1995). The physical activity guidelines emphasise a moderate intensity of activity that is defined much more loosely than the ACSM exercise prescription. For example, walking at a 'normal' pace qualifies as moderate intensity physical activity. In addition, such moderate intensity physical activity can be accumulated through several 'bouts' during the day. For example, one can engage in three bouts of 10 minute exercise during the day to accumulate his/her daily 30 minutes of activity. Such 'bouts' of moderate activity allow for physical activity to be implemented within a lifestyle and in addition, more everyday 'chores' such as gardening, cleaning or washing can now count as physical activity. Following these recommendations, it is possible to be physically active frequently, preferably every day (Hardman and Stensel, 2003). Although scientific research shows support for this new public health physical activity approach, it is still generally acknowledged that physical activity is a helpful starting point, but physical fitness is a better guarantee of securing the absence of illness.

Therefore, engagement in physical activity should only serve as a first step toward becoming physically fit and consequently, illness free.

Conclusion

In this chapter we have traced the construction of the 'healthy' body as it is constituted by the discourse of fitness. To illustrate Foucault's methodology, we divided our discussion quite categorically into sections of archaeology and genealogy. Considering that Foucault referred to his methodology singularly as genealogy in his later works, such clear separation is not necessary. However, treating his methodology as two phases can effectively illustrate how to analyse the formation of discourses step by step as such a technique is not often detailed in Foucauldian studies of sport. Through an archaeology, we first identified what concepts were connected in the 'scientific' enunciations of fitness and discovered that 'health', fitness and physical activity characterised the discussions of the 'healthy body' in the literature of sport and exercise science. This group of concepts enabled a formation of 'health-related fitness': a theoretical formulation about the fit body that then defined an actual practice, the exercise prescription, to obtain the fit body. We further engaged in a genealogy to examine the possible impact of this discourse on the individual exercisers. We first embarked on a detailed analysis of the exercise prescription to conclude that it had a tendency to build disciplined, normalised bodies through its requirement of continual improvement evidenced by specific fitness test results. To obtain physical fitness meant engaging in regular, ever increasing amounts of exercise. When we interrogated the meaning of health in the exercise science literature, a 'healthy' body came to mean an illness-free body that required a level of physical fitness. A scientific, medically based knowledge constituted the preferred 'statements' regarding this body. Therefore, the discourse of the fit, illness-free body has become a part of what Foucault (1980h) labelled a field of scientificity or an *episteme* (see Chapter 2) that enables certain knowledge to be separated out as the 'true', acceptable understanding of the healthy body among all the available statements.

We further noted that by imposing a regime of physical fitness on a population, it is possible to govern individual bodies. Such governance is closely connected to medical knowledge with its rather narrow definition of health. Of course, while a population's improved physical fitness might re-duce health care costs, there are other factors causing illness that might need even more attention (e.g. the junk food industry, pollution, stress caused by overworking). However, by individualising the connection between health and physical fitness, it is possible to divert the surveillance of health risks to the deficiencies of individual bodies. Therefore, health-related fitness practices act as a disciplinary technique that 'fixes' individuals: it creates an 'organised multiplicity' by normalising individual differences into one healthy population. Evidently, the dimension of power – the governance of the individual by requiring a fit, illness-free body – embedded in the health apparatus is formed out of knowledge. Health related physical fitness, therefore, has become part of a 'political anatomy' that together with other apparatuses and political regimes form the 'modality of disciplinary power' (Foucault, 1991a: 221) in society.[1]

There is very little research that has examined the power or social effects that stem from the workings of bio-power. For example, we know little about how specific groups, such as teenage girls or Pacific Islanders, feel about being the target in activity promotion or anti-obesity campaigns. More generally, we know little about the types of subjectivities, modes of domination, social hierarchies and divisions that might occur through campaigns that primarily promote 'fatness' and sedentary lifestyles as social and health problems. We suggest, however, that governmental exercise promotion schemes, as forms of bio-power, are not inherently good or bad but deserve critical reflection given that they aim to regulate behaviour and produce normalised subjectivities.

It is noteworthy, however, that the health-related fitness discourse has been unsuccessful in its mission to constrain individual bodies to take on exercise. Other practices exist within the discursive field of fitness that, similar to the health-related fitness practices, aim to shape individual bodies. In Chapter 4 we discuss whether these alternative practices have been successful in terms of producing bodies that are both docile and useful.

Exercise

Disciplined into docile bodies

Upon entering the Fitness Centre in the Town, one first finds a vast parking lot. The rows of parking spots nearest to the door are filled with SUVs that barely fit within the white lines painted to mark each space. A double glass door leads to the large single-storey building. Windows run high up the white brick walls. The building has an industrial look. Inside we meet a turnstile and on its left a glass-walled office and a service counter. No member can enter without first handing her membership card to the receptionist, and to gain entry to her group exercise class she must obtain a special card. The receptionist checks the client's name on a list – it is imperative to reserve a space in advance. People are sitting on bar stools around tables on the other side of the turnstile drinking sport drinks or café lattes. Immediately to the right one finds a large stretching area. Nearest to the entrance, behind a row of plastic, green plants, there are white exercise machines which some clients use while others sit on the black seats of these machines staring absently to the ground. Further away one sees rows of treadmills, steppers, rowing ergometers, versa climbers and exercise bikes arranged in straight lines all facing the television monitors stretching across the entire length of the back wall. To proceed deeper into the building one passes the sunbed room before coming to the exercise studio. Exercisers stand behind the door that leads to the studio partitioned from the rest of the space by two glass walls. Vertical blinds are meant to prevent anyone from seeing into the studio space. Regardless of the blinds, we can observe that there is an exercise class taking place. An instructor stands in front of a large mirror that covers the entire back wall. She has her back to the mirror as she is facing the exercisers who lie on the floor facing the mirror. The exercisers outside the studio are equipped with small drink bottles and many carry large mats and towels. They are mostly women dressed in sweat pants and T-shirts. The timetable outside the studio door indicates that a Pilates class will take place immediately after the end of the Body Pump class currently in the studio. A flight of stairs leads upstairs where there are separate locker rooms for women and men. At the end of this corridor is another studio with stationary bikes and exercise equipment. The timetable outside the door names this as the space for circuit and spinning classes.

Arguably, the most commonly cited of Foucault's texts in sport studies is *Discipline and Punish: The Birth of the Prison*. As we explained in Chapter 2, here Foucault (1991a) analysed eighteenth-century practices of discipline and punishment, and how these developed into techniques of power. He concluded that power operated by fabricating individual bodies into social order. This fabrication, according to Foucault, was done by disciplinary practices that normalised individuals into useful, docile bodies. The entire arrangement was secured through what he labelled, Panopticism. However, he also noted that our contemporary society similarly carries out these techniques of power. Therefore, discipline in today's society can be said to be 'a type of power, a modality for its exercise, comprising a whole set of instruments, techniques, procedures, levels of application, targets; it is a "physics" or an "anatomy" of power, a technology' (Foucault, 1991a: 215). Several sport scholars have examined how the sporting body has been disciplined into a docile body (e.g. Cole, 1998; Chapman, 1997; Duncan, 1994; Dworkin and Wachs, 1998; Heikkala, 1993; Markula, 2000; White and Gillett, 1994). In this chapter, we attempt to establish how localised discipline builds docile bodies through commercial group exercise practices, and how the media, in the macro-context of fitness, functions as a part of the apparatus for technologies of domination. We conclude by examining how individual exercisers react to such disciplinary techniques.

Docile bodies

According to Foucault (1991a), the body as an object and target of power has already been formulated during classical times. However, the eighteenth-century's disciplinary practices increased the scale of bodily

control over each individual's active body: the efficiency of its movements and its internal organisation. The activities of the human body
were submitted to constant control. Such meticulous control was achieved
through 'discipline' that, according to Foucault, has become an even more
widespread means of practising power over individual bodies in today's
society. Foucault used the notion of docility to demonstrate how bodies become manipulable and effective means for discipline: 'A body is
docile that may be subjected, used, transformed and improved' (Foucault,
1991a: 136). In other words, when docile, the body becomes useful as
it can be moulded as a vehicle for the technologies of domination. As
we discussed in Chapter 2, Foucault demonstrated how docile bodies are
created through the use of space, through selection of suitable activities,
through organisation of time and through the composition of forces. In
the opening passage of this chapter we have shown how a health club
space allows for the timetabling of selected activities. In what follows,
we aim to analyse in more detail if today's fitness practices produce such
docility–utility.[1]

The art of distribution of space

Foucault (1991a) first pointed out that to enable effective disciplinary practices, the spaces accommodating such practices were needed. He noted that
discipline requires an enclosure that 'is the protected place of disciplinary
monotony' (Foucault, 1991a: 141). Prisons were, of course, examples of
such enclosures but so were schools, army barracks, factories or hospitals.
Similarly, there is a special enclosure to practise fitness, the health club or
the fitness centre as we described at the beginning of this chapter. But just
because it is an enclosed space dedicated to physical conditioning, can we
conclude that it is an enclave for discipline? Foucault noted that the principle
of enclosure was not, indeed, sufficient to operate a disciplinary machine.

  In addition to an enclosed space, the art of distributing discipline required
'partitioning' (Foucault, 1991a: 143): To avoid group formations that were
difficult to control, the disciplinary enclosure separated individuals from
each other. Therefore, the space was organised analytically: to eliminate un-
controllable aspects of human bodies gathered together, but at the same time

> to know where and how to locate individuals, to set up useful commu-
> nications, to interrupt others, to be able at each moment to supervise
> the conduct of each individual, to assess it, to judge it, to calculate its
> qualities or merits.
>
> (Foucault, 1991a: 143)

Foucault further argued that disciplinary space was always 'cellular'. An
example of a cellular division of space can be an office where each individual,

while located in a common enclosure, is separated from the other with partition walls that form small cubicles. A health club follows a slightly different spatial logic. As our description at the beginning of the chapter demonstrates, a typical health club is indeed organised as a large enclosure that is then divided into sections for cardiovascular machines, resistance training machines and free weights. This spatial distribution of fitness clubs appears to be a global trend. There are no walls between these areas and upon entering one could glance over all these areas uninterrupted. However, partitioned from this large space are the studios for group exercise. In addition, upon taking a closer look at the activities, either in the studio or in the other areas, each exerciser is claiming his or her own space instead of being engaged in a group task. Even in the group exercise studio, exercisers like to reserve their 'own' space. For example, in their study of women's aerobics classes Maguire and Mansfield (1998) discussed how women liked to 'own' certain spaces on the studio floor and became very agitated if someone invaded, on purpose or by accident, their private exercise space. These participants were effectively exercising alone in a group (see also Markula, 1993). Such observations parallel Foucault's next characteristic for disciplinary spaces: functionality.

Disciplinary spaces were not only partitioned, but they were divided to create a useful space. For example, a factory space began to be divided in terms of tasks or stages required for production, and the individuals who carried out each task. As a consequence, 'each variable of this force – strength, promptness, skill, constancy – would be observed, and therefore characterized, assessed, computed and related to the individual who was its particular agent' (Foucault, 1991a: 145). This allowed an analysis of the entire workforce into individual units. Fitness club members do not contribute to a common production, but are rather part of a service industry as its clients. Nevertheless, it is easy to observe the employees' performance in such an environment. In the fitness club we described, there is a separate office for the manager and even that has glass walls. Contracted personnel such as the personal trainers or fitness instructors wear exercise uniforms when they appear on the fitness floor with their clients. The reception staff operates behind a vast open counter. Foucault also pointed out that hospitals started to keep better track of their patients to obtain better administrative control 'over remedies, rations, cures, deaths, simulations' (Foucault, 1991a: 144). Such control over the fitness club's clients is obvious: one can only enter the club by showing one's membership card that has to be obtained through an individualised assessment with a staff member who, after obtaining a sufficient amount of personal details, will sign in the new clients. Through such tracking, control of how each individual uses the space becomes possible.

Finally, as a result of individualising the space, the rank – 'the place one occupies in a classification' (Foucault, 1991a: 145–146) – became an important aspect of discipline. 'Discipline is an art of rank', Foucault (1991a) asserted, 'a technique for the transformation of arrangements. It individualizes bodies by a location that does not give them a fixed position, but distributes them and circulates them in a network of relations' (146). Such an organisation made it possible to supervise each individual while at work. In addition, each individual had the possibility of moving through ranks instead of being allocated a permanent position in the classification. Such ranking is, of course, common place in any workplace in today's society and a fitness club is no exception. The occupational rank for our hypothetical club would be typical of any nationwide chain. It can consist of several tiers at the regional level ranging from low level positions such as 'a motivator', fitness instructor and receptionist through several levels of national and international management positions. The actual fitness workers, the instructors, tend to be located at the bottom level of this hierarchical management structure. In addition, there are 'rankings' between the clients. For example, Maguire and Mansfield (1998) distinguished between 'established insiders' that were a dominant 'elite clique of individuals' and outsiders. The insiders demonstrated their higher 'rank' by establishing a personal exercise space in the front of the exercise studio and by displaying exercise competency, fashionable exercise clothing and an ideal exercise body. Alan Aycock (1992) observed that among casual bodybuilders, there is a subtle hierarchy based on the perceived level of 'seriousness' in training. At the university gym, 'beefy', built-up trainers claim equipment over leaner clients and women; and athletes are over everyone else. Based on its spatial organisation can we conclude that commercial fitness facilities foster discipline that produces docile bodies?

Foucault concluded that 'in organizing "cells", "places" and "ranks" the disciplines create complex spaces that are at once architectural, functional and hierarchical. It is spaces that provide fixed positions and permit circulation' (Foucault, 1991a: 148). Given such a conclusion, a fitness centre or a health club certainly bears the characteristics of a 'disciplinary' space. In addition, it is a space where individuals come together to exercise alone in a group setting. It appears then that the spatial organisation that allows for such individualisation within a group embeds disciplinary tactics that are 'situated on the axis that links the singular and the multiple. It allows both the characterization of the individual as individual and the ordering of a given multiplicity' (Foucault, 1991a: 149). If spatial organisation is the first element for disciplinary control of an individual's body, the second characteristics is the control of the actual activity done in the space.

The control of activity

Foucault (1991a) observed that the first way of controlling any activity in the provided space was to timetable it. Timetables, he argued, established rhythms, imposed particular occupations, and regulated the cycles of repetition that have long been found in schools, workshops and hospitals. Timetabling ensured an effective use of space in the provided time and it was, therefore, an attempt to 'assure the quality of the time used' (Foucault, 1991a: 150). Time was scheduled for useful purposes: 'Time measured and paid must also be a time without impurities or defects; a time of good quality, throughout which the body is constantly applied to its exercise' (Foucault, 1991a: 151). Moreover, Foucault noted that timetabled activities have been further broken down into smaller elements to increase the effectiveness of the time used and consequently the control of the bodies involved.

In fitness centres, timetabling concerns mainly the studio areas that cannot be used simultaneously for multiple purposes. While there are several types of group exercise classes, most classes are of 60 minutes' duration (yoga classes can also be scheduled for one and a half hours). Recently, however, shorter duration classes such as 30 minutes have gained popularity as clients find it difficult to fit longer work-outs in their working day. These classes, then, require even more effective use of time: 'one must seek to intensify the use of the slightest moment, as if time, in its very fragmentation, is inexhaustible' (Foucault, 1991a: 154). In addition, most classes are further broken down into segments: warm-up, activity, cool-down. This structure is designed to use the time effectively – to provide fitness benefits – in the shortest possible time without injuring the participants. For example, an aerobics class is designed as an effective package to improve all four of the health-related fitness practices: cardiovascular fitness, muscle strength and endurance, flexibility and body composition. To do this an aerobics class is further divided into components with detailed descriptions of timing and contents for each component.[2] In addition to the precise and detailed instructions for composing an aerobics class, there are further details for the correct execution of each exercise.

For example, to ensure cardiovascular benefits, it is imperative to perform each movement properly: using a full range of motion, executing movements continuously and engaging as many body parts as possible. Music accompanies this performance. All participants follow the choreography to music and repeat their exercises identically to each other. The instructor 'cues' each exercise in a concise and precise manner. A well-conducted aerobics class is as precise as an army in its exercise sessions. Such instruction, according to Foucault, aims for the correct use of the body, 'which makes possible a correct use of time, nothing must remain idle or useless: everything must be called upon to form the support of the act required. A well-disciplined body forms the operational context of the slightest gesture' (Foucault, 1991a: 152). Consequently, effective use of time, in addition to optimal use of space, is an integral aspect of disciplinary techniques.

The organisation of genesis

Foucault contended that '[t]he disciplines, which analyze space, break up and rearrange activities, must also be understood as machinery for adding up and capitalizing time' (Foucault, 1991a: 157). This was done in four ways: by dividing a duration of time into successive or parallel segments, by increasing complexity, by deciding the length of each segment and by having an examination of each segment. It was, finally, possible to draw up a 'series of series of exercises' to educate the body. A group exercise class, similar to a standard exercise prescription for resistance training and cardiovascular work (see Chapter 3), follows such a logic of progression: there are successive segments for each component of fitness, each segment is of a certain predetermined length and contains elements of progression from one lesson to the other. Alternatively, modifications for each participant to increase the intensity can be offered in each class to ensure progression at the individual level. Therefore, an exercise programme, a series of series, is developed to ensure a linear progression of the participants' fitness levels. Foucault further observed that:

> at the centre of this seriation of time, one finds ... 'exercise'. Exercise is that technique by which one imposes on the body tasks that are both repetitive and different, but always graduated. By bending behaviour toward a terminal state, exercise makes possible a perpetual character- ization of the individual either in relation to this term, in relation to other individuals, or in relation to a type of itinerary. It thus assures, in the form of continuity and constraint, a growth, an observation, a qualification.
>
> (Foucault, 1991a: 161)

Group exercise classes then, similar to exercise prescription (see Chapter 3), are deeply embedded in disciplinary techniques of power as they assure, through repetitive, progressive programmes, a continual growth of control over the body. In this way exercise becomes an element of 'a machine whose effect will be maximized by the concerted articulation of the elementary parts of which it is composed' (Foucault, 1991a: 164). Exercise classes can be seen as potential sites for disciplining individuals into docile bodies: the space, the gym, is constructed to allow disciplinary control over fit bodies. Robert Rinehart (1998) observed a parallel construction of disciplined bodies in swim training. As he concludes, the pool becomes a space where discipline is instilled in the young bodies of the swimmers through repetitive training of the 'ideal' technique with detailed cues offered by the coaches to correct individual swimmers' ineffective performance and training programmes to ensure progressive improvement. Such activities, including group exercise classes, carry the characteristics of activities for making docile bodies: they are exercises prescribed and imposed on individ- ual bodies. In swimming lessons and in exercise classes discipline arranges 'tactics' by ordering space, time and organisation of the activities in a cer- tain manner. Tactics, Foucault (1991a) asserted, are 'the art of constructing, with located bodies, coded activities and trained aptitudes' (167). They are 'mechanisms in which the product of the various forces is increased by their calculated combination' and consequently, they are 'no doubt the highest form of disciplinary practice' (Foucault, 1991a: 167). Foucault next examined what kind of power arrangement is necessary for the tactics of discipline. In Chapter 2 we introduced Foucault's concept of Panopticism which functions as a disciplinary arrangement. In this chapter, we expand our previous discussion by first looking at Panopticism at the microcosmic level of a fitness club before attempting to broaden our analysis to power relations that sustain docile bodies at the broader societal level.

Panopticism

As we established in Chapter 2, Panopticism is a machine for creating and sustaining a power relation independent of the person who exercises that power. Foucault (1991a) found Jeremy Bentham's design for a prison, the Panopticon, as the architectural figure for such a power relation. His design was based on two principles: power should be visible (i.e. the inmate will constantly see the central tower from which s/he is spied upon) and unverifiable (i.e. the inmate must never know whether s/he is being looked at; but s/he must be sure that s/he may always be so) (Foucault, 1991a). Furthermore, because the 'supervisor' is invisible, unidentifiable, individuals could be randomly assigned to operate the panoptic power arrangement. On the other hand, as the inmates do not see who supervises them (the tower might as well be empty) yet know that there is constant supervision over them, they take responsibility for their own supervision.

Fitness centres or health clubs are not designed architecturally as Panopticons. There is not, at least not usually, an enclosed observation tower for supervisors. However, a fitness club lays itself out as a large field of visibility: anything one is doing can be observed by multiple others. These observers are mostly fellow exercisers who do not assume the role of a visible, unmoving guard. One never knows who is observing and what, but one is definitely exposed to such constant, yet invisible observations. Health clubs typically have mirrors, usually both in the weight training area and in the studio. This adds a further opportunity to gaze and to be gazed upon by the others. For example, Aycock describes the role of mirror in men's weight-training practices:

> the arrangement of machines, weights, and mirrors demands a supervision of oneself, and that of others, as actions are monitored continuously by users. Persons are not only the objects of a gaze, but the subjects of incessant surveillance that constitutes the body as a figure of discipline.
> (Aycock, 1992: 349)

Such surveillance results in a rather bizarre situation where

> [a]t once, one must see oneself in the mirrors, see others looking at oneself, and not see others who are themselves not being seen; all this while constantly appraising performances even to the extent of imitating the persons who are presumptively invisible.
>
> (Aycock, 1992: 354)

Unlike the open space of the weight training area, fitness studios are usually enclosed from the larger gym floor. Therefore, group exercisers could be argued to be exposed to a lesser degree to the supervising gaze from the other gym users. In our example, the fitness centre we described at the beginning of the chapter, the studio had glass walls that could be closed off by vertical blinds. This allows outsiders to peek through them, yet it is difficult to see outside from within the studio. Therefore, despite the promise of invisibility, studio exercisers are exposed to the gaze of fellow exercisers who, like Bentham visioned, are made further unobservable with the help of the blinds. During their exercise sessions, each participant is exposed to the controlling gaze of his/her fellow exercisers as well as their own gaze reflected by the mirror. In a way similar to weight-training sessions, the mirror in aerobics classes facilitates the unidentifiable gaze that at the same time every participant possesses. For example, in Markula's (2003a) study, many of the exercisers found themselves comparing their bodies and abilities to those of other participants (see also Maguire and Mansfield, 1998). Therefore, in the presence of the mirror there is no need for any external, outside supervision. Being subjected to the field of such visibility while engaged in physical activity, the exercisers have cast the ever-seeing, controlling eye upon themselves: they take on both the role of the invisible supervisor and the visible inmate. We question now, however, for what purpose these individuals are engaged in such constant control.

While Panopticism works to exercise power within enclosed spaces such as prisons or fitness clubs, Foucault (1991a) argued that it also allows the exercise of power to be supervised by society as a whole. As the supervision, the controlling power, is not visible, not assigned to a certain person(s), anybody can take on such a task. This allows power relations 'to function in a diffused, multiple, polyvalent way throughout the whole social body' (Foucault, 1991a: 208–209). Therefore, if the participants in the gym have assumed the role of supervisors to control and discipline their bodies, we can still ask what exactly do they try to supervise. We established already earlier that the gym space and exercise practices are designed to discipline our bodies toward 'normalcy'. Any deviation from 'normal' is a punishable crime (Foucault, 1991a). We focus next on what is considered 'normal' in terms of the observable body in the gym and where we might have gained our idea of a 'normal gym body'.

Foucault (1991a) maintained that discipline takes 'functional inversions' across several institutions that then work together as sites for disciplinary techniques. One institution working closely together with the fitness industry is the media that produces multiple sources (fitness manuals, fitness magazines, exercise videotapes, television programmes, commercials) to further sell fitness to individuals. The media observes fitness trends and at the same time circulates fitness images throughout society. Therefore analysing how the media presents the fit body can help us to consider what is a 'normal' fit body in contemporary society.

Media and fitness: the 'normal' body

> Basically it was journalism, that capitalist invention of the nineteenth century, which made evident all the utopian character of this politics of gaze.
>
> (Foucault, 1980b: 162)

Health and Fitness, a popular women's fitness magazine in the UK, devoted its July 2005 issue to summer toning. It offered a 14-page shape-up special, 25 top tone-up tricks to beat cellulite, and reader testimonials that one *can* change one's body shape. Also discussed were eight ways to slow down one's hectic life, advice on how to beat cystitis, detox recipes, and 'amazing stories' of how exercise has saved women's lives. In the popular consciousness, the boundaries between health (how to avoid cystitis or stress), beauty (changing one's body shape) and fitness (toning exercises) are blurred. While the name of the magazine suggests a connection between fitness and health, we get the impression that healthy, fit people are also beautiful people. The cover portrays a tanned, young and thin model in a bikini smiling at the camera on a summer beach. In popular culture, health ideals and physical beauty ideals have become congruent, as health has increasingly become inscribed on body shape (see also Featherstone, 1991). This, however, is not necessarily a contemporary phenomenon. For example, the connection between a fit body and an ideal male body began to emerge already a century ago.

In early twentieth-century Europe, a man named Eugen Sandow displayed his body in public shows. Because of his beautifully proportioned body, Sandow became a celebrity touted as the most famous man in the world. Sandow's physique resembled the slender, yet visibly muscular appearance of the Ancient Greek statues and he often posed in photographs (nearly) nude copying the classic Greek poses. Sandow's ideal, then, was to be the world's best developed (not the strongest) man and his success foregrounded an idea of building aesthetic muscularity for its own sake (Stothart, 1994). Settled in London, Sandow established a chain of gymnasiums, designed training apparatus and published his magazine *Physical Culture* (Stothart, 1994).

As Sandow toured the world, his physical culture movement took hold in the USA. There its proponents included Bernarr MacFadden who later became the editor of *Physical Culture* in the USA. He promoted the body as the means and the goal of adoration with such enthusiasm that he gained the nickname 'Body Love'. The body was an object of care in its own right: 'a strong and beautiful body has become a thing of honor and glory, and the proper feeding of the body a duty recognized and a pleasure to be enjoyed by all' (in Mrozek, 1989: 34). MacFadden's *Physical Culture* magazine promoted the male ideal body of broad shoulders, deep chest, trim waist, and beautiful proportions. Charles Atlas was one such a body when he obtained the title, 'World's Most Handsome Man' in MacFadden's *Physical Culture* magazine. Atlas became one of the celebrated images of perfect manhood in 1930s and 1940s America with his philosophy that the body was to be trained and shaped into a pleasing appearance. There was an added element of male confidence deriving from the well-built physical self. As a source of confidence the look of the body was considered more important than what one did for work. In today's popular literature, men's ideal body shape has not changed a great deal. Men's fitness programmes are commonly designed to improve upper body strength and size through weight training. In addition, exercises such as sit-ups for abdominal definition ('the six pack') feature prominently. White and Gillett (1994) point out that upper body muscularity or strong abdominals are of little use today as many men's work involves little physical strength. However, they add, muscles have increasingly important social value for men in today's changing society. Building muscles helps some men to re-define themselves as males in an environment where other opportunities for 'traditional' masculinity have become increasingly scarce. These researchers claim that muscles are markers of embodied masculine power: muscles are used as a sign of dominance, control, authority, physical strength and power. Because men's body ideal is also lean, in order to display maximum muscle definition, weight loss exercises, often running or cycling, are an important part of men's fitness programmes. As a separate strand, there is also men's popular bodybuilding literature which has inherited some features from the physical culture movement (e.g. Aycock, 1992; Klein, 1993; White and Gillett, 1994). The fit feminine body, however, has evolved through a slightly different route.

When men were building the bodies of the Greek Gods, women's ideal body was still corseted into a shape of an hour glass. Since the beginning of the nineteenth century women's body ideal has been constantly redefined. Women's body ideal has evolved from the curves of the 1950s ideal Marilyn Monroe to the lankiness of super model Twiggy in the 1960s and extreme thinness of Kate Moss today. The fitness movement has surfed on the wave of this change. In the 1960s the father of the aerobics running programme, Kenneth Cooper, already felt that women's exercise should primarily improve bodily appearance: 'The way it works out, women earn a double payoff from aerobics; they go to the program to improve their looks and they get fitness and health as fringe benefits' (Cooper, 1970: 134). In the 1970s and early 1980s when women were increasingly urged to exercise to take care of their bodies, the ideal body was described as slim and softly curvy (Markula, 1993). When Jane Fonda published her *Workout Book* in 1981 a new ideal, a fit, trim and toned body, stepped into women's fitness movement.[3] Among other feminist researchers, Foucauldian feminists (e.g. Bartky, 1988; Bordo, 1993; Markula, 1995) have identified this fit body as the ideal feminine body that permeates contemporary western society. Sandra Bartky (1988) summarised the characteristics of today's feminine body ideal: 'The current body of fashion is taut, small-breasted, narrow-hipped, and of a slimness bordering emaciation; it is a silhouette that seems more appropriate to an adolescent boy or a newly pubescent girl than to an adult woman' (64). In addition, Susan Bordo (1993) observed that it is no longer enough to eliminate excess fat, but fit, healthy looking bodies, in addition to appearing thin, should look tightly toned. While muscle tone is an important aspect of the women's body ideal, too much muscle mass is considered repulsive (Markula, 1995). Similar to the physical culture movement, women build self-confidence through the aesthetics of a thin and toned body: the attractive female body has come to signify a controlled mind and healthy self-confidence (Markula, 1995, 2001).

It is obvious that most women do not naturally possess the ideal body shape, because most women simply do not have the biological make-up for the ideal body. For example, it has been estimated that only 5 per cent of women are born with the right genes for the contemporary slim ideal. Nevertheless, this body shape is celebrated as the 'normal' body which women are incessantly encouraged to build despite the likelihood of never obtaining it. How is it possible that women are persuaded to keep up with this game that can never be won? Here we return to Foucault's concepts of discipline and self-surveillance and how these are aligned with the confessional technique.

Confessional technique of the disciplined body

Foucault argued that within Panopticism 'power becomes less individualized, more functional, more anonymous, but those upon whom it is exercised become more individualized – particularly the ones out of the norm' (Foucault, 1991a: 193). More interestingly, he continued, it is important to also submit the 'normal' to the controlling gaze of this power.

This is done by questioning their normalcy: 'if one wants to individual-
ize the "healthy", the "normal" one asks how much abnormality might
secretly lie in them. Therefore, power produces the truth about the individual, it produces the individual and knowledge about him' (Foucault,
1991a: 193). The fitness media have an advantage in this game because the
majority of consumers fall outside the 'normal' ideal body and are, thus,
bound to find themselves outside the norm. The media, however, individ-
ualise the quest for the fit body through confessionality that, combined
with scientific knowledge, further locks individuals into the disciplinary
Panopticon. Foucault's examination of the concurrent development of sexuality and confession parallels the construction of the ideal body as a
'normal' body.

Foucault examined how sex became 'Scientia Sexuality': a set of practices
moulded through 'interference of two modes of production of truth: procedures of confession and scientific discursivity' (Foucault, 1978: 64–65).
Similarly, the fit body can be seen at the interface of scientific discourse of
the fit body and individual confession of not fulfilling the requirements for
such a body. Here it is important to observe that the scientific discourse of
'health' has been seamlessly woven together with the discourse of a body
beautiful in the popular media. While Foucault detailed confessionality
through a historical genealogy, we analyse whether such a process operates
in today's fitness mediascape and whether it operates as a disciplinary technique via an article titled 'Slash Your No. 1 Health Risk – Today' (Bird,
2005) for the British women's fitness magazine ZEST. The magazine's
slogan 'Health, diet, fitness, looks: A better body guaranteed' embodies
the concerns we have discussed so far in this chapter: the seamless mixing
of health with the looks of the body. Such a mix also allows the scientific discourse of health to be combined with the ideal body and allows
us to examine confessionality at the interface of these two disciplinary
techniques.

According to Foucault (1978), confession became an acceptable scientific
observational technique through the combination of physical examination
and personal history regarding the signs and symptoms of any illness: 'the
interrogation, the exacting questionnaire, and hypnosis, with the recollec-
tion of memories and free association: all were ways of reinscribing the
procedure of confession' (Foucault, 1978: 65). In today's fitness magazines,
interrogation takes the form of a questionnaire. For instance, our sample
article urges the reader to 'use our tests to assess your real risks' (Bird, 2005:
43) of such serious diseases as heart disease, breast cancer, depression or
osteoporosis. Answering the questionnaire, that consists of routine yes or no
questions regarding one's personal history and personal lifestyle habits, is
the first of the 'simple steps' offered by our sample article.

Second, Foucault noted that providing such detailed personal accounts
allows for the establishment of causality:

> The most discrete event in one's sexual behavior ... was deemed capable of entailing the most varied consequences throughout one's existence; there was scarcely a malady or physical disturbance to which the nineteenth century did not impute at least some degree of sexual etiology.
>
> (Foucault, 1978: 65)

Such limitless dangers justified meticulous confession of the details regarding one's sexual behaviour. In contemporary society, sexual activity is still considered to come with certain risks such as being infected by HIV or sexually transmitted diseases. However, it appears that other behaviours have occupied equally alarming status. For example, it is striking that there seems to be no major illness without a causal link to sedentary behaviour (see also Chapter 3). We have perhaps moved into a society of limitless dangers of the inactive, fat and unfit body. Our example article illustrates such potential, hidden dangers of the unfit body as the questionnaires inquire incessantly about the reader's level of inactivity or overweightness. Only questions about smoking or binge drinking are more numerous. Obviously, the body is, through such interrogation, capable of detailing the most varied consequences to the rest of our lives – the risk of serious illnesses. We also note that the magazine questionnaire on the risks of each illness consists of five to seven generic questions (such as 'Are you overweight?') and apparently the author claims that the most serious and longitudinal consequences to one's life can be determined based on such a generic interrogation.

Foucault (1978) concluded that through the scientification of confession, it became possible to know issues unknown even to the confessing individual. Therefore, the idea was not to make one tell things that one was trying to hide, 'but what was hidden from himself, being incapable of coming to light except gradually and through the labor of a confession in which the questioner and the questioned each had a part to play' (Foucault, 1978: 66). Such a sentiment is obvious in our example article: the reader is caught unaware of the dangers of her unfit body, but can now 'stop fretting needlessly' (Bird, 2005: 41) because one is able to discover one's number one health risk through the questionnaire assessment.

Because the confessor was unaware of the danger of his/her behaviour, Foucault (1978) observed that s/he could not understand what the resulting dangers were. Therefore, one needed an interpreter of the results. Such results also needed to be scientifically validated to become part of the scientific truth – to mean anything in terms of the consequences: 'The truth did not reside solely in the subject who, by confessing, would reveal it wholly formed ... the revelation of confession had to be coupled with the decipherment of what is said' (Foucault, 1978: 66). In the *ZEST* article, an interpretation of one's results follows the confessional questionnaire. The interpreters are, of course, medical doctors who detail the risks of each behaviour to which the reader has confessed.

Finally, Foucault (1978) asserted that through the development of the confessional technique, sexual behaviour was medicalised: normal and pathological behaviours were determined and characteristics of sexual morbidity were identified. In addition, 'sex would derive its meaning and its necessity from medical interventions: it would be required by the doctors, necessary for diagnosis, and effective nature in the cure' (Foucault, 1978: 67). Similarly, the fit body becomes pathologised through our article: physical inactivity and obesity are identified as unhealthy (although inactivity and obesity are not defined as terms). Interventions for the unhealthy are offered: take regular weight-bearing exercise, eat sensibly by overhauling your diet. As the questionnaire concerns our everyday behaviours such as eating, drinking and the effects of a stressful life, the confessor is bound to tick at least a couple of boxes to identify herself as abnormal beneath the surface. The 'normal' have become targets for the controlling gaze of the Panoptic power that questions their normalcy. As a consequence, individuals are produced in power relations based on what knowledge is produced about them.

Why is the confessional technique effective? Carol Spitzack's (1990) evocative study of women's dieting can be informative here. She argued that the discourse of dieting entails a curious contradiction. Women are persuaded to diet by being offered their liberation through body reduction: women will have control of their lives, they will be free to pursue many tasks once they have lost their excess weight. Such a promise of liberation presupposes a confession of being too fat, and the willingness to take one's life in control and make a change. As this confession mentality necessitates ongoing confession, Spitzack argued, women are made to do the watching themselves; the female body, therefore, becomes a site of constant scrutiny and women internalise their concern about their body shapes. Similarly, our example article (Bird, 2005) assumes that women have internalised a fear of serious diseases and promises to liberate them from this fear by providing rather common-sense, loosely formulated advice on how to reduce their health risks. The exercise advice offered by the article – regular exercise by taking 10,000 steps a day (equivalent to walking five miles) to reduce the risk of cardiovascular disease, or running outdoors – is relatively unrealistic advice to follow for most women. In addition, like dieting, having to confess one's previously unrecognised risky health behaviours reveals yet another set of activities to carefully observe and control in one's life. The article on health risks (Bird, 2005) pictures a large photograph of a naked, oiled, perfectly toned, thin, young woman further cementing the link between healthy behaviour and looking good. The body is exposed to confess the ills previously hidden from the examining gaze. In addition, the picture promises a transformation from a health slob into an ideal beauty once confession and the necessary activities toward improved health are taken.

It is quite likely that exercise can turn us into docile bodies and act as a disciplinary technique of power. The disciplinary effect is strengthened through the media presentation of the perfect body. Even 'normal' individuals can be pathologised to confessing the bodily flaws or 'unhealthy' behaviours that result in a less than ideal body shape. Such a body shape, again, can present a serious health risk. For example, the *ZEST* article suggests that 'bodyshape is a better indicator of cardiovascular risk than body weight, and that being an apple shape puts you more at risk' (Bird, 2005: 43). In this sense, the fitness industry can be seen as part of the disciplinary machine in society today similar to the prison, hospital, school or factory that Foucault identified as eighteenth-century disciplinary institutions. In his work on discipline and punishment, Foucault (1991a) was mainly concerned with establishing how control over individuals or the social body changed from spectacular punishment by the sovereign, identifiable power to exposing individuals to an invisible, unidentifiable constant surveillance that aimed to govern by individualising people through disciplinary techniques of space, gaze, and controlled exercise. He collected evidence from historical texts on punishment, prison plans and military exercise forms, but was accused of ignoring how the individuals reacted to such uses of power. While he did not consider this the exact aim of his own study, he was aware that Bentham himself excluded 'the effective resistance of people' (Foucault, 1980b: 162) in his model of Panopticon. Foucault did not want to disregard 'resistance' to the disciplinary power arrangement:

> resistances to the Panopticon will have to be analysed in tactical and strategic terms, positing that each offensive from the other side serves as leverage for a counter-offensive from the other. The analysis of power-mechanisms has no built-in tendency to show power as being at once anonymous and always victorious. It is rather a matter of establishing the positions occupied and modes of actions used by each of the forces at work, the possibilities of resistance and counter-attack on either side.
>
> (Foucault, 1980b: 164)

Foucault embarked on his own examination of people's reactions to disciplinary power in his three volumes of *History of Sexuality*. We will examine this in more detail in the last section of this book, but will presently consider exercisers' reaction to the media-fitness industry machinery to consider this aspect of power relations. This section includes data from several studies examining individual exercisers' responses to the construction of the ideal body.

Exercisers' reactions: a counter-offensive?

Because resistance is a common concept used by sport studies scholars, it is necessary to revisit the way Foucault visions this concept within his theoretical schema of power relations. Foucault's notion of resistance differs fundamentally from the idea of agency directed against a visible authority of state, class or other clearly identified 'dominant' group advocated by the theory of hegemonic power. As we described in Chapter 2, the opposition of agentic individuals resisting the dominant groups is based on the binary between individuals denied any access to power, who thus exist outside privilege, and individuals who are fully embodied with power and use it purely to maintain their dominance (a structure similar to a King, an absolute sovereign, holding power over his citizens). Throughout his work in *Discipline and Punish* and *History of Sexuality*, Foucault saw power operating through a different premise to the dualistic oppressed–oppressive hierarchy. Instead of a visible, identifiable source of power, Foucault assumed that power relations operate through disciplinary tactics while remaining invisible. As it is more complex to identify how power operates, it is also more difficult to detect who, what and how individuals resist. In addition, as every individual is a part of power relations, resistance cannot exist outside of these relations. Therefore, we can no longer observe a clearly identified 'powerless' resisting the evil power to overturn it. Instead we need a recognition of points of resistance throughout the relations of power. Therefore, Foucault (1978: 96) asserted that rather than 'violent ruptures' that overturn power, there are 'cleavages' – points, knots, or focuses of resistance – that are distributed in irregular fashion over power relations at multiple points. It is worth quoting Foucault at length here before embarking upon an analysis of 'resistance' in exercise:

> one is dealing with mobile and transitory points of resistance, producing cleavages in a society that shift about, fracturing unities and effecting regroupings, furrowing across individuals themselves, cutting them up and remolding them, marking off irreducible regions in them, in their bodies and minds. Just as the network of power relations ends by forming a dense web that passes through apparatuses and institutions, without being exactly localized in them, so too the swarm of points of resistance traverses social stratifications and individual unities.
>
> (Foucault, 1978: 96)

To tackle these transitory points of resistance, Foucault advised an investigation of the most local power relations at work to identify how discourses such as 'the healthy looking body' are made possible. There are several studies that focus on individual exercisers' relationships to the construction of the ideal body in exercise classes. To highlight a possible fracturing or remoulding of this particular discourse we will now map exercisers' reactions to their practices to detect how effectively they function as disciplinary techniques to produce docile bodies.

Several studies record women's exercise experiences (e.g. Dworkin, 2003; Haravon, 2002; Maguire and Mansfield, 1998; Markula, 1995). There is a general consensus that women exercise to obtain the ideal body shape. For example, in Markula's (1995) study the participants discussed particularly the role of the so-called 'toning exercises' in body shaping. These exercises target one muscle group – or body 'spot' – at a time to effectively tone the intended, isolated body part. This is an efficient use of time: the particular muscle is toned without wasting time and energy in conditioning any unintended muscles. Only few exercisers question the rationale for performing uncomfortable toning exercises for the sake of body shaping: these workouts do, indeed, effectively tone the body and the participants found it a necessary – yet uncomfortable and difficult – way to achieve muscle tone. While they admire tone, women do not desire visible muscularity.[4] Shari Dworkin (2003) recorded similar responses in her ethnographic study of women's exercise patterns. Women in her research wanted to become strong without sporting bulging muscles. Even the women who lifted weights wanted to become thin, lean and hard, not bulky. Dworkin continued that as a matter of fact only a minority of women lift weights, while all engaged in cardiovascular exercise (aerobics or cardio machines) to lose or maintain weight. The exercisers noted that while low weight was not natural for them, they were willing to do whatever it took (e.g. long cardiovascular workouts up to seven days a week) to obtain the thin and toned look. Women in Markula's (1995) study also claimed that first and foremost they worried about being thin and once sufficiently thin, worked on muscle tone. Some aerobicisers completed their toning exercises based on this rationale: toned muscles actually will make one look smaller. As the ideal female body is also a youthful body some women turned to aerobics to specifically fight the effects of age. Age exacerbates problems with the body shape and the exercising women felt pressure to work increasingly hard to obtain the ideal figure.[5]

Based on the results from Dworkin's (2003) and Markula's (1995) studies, female exercisers chose to engage in practices that aided them in the construction of an ideal, healthy looking body. They were well aware of an invisible gaze that somehow forced them into 'normalising' their bodies toward the ideal body. Some claimed the gaze as male; others did not really recognise its source claiming it is just ubiquitously 'societal' (Markula, 1995). This gaze set the standard of the desirable female form and supervised the transformation toward the 'normal'. The exercisers accepted, albeit grudgingly, the bodily discipline required for this process (see also Dworkin, 2003) and did not challenge the body ideal itself in their exercise classes. Leslea Haravon (2002), on the other hand, examined the strategies used by feminist aerobicisers, because these women, she assumed, should reflect on the disciplinary practices of building the beautiful body.

Haravon (2002) observed that the feminist participants were indeed aware of the 'objectification of the female body' and the emphasis on obtaining the perfect body through aerobics. The feminist aerobicisers responded to this emphasis by distancing themselves from the practices of promoting the body beautiful; by reclaiming the disciplinary aspects of exercises (following the precise instruction, repetition and fragmentation) as positive, enjoyable and helpful; by refusing to participate in exercises that made them uncomfortable; or by justifying their participation through claiming that 'There's no perfect class' (Haravon, 2002: 105). Consequently, Haravon recorded that even the feminist participants did not imagine a group exercise class without the ills of disciplinary body practices, and even less did they imagine creating a class based on a different logic themselves. Therefore, while they reflected on the perfect body and their own practices towards building it, they did not actively engage in any counter-attack by creating alternative practices for a group exercise class.

Women's ideas about exercise often resonate with the fitness discourse in the media: they work on their problem spots; they long for a toned body, but not for visible muscle definition; they struggle to fight fat and age, exactly as urged by the media texts (e.g. Dworkin, 2003; Cole, 1998; Cole and Hribar, 1995; Duncan, 1994; Eskes et al., 1998; Markula, 2001; 2003a). However, the same aerobicisers criticised the portrayal of the exercisers in the media as unreal and even irritating (Markula, 1995). They suspected that the model exercisers were selected because of their looks, not because of their expertise. They were irritated having to continually read how to reshape their bodies and questioned whether such exercises 'really work'. Some exercisers had stopped paying attention to such exercise columns or buying magazines after finding out that the exercise information was always about improving the same body spots. Some women also wrote letters to the editors of women's fitness magazines to complain about the one-sided depiction of the thin and toned ideal in those magazines (Markula, 2001). Exercisers viewed videotapes with a particularly strong suspicion: the video exercisers appeared too perfect to be real. Therefore, some aerobicisers in Markula's (1995) study urged women to move their bodies from infront of the television to the class where it was possible to get individual feedback from the instructor and support from the group. Many women also believed that the media only display perfect bodies, and they accepted that the body ideal was 'unhealthy' and unrealistic, yet at the same time, they longed to possess such a body themselves.

From a Foucauldian perspective we conclude that by becoming aware of the defects of one's body, aerobicisers follow the disciplinary exercise practices. Under the disciplinary technology, Foucault stated, 'one's own body can be acquired only through the effect of an investment of power in the body' (Foucault, 1980f: 56). The desire to obtain the ideal thin and toned body reflects the 'insistent, persistent, meticulous work of power on the bodies ... the healthy bodies' (Foucault, 1980f: 56). Therefore, it is no wonder that women exercisers feel pressured to continuously work towards an ideal body. However, as we have discussed, there are women's voices that speak openly against disciplining one's body in exercise classes and criticise the pervasive narrowly defined ideal, healthy looking body in the media (e.g. Haravon, 2002; Markula, 1995, 2001). These can be read as signs that '[p]ower, after investing itself in the body, finds itself exposed to a counter-attack in that same body' (Foucault, 1980f: 56). The exercisers' actions of refusal can be considered clevages that break the dominance of the bodily discipline. 'But,' as Foucault (1980f: 56) concluded, 'the impression that power weakens and vacillates here is in fact mistaken; power can retreat here, re-organise its force, invest itself elsewhere ... and so the battle continues.' Although critical of the ideal, the exercising women do not work to change the healthy looking body, but rather continue to adopt practices to cope with it. Neither do they suggest ways of changing exercise practices, yet they might modify the existing ones or demand detailed instructions for the 'correct' execution of them. Therefore, any knots of resistance have not been able to organise into a force with enough leverage to compel a change in the disciplinary logic of the body beautiful. Foucault also emphasised that resistance can take place anywhere within power relations. Interestingly, the studies looking at 'resistance' to the feminine body ideal through exercise, have only focused on participants' reactions. However, are these the only 'positions occupied' and 'modes of actions' that can be used to strategically disrupt the disciplinary dominance? Does the dualistic assumption of powerless agents (the individual exercisers) resisting the dominant groups (the media?) still underlie our research logic? To identify further knots of resistance, we believe that researchers need to reach beyond participants' experiences and examine also other levels of power relations. Foucault introduced his concept of the technologies of the self to further examine how a variety of individuals operate within power relations. In the final section of this book, we consider the technologies of self and ask: Can fitness adopt a new ethics as a result of modified power relations? And if so, how does power re-organise itself? Where does it invest? Before answering these questions we will first continue our examination of how physically active bodies are constructed within a web of discourses that structures sport. In Chapters 5 and 6 we focus specifically on how sporting identities are formed through practices of heavy contact sport, namely rugby.

Chapter 5

Sport and the discursive construction of gendered bodies

The links between sport, identity construction and gender relations has been one of the most researched topics within the relatively brief history of the sociological study of sport. The numerous researchers who have examined sport and gender tend to agree that sport has long been valued as a masculinising practice and, accordingly, it is vitally important in how males *and* females 'define and differentiate the meaning and practice of masculinity' (Rowe, 1995: 123). The relationship between sport and masculinities has, however, been a cause of concern for a number of critical sport sociologists. Concerns have been raised, for example, that sport helps to produce a dominant but problematic form of masculinity that acts to marginalise alternative masculinities and to subordinate females (e.g. Connell, 1990; Messner, 1992, 2002; Messner and Sabo, 1994; McKay *et al.*, 2000). Previous research from multiple feminist perspectives has similarly demonstrated that the knowledge of sport as a masculinising practice has resulted in on-going struggle for legitimation and equity for sportswomen (e.g. Cahn, 1994; Cole, 1994; Duncan and Hasbrook, 1988; Hargreaves, 1994; Hall, 1996; Lenskyj, 1986; McKay, 1997; Willis, 1982). Sport, therefore, has typically been positioned as a producer of problematic identities and inequitable gender relations within sociological literature.

In this chapter (and the following one) we contribute to this academic debate by examining the discursive links between sport and gender. We first discuss how previous research locates the construction of gendered sporting identities. Second, we introduce a Foucauldian approach for investigating the production of identities in sporting contexts. Finally, we examine how individuals actively participate in the construction of disciplined and gendered sporting identities.

Within this section we focus on the social importance of rugby union in New Zealand. Rugby, a sport played by males and an increasing number of females, provides one discursive context for examining how individuals negotiate understandings of gender and self, while simultaneously participating in the construction of gendered identities. In our investigation, we were particularly interested in (1) how men's experiences of rugby shape their negotiations of self and masculinities, and (2) how female identities are (re)produced by men 'making sense' of women's participation in rugby. Our research project was, accordingly, concerned with understanding the discursive links between male *and* female rugby participation and the production of gendered identities. The research findings are subsequently presented in Chapter 6.

The construction of gendered sporting identities: a review

Young males in western countries have for many years been encouraged or required to play sport, particularly the so-called masculine sports, such as football, ice hockey and basketball. In contrast, many females have been actively prohibited or discouraged from participating in a range of sporting activities. To understand why these differences have occurred and the contemporary relationships between sport and gender, it is relevant to examine the arguments of sport historians and sociologists.

Historians typically suggest that modern sport (when sport is defined somewhat *narrowly* as secular, rule-bound, institutionalised and competitive physical activities that contain a ludic element) developed in the eighteenth and nineteenth centuries in England (e.g. Dunning and Sheard, 1979; Guttman, 1978; Hargeaves, 1986). Critical historians suggest, more specifically, that sport emerged within this era from the male-only contexts of the English public schools and in relation to Victorian concerns about social order, sexuality, morality, health and industrialisation (e.g. Burstyn, 1999; Chandler, 1996; Collins, 1998; Crosett, 1990; Dunning and Sheard, 1979). Tim Chandler (1996) argued, for instance, that from 1860 onwards educators encouraged male participation in sport as an appropriate means of instilling manly character and to help produce 'muscular Christians'. The discourses associated with muscular Christianity reciprocally shaped the Victorian notion of sportsmanship, which emphasised fair play, modesty, and the following of rules, but also encouraged males to participate in a 'redblooded, aggressive and virile' manner (Morford and McIntosh, 1993: 61). The growth of sport, according to Varda Burstyn (1999: 74), was also connected to the development of urban industrial centres and the belief that sport 'trained males in the values and conventions of the workday world of factory or office'.

The Victorian interest in regulating sexual practices (see Foucault, 1978) has similarly been deemed important in the construction of sport as a moral and manly endeavour (Crosset, 1990). Many Victorian educators, for example, believed that by encouraging school-boys to be active in sport, little energy would be left for sexually immoral practices (Chandler, 1996). Sport was, therefore, assumed to build moral character by preventing immoral thoughts and actions: 'Weak, intellectual boys were thought to suffer from perverse thoughts and actions' (Crosset, 1990: 52). In contrast, 'strong, athletic boys were thought to be in control of their passions' (Crosset, 1990: 52). Crosset, accordingly, contended that within the Victorian context, males who did not participate in sport indirectly risked becoming known as effeminate and unhealthy. Relatedly, weaker and non-sporting boys were marginalised as saps or sexual/gender deviants.

In sum, the prime historical argument to explain why young males have been typically encouraged to play sport, rests on the assumption that participation will produce healthy, virile, hard working, rule-following, competitive, courageous and moral men. Burstyn (1999) further argued that these particular 'masculine' attributes have been highly valued, not because they have intrinsic value, but because they prepared young males for 'manhood' and their ensuing roles as workers in capitalist economies, patriarchs in traditional forms of the family, and in 'exercising violence in the service of nation and empire' (74). The subsequent popularity of (male) sport throughout the twentieth century has, therefore, been linked to its ability to reaffirm a seemingly practical and respected form of masculinity. Sport, in this manner, has been conceptualised as a masculinising practice and as a producer of inequitable power relations between males. If sport has been predominantly known as a manly activity, how has this understanding shaped the story and experiences of female involvement in sport?

In contrast to the history of male participation in sport, the discursive understanding of sport as masculinising, has helped to produce a very different feminine identity. Far from being encouraged to participate in sport, females have had to struggle for sporting legitimacy. Richard Giulianotti (2005), for example, stated that 'women's advances in sport were often controlled and curtailed by men in accordance with patriarchal norms' (83). Despite the unfairness and injustice of these sexist discriminations females did 'participate in the great athleticization of late nineteenth-century society' (Burstyn, 1999: 49); although typically in sporting activities independently organised by females and in venues on the periphery of society (Lenskyj, 1986).

In spite of women's more recent athletic progress, many researchers have illustrated an assortment of contemporary gender inequalities, such as the marginalisation and trivialisation of women's performances, and the sexualisation and infantilisation of their athletic bodies (e.g. Cahn, 1994; Cole, 1994; Duncan and Hasbrook, 1988; Hargreaves, 1994; Hall, 1996; Lenskyj, 1986; McKay, 1997; Willis, 1982). More generally, the discursive positioning of sport as a masculinising practice can still create 'gender troubles' for sportswomen (e.g. Chapman, 1997; Cole, 1993; Duncan, 1994). Many females, for example, are aware that participation in sport, particularly the aggressive body-contact sports, can lead to questions about their femininity and sexuality, and risk harassment and isolation (Caudwell, 1999, 2002).

Subsequently sportswomen can become subject to the control of compulsory heterosexuality and the associated fear of 'gender deviance' (Shogan, 1999: 59). These fears can manifest in various ways. Some sportswomen, for example, attempt to avert them by displaying overt signs of femininity while participating (Bolin, 1992), whereas others succumb and withdraw from sport. Many sportswomen, however, successfully 'work out the incongruity between their female bodies and their "masculine" performances' (Shogan, 1999: 62) despite being subject to strict gender surveillance.

Our succinct examination of the history of sport and gender relations offers a plausible explanation – that sport has been discursively constructed as a masculinising practice – to help understand why the contemporary sporting world is far from a level playing field for females *and* males. It was, however, not until the early 1990s, aided by the promotion of feminist theorising (e.g. Bryson, 1987; Hall, 1982; Hargreaves, 1982; Theberge, 1981, Willis, 1982), appropriation of neo-Marxist understandings of power/hegemony (e.g. Carrigan *et al.*, 1985), and the influential work of Michael Messner and Don Sabo (e.g. 1990, 1994), that concern about the relationships between masculinities and sport became prominent within sociological studies of sport. This research has been typically underpinned by the concepts of hegemonic masculinity and gender order, as popularized by R. W. Connell (1987, 1995, 2001). In the following section we introduce these concepts and critically examine the associated sport and gender research.

Polemics surrounding sport, gender and hegemonic masculinity

Connell argued that hegemonic masculinity, as a state or condition of ideology, frames understandings of how particular ways of performing maleness seem natural and normal, but simultaneously sustains problematic relations of dominance within an assumed structure or *order* of gender. Connell (2002: 28) described the hegemonic form of masculinity, as the 'most honoured or desired in a particular context' and, more specifically as 'the configuration of gender practices which embodies the currently accepted answer to the problem of the legitimacy of patriarchy, which guarantees (or is taken to guarantee) the dominant position of men and the subordination of women' (Connell, 1995: 77). Connell, as inspired by Gramsci's (1971) understandings of power, connected the constitution and promotion of hegemonic masculinity with the actions of ruling classes or groups, economic activities and a hierarchical structure of power:

We might propose ... that the hegemonic form of masculinity in the current world gender order is the masculinity associated with those who control its dominant institutions: the business executives who operate in global markets, and the political executives who interact (and in many contexts merge) with them. I will call this 'transnational business masculinity'.

(Connell, 2002: 39)

Connell prudently refused to provide a definitive list of the traits or behaviours representative of hegemonic masculinity. He stated, however, that contemporary forms of hegemonic masculinity link exalted notions of manliness with toughness and competitiveness, and current exemplars are male participants in the popular winter football codes, such as 'those who run out into the mud and the tackles themselves' (Connell, 1995: 79). Connell more specifically linked this hegemonic form of masculinity with the ostensibly divergent form of 'transnational business masculinity' (Connell, 2002: 32):

> Transnational business masculinity does not require a powerful physique, since the patriarchal dividend on which it rests is accumulated by impersonal, institutional means. But corporations increasingly use images of the exemplary bodies of elite sportsmen as a marketing tool (as seen in the exceptional growth of corporate 'sponsorship' of sport in the last generation), and indirectly as a means of legitimation for the whole global gender order.
>
> (Connell, 2002: 39–40)

Connell's concepts of hegemonic masculinity and the gender order as heuristic devices for understanding relationships between sport and gender have been widely acknowledged as useful. Indeed, the critical analyses concerning sport, gender and the concept of hegemonic masculinities were quickly and widely accepted within the sociology of sport; 'some might even say, canonized' (McKay et al., 2000: 3). Many critical commentators have subsequently drawn on this theoretical framework and argued that sport, particularly the popular winter football codes, problematically link violence, tolerance of pain, competition and physical skill with masculinities (e.g. Hickey, et al., 1998; Lynch, 1993; Miller, 1998; Nauright and Chandler, 1996; Rowe and McKay, 1998; Trujillo, 1995; Young et al., 1994). Sport has, accordingly, been represented as the prime social institution that promotes the construction of hegemonic masculinity and male privilege in society (Bryson, 1990; Messner, 1992; Young et al., 1994), the relative poor health of males (Sabo, 1998; Sabo and Gordon, 1995), the marginalisation and denigration of other masculinities (Connell, 1987; Whitson, 1990; Young et al., 1994) and actions of violence, particularly against women (Curry, 1998; Loy, 1995; Sabo et al., 2000).

A number of researchers, however, have also raised pertinent questions about the analyses of sport and masculinities. Commentators, for example, have questioned the salience of focusing reductively on masculinities for examining understandings of pain or processes of male identity formation in sporting contexts (e.g. Albert, 1999; Curry, 1993; de Garis, 2000; Hunt, 1995; Pringle, 2003; Young and White, 1995). Others wonder whether the critical analyses have unduly focused on negative aspects and correspondingly trivialised the positives (e.g. de Garis, 2000; McKay *et al.*, 2000). Jim McKay and colleagues, for instance, asked: 'Have sport studies scholars overstated the extent to which sport is a conservative institution that largely reproduces existing inequalities, while ignoring or downplaying the range and diversity of existing sport activities?' (McKay *et al.*, 2000: 6–7). In addition, others have questioned the effectiveness of the concept of hegemonic masculinity for examining the complexities and contradictions associated with power and gender (e.g. de Garis, 2000; Donaldson, 1993; Giulianotti, 2005; Martin, 1998; Miller, 1998; Pringle, 2005; Speer, 2001; Star, 1999a; Tomlinson, 1998; Wetherell and Edley, 1999).

Alan Tomlinson (1998) argued, for example, that hegemony theorists have tended to focus on power as a form of domination that operates in a top-down manner that subsequently encourages representations of sport as part of an 'all-pervasive power structure' (237). Similarly, Giulianotti (2005) commented that if the concept of hegemonic masculinity is used inflexibly the resulting research can appear, to its detriment, as 'simple *dietrologia*' (96), where *dietrologia* is the Italian word for the art of finding sinister explanations for the most obvious of decisions. Michael Donaldson, in contrast, was pragmatically concerned that the definition of hegemonic masculinity was too 'slippery' (Donaldson, 1993: 647) and, accordingly, difficult to conceptualise and use. He also raised questions about the viability of using elite male sport participants as exemplars of hegemonic masculinity.

> A football star is a model of hegemonic masculinity. But is a model? When the handsome Australian Rules football player, Warwick 'the tightest shorts in sports' Caper, combined football with modeling, does this confirm or decrease his exemplary status? When Wally ('the King') Lewis explained that the price he will pay for another 5 years playing in the professional Rugby League is the surgical replacement of both his knees, this is undoubtedly the stuff of good, old, tried and true, tough and stoic, masculinity. But how powerful is a man who mutilates his body, almost as a matter of course, merely because of a job? When Lewis announced that he was quitting the very prestigious 'State of Origin' football series because his 1-year-old daughter had been diagnosed as hearing impaired, is this hegemonic?
>
> (Donaldson, 1993: 647)

To overcome these limitations a growing number of researchers have drawn on Foucault to examine the influence of sport in the production of disciplined female bodies (e.g. Chapman, 1997; Cole, 1994; Duncan, 1994; Eskes *et al.*, 1998; Markula, 1995, 2003b; Shogan, 1999; Theberge, 1991) and, to a lesser extent, masculine subjectivities (e.g. Heikkala, 1993; Pringle, 2005; Pringle and Markula, 2005; White and Gillett, 1994). We examine next how Foucault's tools can be used to understand the influence of sport in the production of gendered identities.

Foucauldian theorising and the discursive construction of identities

To introduce a Foucauldian understanding of the construction of gendered identities via sport we recap, and then expand, on Foucault's ideas on the constitution of the subject (as detailed in Chapter 2). Foucault (1983a) retrospectively explained that his prime research aim had been to investigate the different ways in which human beings have been transformed into subjects. Within his earlier archaeological work Foucault primarily examined the discursive influence of the human sciences with respect to how these sciences classified and divided people, both spatially and socially, into various categories. Foucault's early focus, therefore, was the controlling influence of scientific discourse in the constitution of identity and individuals. Within *The Archaeology of Knowledge* he then attempted to 'bracket off' the workings of discourse from social practices and institutions to map the apparent autonomy of discursive formations. Yet Foucault was not entirely happy with the results of his somewhat structuralist experiment. Indeed, he later acknowledged that the workings of discourse were always tied to human actions and the workings of power. Foucault was relatedly critical, as Paul Rabinow (1984: 10) stated, of analyses that treated 'discourse (or ideology) as reflections ... of something supposedly "deeper" and more "real"'. Foucault's subsequent turn to genealogy redirected his focus back to social institutions, material practices and towards the analysis of specific *forms of power*. Foucault (1983a) was particularly interested in forms of power 'which make individuals subjects' (212) and tie them to specific identities. Foucault maintained that power is always present within human relations and he located the body as the site for the workings of power. The productive effects of power, he elaborated, produced 'certain bodies' (Foucault, 1980e: 25) and also the desires, postures and interactions of those bodies.

Foucault was, then, interested in the social processes that connected relationships of power within specific discursive contexts. These, he believed, produced differentiated experiences and created specific identities. In his later works concerned with sexuality and ethics, Foucault further emphasised the importance of studying *experiences* to help understand processes of identity creation. He asserted within the preface to *The Uses of Pleasure* that his 'object was to analyze sexuality as a historically singular form of experience' (Foucault, 1997e: 199). Moreover, he asserted that he treated sexuality as a 'complex experience' (200): an experience that,

> conjoins a field of knowledge . . . (with its own concepts, theories, diverse disciplines), a collection of rules . . . and a mode of relation between the individual and himself [sic] (which enables him to recognize himself as a sexual subject amid others).
>
> (Foucault, 1997e: 200)

Consequently, from a Foucauldian perspective, identity can be understood as constructed via *experiences* that are linked to the workings of discourse, power relations, disciplinary techniques and processes of active self-negotiation. This focus on 'experiences' as constituting subjectivities has been largely overlooked within sporting research. Debra Shogan (1999) stated, for example, that researchers who study identification processes within sporting contexts typically select a category of people, such as female athletes, and then proceed to examine the experiences of this group. Yet the weakness of this approach, she argued, is that 'the social scientist already presumes to know who a female athlete is, thus contributing to the solidification of the category "the female athlete"' (47). Shogan explained further:

> Experiences of 'female athletes' don't just happen. These experiences are the consequences of certain sets of discourses and technologies that make possible these experiences and not others. Tracing discourses and technologies of disciplines that have produced experiences of 'athlete,' 'female,' and, say, 'white,' 'able-bodied,' or 'heterosexual,' make it possible to explore how these discourses and technologies differentiate and how they create the fact of different social groups in the first place.
>
> (Shogan, 1999: 47)

A Foucauldian investigation of the production of sporting identities, accordingly, would not presume that an athletic or even a female or male identity was pre-existing within a particular body. In a related manner, a key difference between Foucauldian studies of gender construction and the studies deriving from Marx concerns the assumption about the existence of an authentic or true self. Studies that have drawn on the Marxist inspired concept – *ideology of masculinity* – accept that identities are socially constructed, but underpinning the ideologically constructed 'false' identity lays a true self: an 'un-alienated' self that can be discovered in its true authenticity once repressive forms of power are removed.

Foucault, following his anti-humanist stance, was sceptical of the notion of a 'true self' for two prime reasons. First, he did not view power as operating repressively but productively. He asked rhetorically: 'if power were never anything but repressive, if it never did anything but to say no, do you really think one would be brought to obey it?' (Foucault, 1980d: 119). Moreover, he accepted that one can never escape the workings of power, thus, the subject is constantly produced in relations of power and related social practices. Second, he argued that the concept of ideology was dependent on the humanistic notion of authentic consciousness, given that ideology 'stands in virtual opposition to something else which is supposed to count as truth' (Foucault, 1980d: 118). Foucault further explained that if this ideological 'truth' was *not* socially constructed it must rest on the assumption of an authentic consciousness or, in other words, a human essence.

Foucault's genealogies aimed, in part, to illustrate how the notion of a human 'nature' was in itself a discursive construction. The task of genealogy, for example, was 'to expose a body totally imprinted by history and the process of history's destruction of the body' (Foucault, 1977c: 148). Thus, under a Foucauldian lens, gender (just like sexuality) is not considered a 'natural feature or fact of human life but a constructed category of experience which has historical, social and cultural, rather than biological, origins' (Spargo, 1999: 12). A Foucauldian perspective, accordingly, would examine how understandings of sexuality or gender developed over time and, reciprocally, how these understandings shape *experiences* of being human.

Drawing from Foucault, Shogan highlighted that athletic bodies are by no means results of natural processes. She asserted: 'Disciplined athletic bodies are not "natural" or "normal," and there is nothing "natural" or "normal" about a body disciplined as feminine or masculine. Femininity and masculinity, like sport skills, are acts or performances that must be learned' (Shogan, 1999: 51). In other words, we should not think that male athletes who display aggression and ignore pain in the pursuit of victory are somehow revealing the true essence of maleness or, reciprocally, that female athletes who display grace, rhythm and flexibility are exhibiting the inherent qualities of femaleness. In contrast, we conceptualise athletes as produced via their sporting experiences that are structured within relations of power and discourse, in their respective sporting 'disciplines'. Sport in this sense can be thought of as a *modern discipline*; it is 'both an exercise of control and a subject matter' (Shogan, 1999: 11). This 'discipline' is also assumed to *help* produce the modern gendered identities where the masculine and feminine bodies are both docile, yet different.

Foucauldian analyses of sport and gender

Researchers who have drawn on Foucault to understand sport and the construction of multiple identities have commonly examined female experiences in sport and exercise contexts in relation to disciplinary techniques (e.g. Cole, 1994; Duncan, 1994; Eskes *et al.*, 1998; Markula, 1995, 2000; Theberge, 1991). These researchers typically concluded that 'physical activity acts as a technology of domination that anchors women into a discursive web of normalizing practices' and 'disciplines women into docile bodies" (Markula, 2003b: 88). Yet other researchers have more recently drawn on Foucault's concerns with the technologies of self to examine how sportswomen negotiate their experiences and potentially subvert the docility–utility dichotomy to undertake sporting practices for personal gain (e.g. Chapman, 1997; Guthrie and Castelnuovo, 2001; Johns and Johns, 2000; Shogan, 1999; Wesely, 2001).

Gwen Chapman (1997), for example, drew on Foucault to examine how sporting women's bodies are constructed in relationships of power in the context of lightweight rowing: a sport demanding that competitors meet weight restrictions. Her analysis revealed that many of the athletes experienced tension in relation to the intersection between biomedical, 'gender and sports discourses' (221); discourses that crystallised in the minds of the athletes to reinforce 'the importance of creating an idealized physical body' (221). The rowers subsequently struggled with their own bodies and 'their relationships with themselves' (221). Chapman concluded that 'at the same time that sport offers women discursive tools to oppose oppressive power relations, it also further enmeshes them in normalizing discourses that limit their vision of who and what they can be' (Chapman, 1997: 221).

A smaller number of researchers have also examined the production of masculinities from a Foucauldian perspective. Juha Heikkala (1993) for example, illustrated that athletic bodies (male or female) are normalised by the disciplinary techniques of modern sport and the logic of competition so that they develop 'productive bodies' (398) and a 'will to win' (397). Sporting bodies, therefore, need to gain pleasure in 'training, sweat, and muscular pain' (400) to produce their athletic (i.e. masculine) identity. Similarly, White and Gillett (1994: 20) suggested that the disciplinary practices employed in sport could be understood as 'truth games' or techniques 'that some men use to understand themselves as masculine'. Athletic identity can, accordingly, be understood as produced via technologies of dominance and of self within the discursive context of sport. Heikkala explained:

> in sport, external control by authorities is only half of the story. Sport is not forced labour; it must and does include a strong voluntary flavour. Significantly, the will to do better must also carry a strong internalized feeling of a 'need' of discipline and conformity to the practices necessary for achieving the desired goal. The eye of an external authority is accompanied with an internalized 'bad conscience', which sounds an alarm whenever tasks are not properly executed or the columns of training diaries are not adequately filled. ... This bad conscience is a

consequence of normalizing techniques and is the instrument of control, internal or external.

(Heikkala, 1993: 401)

The cumulative result of successful disciplinary training, according to Foucault (1977a), is the production of a docile but 'efficient machine' (164). Within a sporting context, a well-disciplined body conforms to instructions and rules, works in unison with other trained bodies, performs with minimal error, displays appropriate skills, tolerates discomfort, follows prescribed tactics and exhorts maximum efficiency in the performance of its duties. Such disciplined bodies have become sought after commodities in professional sport. We suggest, relatedly, that the subsequent celebration of these 'champion bodies' can be partly understood as a celebration of disciplined work and normalisation or conformity (Heikkala, 1993). The high performance athlete, for example, conforms by not questioning the umpire or coach, the value of competing, nor the rationality of arduous training requirements.

Not all sporting bodies, however, are celebrated and not all that undergo disciplinary training become high-performance machines. Foucault (1991a) recognised that disciplinary power is not always successful in determining the shape of people: 'instead of bending all its subjects into a single uniform mass, it separates, analyses, differentiates, carries its procedures of decomposition to the point of necessary and sufficient single units' (170). In this manner he suggested that: 'discipline "makes" individuals' (170). The disciplinary techniques employed within sport settings, for example, can help create normalised athletes and champions, but can also produce a multitude of subject positions such as: losers, benchwarmers, social players, tomboys, queers, sports drop-outs, cheats, the lackadaisical, unfit, unskilled, disabled, injured and, of course, ill-disciplined.

In contrast to studies of masculinities that have employed hegemony theory – which tend to conclude that sporting activities primarily help produce a dominant form of masculinity – Foucauldian based studies accept that sport, as a modern discipline, creates a plethora of identities that can reaffirm but also challenge dominant understandings of masculinities (Pringle and Markula, 2005). In a related manner, Foucauldian studies would not necessarily deduce that sport primarily acts as a tool for the 'ruling groups' to maintain hegemony. Regardless of these differences, examinations of sport via Foucauldian or hegemony theory typically recognise sport as a *masculinising practice* that organises various knowledges about bodies and shapes relations of power between multiple 'subjects'.

Having discussed Foucauldian analyses of sport and gender, we now examine a specific sporting context to explore the interplay between sport disciplines and the production of multiple subjectivities and power relations. While there are numerous sporting disciplines we have chosen to draw on

Foucault to examine how the social dominance of rugby within New Zealand is linked to the constitution of male *and* female athletic identities.

Contextualising rugby and introducing our research problem

Rugby was selected as the sport of analysis due to its reputation within New Zealand as a rough sport played predominantly and traditionally by males but also, in more recent years, by a relatively small yet growing number of females. The sport is characteristically regarded as New Zealand's national sport and even as a way of life or secular religion (Laidlaw, 1999; Richards, 1999). Rugby's privileged socio-cultural position is reflected in the extensive sportsmedia coverage devoted to the sport (McGregor, 1994), and rugby's prominent place within New Zealand schools (Pringle, 2002; Star, 1999b; Thompson, 1988). Several sport sociologists have been concerned with the links between violent sports like rugby, masculinities and gender relations (e.g. Dunning and Sheard, 1979; Messner and Sabo, 1990; Sabo and Runfola, 1980; Sheard and Dunning, 1973). For example, Schacht (1996) in his ethnographic examination of rugby in North America concluded:

> Rugby players situationally do masculinity by reproducing rigid hierarchical images of what a 'real man' is in terms of who is strongest, who can withstand the most pain, and who relationally distances himself from all aspects of femininity through forms of misogynistic denigration. ... Rugby, like other sporting events, is literally a practice field where the actors learn how to use force to ensure a dominant position relative to women, feminine men, and the planet itself.
>
> (Schacht, 1996: 562)

We regarded rugby as an important but potentially problematic discursive space within which people participate in the construction of gendered identities and games of power. This conceptualisation of rugby, accordingly, encouraged our desire to examine the influence of rugby in the production of gendered bodies. Our subsequent examination was guided by two prime research questions. First, we wanted to understand: 'How do men's rugby *experiences* of fear, pain, and/or pleasure articulate with understandings of self and masculinities?' And second: 'How do men participate in the discursive construction of female athletic identity?' To answer both of these questions we interviewed a diverse group of 14 New Zealand men.

Men's subjective *experiences* of rugby fear, pain and/or pleasure have been rarely examined, yet they are meaningful and significant aspects of participation in sports of risk. Heavy-contact sports, for example, are recognised to be as 'much about dealing with fear and anxiety in oneself as it is about dominating an opponent' (Fitzclarence and Hickey, 2001: 129).

It has also been postulated that a male athlete's performance of masculinity is vulnerable if he cannot sustain a display of fearlessness in times of corporeal risk (Sabo, 1986; Young *et al.*, 1994). We assumed, therefore, that an analysis of men's experiences of rugby fear would help highlight the discursive links between sport and masculinities. Similarly, we thought it might be advantageous to examine men's embodied experiences of rugby pleasure. Michael Gard and Robert Meyenn (2000), for example, argued that if critical researchers want to change the social influence associated with heavy-contact sports, there is a need to examine the discourses of sporting pleasure. Indeed, despite the significant risks of injury and pain, many males and a growing number of females enjoy actively participating in rugby.

Our interest in examining female athletic identities stemmed from the recent phenomenon of females participating in a broader range of sports, such as rugby, and the related concern that some men have lost their sense of identity due to women's 'intrusion' into sport. Mariah Burton Nelson (1994) has correspondingly suggested that female advancement in sport has spurred a backlash against feminism and fuelled something akin to a crisis of masculinity. She argued, for example: 'The stronger women get, the more enthusiastically male fans, players, coaches, and owners seem to be embracing a particular form of masculinity: toughness, aggression, denial of emotion, and a persistent denigration of all that's considered female' (Nelson, 1994: 6).

Michael Messner (2002) similarly acknowledged that 'athletic progress for girls and women . . . has not been without costs, questions, and dilemmas' (137). Although this mass movement has 'empowered women in ways that have challenged and destabilized the masculinist center of American sport' (137) it has also prompted a reactionary response to affirm this problematic centre. Despite such claims, little empirical information exists to illustrate how men have reacted to the supposedly recent advent of 'stronger women'. We, therefore, aim to examine the discursive construction of gendered identities through the voices of male rugby participants to reveal something about 'what we are, in this very moment' (Foucault, 1983a: 216) as humans interacting in a complex web of power relations.

Conducting a Foucauldian analysis of sport, gender and power

Data were collected in relation to our focal research questions through in-depth interviews with a purposefully selected group of adult men (Patton, 1990). Our process of selecting appropriate interview participants was designed in response to our recognition that previous masculinities research on sport and pain had overwhelmingly concentrated on the experiences of elite level athletes. Research has examined, for example, the understandings of a champion wrestler (Curry, 1993), an 'iron man' (Connell, 1990:

83), professional footballers (Roderick *et al.*, 2000), rugby union players who are 'highly committed' (Sparkes and Smith, 1999: 78) and men who have retired from 'athletic careers' (Messner, 1992: 8). There have been, however, few empirical examinations of how males who are not elite level athletes encounter and make sense of sports with respect to understanding masculinities. Little was known, therefore, about how so-called 'normal' men negotiate understandings of masculinities in the face of the cultural dominance of heavy-contact sport. More generally, more research was needed to highlight how men construct meanings about strong and aggressive sportswomen. A purposeful sample was collected to help answer our two prime research questions.

We invited 14 men with a diverse range of rugby participation experiences to be interview participants; all accepted this invitation. The interviewees, given pseudonyms here to protect their identity, ranged in age from 21 to 50 years and were selected through personal contacts. Although we attempted to interview men of different social and ethnic backgrounds all indicated that they were heterosexual. Of the 14 men interviewed, one had never played club rugby, five had played briefly as boys, three participated into their teens and five into their twenties: including one who had played professionally. Although this might sound as if we predominantly interviewed rugby participants, it is relevant to recognise that rugby participation was mandatory for all young New Zealand males up until the 1970s (Star, 1999b) and, although no longer compulsory, rugby has remained culturally central.

Through interviewing this range of men we wished to understand the uniqueness of how each interviewee made sense of his rugby experiences and women rugby players, while also examining the broader discursive influence of rugby and gender that cut across their narratives. We, therefore, aimed to connect the unique stories of a range of men with wider socio-political issues. The interviews were audio-taped and transcribed verbatim. We did not remain neutral or passive while conducting the interviews but aimed to construct an environment where the interview participants' interpretive capabilities were 'activated, stimulated, and cultivated' (Holstein and Gubrium, 1995: 17). This interview technique allowed the interview participants to reveal the complexities of their lived experiences, subjective understandings about gender and rugby, and the discursive resources used in constructing these understandings. Accordingly, the in-depth interviews were effective for disclosure of the discursive construction of the men's lived rugby experiences.

The 'free interplay' (Kvale, 1996: 203) of analytical techniques was guided, in part, by Foucault's (1978) strategies for examining the workings of discourse and power relationships. Foucault (1972) used the term 'discourse' in reference to social practices that regulate the production and circulation of statements and perceptions of reality.[1] We were interested,

therefore, to excavate the discourses that systematically formed the interviewees' knowledge of rugby and to explore how these discourses *governed* the
interviewees' statements and perceptions about rugby and gender. To identify the discourses of significance we first distinguished the prime 'objects'
enunciated into existence by the interviewees (e.g. rugby, female rugby players, masculinity). More generally, we looked for regularity in the dispersion
of statements related to these objects and the 'rules of formation' that governed the dispersion of these statements. Foucault, for example, suggested:

> Whenever one can describe, between a number of statements, such a
> system of dispersion, whenever, between objects, types of statements,
> concepts, or thematic choices, one can define a regularity (an order,
> correlations, positions and functionings, transformations), we will say,
> for the sake of convenience, that we are dealing with a *discursive
> formation*.
>
> (Foucault, 1972: 38, italics in original)

Our analysis of the interview transcripts was also guided by Foucault's
(1978) 'cautionary prescriptions' (98) for understanding the workings of
discourse. He warned that it was not a simple task to identify a specific
discourse and, correspondingly, suggested we should not expect 'that the
world presents us with a legible face, leaving us merely to decipher it;
it does not work hand in glove with what we already know, there is
no pre-discursive fate disposing the world in our favour' (Foucault, 1972:
229). He explained that discourses were difficult to decipher, in part,
because a 'multiplicity of discursive elements … can come into play in
various strategies' (Foucault, 1978: 100). We, therefore, thought that the
interviewees' understandings of rugby and gender would not necessarily
be simply 'divided between accepted discourse and excluded discourse, or
between the dominant discourse and the dominated one' (Foucault, 1978:
100) but that numerous and even contradictory discourses would possibly
govern the interviewees' perceptions.

Foucault (1972) further suggested that discourse 'must be treated as a discontinuous activity, its different manifestations sometimes coming together,
but just as easily unaware of, or excluding each other' (229). More generally, he explicated that the tactical function or power effect of discourses,
given their discontinuity, 'is neither uniform nor stable' (Foucault, 1978:
100). For instance, the effect of the same discourse could act to reinforce
but also undermine and weaken the workings of power. In relation to the
discontinuity and instability of discourses, Foucault provided some specific
techniques of analysis:

> It is this distribution that we must reconstruct, with the things said
> and those concealed, the enunciations required and those forbidden,

that it comprises; with the variants and different effects – according to who is speaking, his [sic] position of power, the institutional context in which he happens to be situated that it implies; and with the shifts and reutilizations of identical formulas for contrary objectives that it also includes.

(Foucault, 1978: 100)

Following Foucault's broad suggestions we analysed the interview transcripts to identify the discourses that regulated the interviewees' statements concerning their rugby experiences and understandings of male and female rugby. More generally, we were interested in the 'tactical productivity' (Foucault, 1978: 102) of these discourses. In other words, we wanted to understand how these discourses were drawn upon to (re)produce sporting identities and shape gender relations, but also we wanted to examine how the interviewees *strategically* used these discourses to position themselves and others.

Bridging words

In this chapter, we first provided an overview of how previous research has understood the relationships between sport and the construction of gendered identities. We then examined Foucauldian tools for understanding the constitution of subjectivities and power relations. Foucault highlighted that identity is constructed via human experiences as related to the discursive context, power relations and technologies of domination and self. Drawing from Foucault's work, we designed a research project to investigate the discursive formation of men's *experiences* of rugby and their subsequent participation in the construction of gendered athletic identities. In the following chapter, we present our research findings.

Chapter 6

A discursive analysis of rugby experiences and the construction of gendered identities

In the previous chapter we examined the production of gendered identities within sporting contexts. We highlighted how research has tended to position sport as a producer of problematic identities and inequitable gender relations. We then revealed our desires to expand this debate by drawing on Foucault to examine how individuals actively participate in the construction of gendered sporting identities. To help with this endeavour we, accordingly, detailed Foucault's (1997e) approach for examining human experiences to understand the construction of identities. Foucault advocated that through examining the experiences of humans, via a focus on the workings of discourse and different techniques of power, one could gain understanding of how different social groups, such as males and females, and specific identities are (re)produced. In following Foucault's ideas we detailed our research method to examine two interrelated phenomena associated with the social importance of rugby within New Zealand: (1) how do men's rugby *experiences* of fear, pain, and/or pleasure articulate with understandings of self and masculinities? And (2), how do men participate in the discursive construction of female athletic identity?

In this chapter we present the results from our analysis of rugby experiences and draw tentative conclusions about the discursive links between sport and the construction of gendered bodies. We first discuss the interviewees' subjective rugby experiences and present these in a chronological order, from boyhood to adulthood, to illustrate how their relationships with rugby changed over time. We then discuss the interviewees' understandings of female rugby players. In the final section, we discuss our findings and draw tentative conclusions about the contemporary constitution of bodies within complex webs of power relations suffused by the discursive importance of sport and gender.

Men's subjective experiences of rugby pain, fear and/or pleasure

To examine the discursive links between rugby and the construction of gendered bodies we initially wanted to understand how rugby, as one of our prime 'objects' of analysis, was enunciated into existence by our interviewees. In other words, we wanted to understand how the interviewees 'knew' of rugby. We correspondingly began the interviews by asking each interviewee to talk about their earliest memories of rugby. In response to this invitation and other on-going questions, we heard diverse, complex and, at times, evocative stories of their youthful experiences of rugby.

Reflections on boyhood experiences

All of the interviewees – regardless of whether they held supportive, critical or mixed feelings about rugby – gave accounts of how rugby was a pervasive influence in their youth. This 'pervasiveness' existed to the extent that the majority of interviewees believed they were expected to participate in rugby and most did: 13 of the 14 men participated in organised rugby competitions before their 11th birthday. For many of these men, rugby was a compulsory aspect of their youthful education:

> Rugby was part of the curriculum – the boys would play rugby as part of their schoolwork and the girls would play netball. That was how it was: you milked cows, you went to school, you played rugby, you went home. . . . All the boys did rugby.
>
> (Lionel)

The interview participants suggested that they played not only because it was required but also as 'it was the thing to do' (George), 'it was fun' (Willy) or to simply 'fit in' (Sebastian) and be 'normal' (Colin). Edgar was the only interviewee who did not play competitive rugby while at primary school. He explained his lack of participation in a somewhat defensive manner:

> I was always the smallest kid in class: all the way through. And there wasn't a strong rugby influence in my family. My father was much older, he must have been approaching 50, so he never took me to rugby games or enrolled me at the local rugby club. . . . But the prime reason why I didn't play was because. . . . I was sick a lot with asthma.
>
> (Edgar)

Edgar, however, clearly understood that 'rugby was a prime way of being socially accepted' and poignantly remarked: 'obviously I would have liked to have been good at rugby'. Such is the impact of being subject to a mode of masculinity that implicates: if you are a boy and you do not play rugby, you are different and less valued. Rugby participation, in this respect, was a prime normalising practice for young males; it helped mark boys' bodies as appropriately masculine.

Through our analysis of the interview transcripts it was apparent that the social dominance of rugby was typically governed by three dominating discourses. The first discourse produced rugby as a sport specifically for males. Many of the interviewees simply spoke this 'truth' into existence by proclaiming that rugby was a 'man's game'. George, in typical fashion, stated, 'I believe it's a man's game personally' but also added: 'actually it's a young man's game, but if you want to play it when you are older then that is cool'. George was, therefore, liberal-minded enough to remove the ageism from his statement, but neglected to recognise the inherent sexism. The discourse producing the 'truth' that rugby was a sport specifically for males simultaneously prevented recognition of female involvement in rugby. This example illustrates how discourses not only produce the 'objects' of which they speak, but also constrain what can be thought, expressed and acted upon (Foucault, 1972).

The second prime discourse of rugby positioned the sport as a rough or aggressive sport. This discourse was evidenced by the manner in which the interviewees referred to rugby as a 'hard-contact sport' (Colin), 'good vigorous sport' (Neville) or as a 'bruising-game' (Seamus). The third prime discourse of rugby constituted it as New Zealand's national sport. This discourse was talked into existence by all the interviewees as an indisputable truth: despite the historic fact that half of New Zealand's population were, for many years, actively prohibited from playing rugby.

The discursive knowledge of rugby as New Zealand's national sport, a male-sport and as a rough sport provided a prominent context in which the interview participants negotiated understandings of gender, masculinities and self. Underpinning these three dominating discourses of rugby was the knowledge of rugby as a 'sport' or 'game'. The power effect of this particular knowledge encouraged the majority of the interviewees to view rugby somewhat quixotically.

The knowledge of rugby as a male-sport was reciprocally supported by particular understandings of masculinities. The men's interview accounts revealed, for example, that the cultural significance of rugby helped to promote the belief, within the context of their youth, that males should be tough, relatively unemotional, tolerant of pain, competitive and, at times, aggressive. Moreover, it was apparent from the interview accounts that these discursive understandings were lived into existence and performed with animated vigour primarily on the school rugby fields. It was typically only boys, accordingly, who regularly displayed feats of bravery, skill and aggressive competitiveness, and these actions congealed over time to help constitute the interviewees' youthful understandings that males were *naturally* different from females. Edgar, for example, stated:

> The boys generally played contact sports at lunchtimes, such as rugby ... whereas the girls ... did hopscotch or skipping or just sat around talking. So there was a clear difference in roles and they tended not to play together ... there were clear differences between males and females because they were different.
>
> (Edgar)

The interview participants' understandings of rugby and masculinities were also produced in relation to an array of contingency factors, such as their body shapes, physical abilities and family backgrounds. The disciplinary practices of youthful rugby, therefore, produced a plethora of individual bodies and understandings. For example, Seamus, as an 11-year-old emigrant from England, was acutely aware of how playing rugby helped him feel accepted:

> Coming to New Zealand from England I was a 'pommie bastard', that was what I was called. And so it was a little bit difficult for me to come to terms with it. So being in any team, playing any sport gave me the opportunity to actually fit in and I actually quite enjoyed it. It gave me a chance to conform to a New Zealand standard by participating in a game that Kiwis (New Zealanders) did and it just happened to be the sport of rugby.
>
> (Seamus)

Participation in rugby therefore helped mark Seamus' body as normal. In contrast, Lionel was cognisant of how rugby constituted his body as 'weak and weedy':

> I was the weakest link in the team. I was always the tallest in the class but ... I was very thin and I couldn't run fast. I don't know if I was more afraid of getting hurt or doing the wrong thing. I couldn't really tackle to stop somebody ... it was embarrassing at times.
>
> (Lionel)

The interview participants made sense of their early rugby experiences in a multitude of different ways: the dominating discourses of rugby did not bend all males into a coherent masculinity type. This finding supported Foucault's assertion that disciplinary practices do not shape 'all its subjects into a single uniform mass, it separates, analyses, differentiates, carries its procedures to the point of necessary and sufficient units' (Foucault, 1991a: 170).

Despite this production of individual males, all of the interview participants had to contend with the knowledge that, as males, they were expected to play the potentially damaging sport of rugby and remain overtly fearless throughout. The complex articulations between participating in heavy-contact sports, taking pain and dominant forms of masculinities have been well acknowledged (e.g. Messner, 1992; Hickey and Fitzclarence, 2001; Young *et al.*, 1994). The ability to not give into pain, for example, is typically regarded as 'appropriate male behavior' (Young *et al.*, 1994: 182). Kevin Young and colleagues suggested that although male athletes may not enjoy pain and injury, they continue to participate in an uncritical manner, as 'injury becomes more constituting than threatening' (Young *et al.*, 1994: 188). In this respect, they theorised that male athletes, in their desire to reap the benefits associated with performing the traits of hegemonic masculinity, come to accept sporting pain and injury as normal.

Within this study, the discursive articulations between masculinities, rugby and toughness, were also influential in shaping the men's early rugby experiences. Yet the men tended to respond in divergent modes to these significant articulations. The seven interview participants who prided themselves on their rugby-playing abilities, for example, reported that they gained considerable pleasure in participating in the ruggedness of rugby with its risks and realities of injury and pain. 'Primary school rugby was exciting', Willy informed, 'and I think that the physical contact side made it more exciting, you know: the tackling, the fending – trying to rip the ball off of someone'. He further suggested: 'We felt good about playing rugby at lunchtime ... because we took the hits, scratches, grazes and stuff'. The knowledge that these interviewees played a corporeally dangerous sport and could tolerate pain was primarily meaningful as it linked with their youthful understandings of what it meant to be manly. In this manner, these men's accounts helped to support the theory that pain and injury are, *in part*, masculinising (e.g. Sabo and Panepinto, 1990; Schacht, 1996; Young *et al.*, 1994).

In contrast, the seven interview participants who were typically not confident playing rugby, reported that participation caused considerable tension. This tension stemmed from their knowledge of rugby as a potentially injurious sport, their associated fears of pain, and their conflicting desires to appear normal through playing rugby. Lionel, for example, reported: 'I knew that as soon as I got on the field there was going to be some occasional moments of terror, but I also knew that it was just the way things were'. Lionel, more specifically, defined rugby as a sport of pain: 'I simply didn't like rugby because it hurt. ... In fact everything about rugby hurt'. Lionel's fear of rugby and pain was not unusual, Sebastian, for example, bluntly stated: 'I was ... very fearful of fights and rugby terrified me. Here was a game full of physical contact, fights, and a game that is purely nothing but someone running into you and knocking you over'.

The interview participants who were fearful of rugby reported they did not share this knowledge with anybody, not even their closest friends or family: the topic was taboo. This silencing process would have helped rugby maintain its cultural dominance: silence, as Foucault asserted, is 'a shelter for power' (1978: 101). However, the experiences of rugby trepidation encouraged these interviewees to all quit playing before their teenage years. They quit, in part, because their fear of rugby helped to create a sense of self that was not comforting. Colin, for instance, reported: 'Playing rugby sort of destroyed me ... it made me feel like I wasn't quite good enough, I felt *soft*. Looking back now I can remember it well, it's quite clear, it made me feel soft'. Rugby participation for these interviewees, more specifically, produced a sense of self that caused tension with respect to how they knew their masculine selves. They typically used adjectives, for example, that were antithetical to dominant understandings of masculinities to describe their rugby playing selves, such as: timid, sensitive, soft, weak, non-aggressive, scared, inadequate, bewildered and uncompetitive. This is not to suggest that the interview participants' stories-of-self became scripted by their rugby experiences, as they knew of themselves in multiple ways. Nevertheless, these gender tensions helped fuel – in combination with the realities of embodied pain and their concerns about abilities to perform on panoptic rugby fields – their decisions to quit and avoid future rugby participation. Pain and injury were not masculinising experiences for these men.

The teenage years and reverse discourses of rugby

In the transition from boyhood, where few injuries occurred in rugby and all males were encouraged to participate, to teenage years where participation was no longer mandatory and rugby was played with greater physicality, rugby was discursively transformed from a 'sport for all males' to a 'man's sport'. Rugby was subsequently played by a more select group of males; typically those that were more skilled, confident, faster, stronger and bigger. In the process, the rugby players, particularly those in the school's premier team, the First XV, became positioned as 'men'. Associated with this prized masculine subject position, the First XV players gained significant status. Moreover, this status was augmented by various school practices, including the provision of a distinctive and respected school uniform: the exemplary uniform of businessmen.

> The First XV had a different uniform – different to all the other stu-
> dents – we had ties and a blazer and special long pants. You'd get
> dressed up and walk about the school and people would notice you. It
> was a sort of special thing, and you felt good about being in the team.
> It gave you status.
>
> (Tom)

The secondary school's promotion and organisation of rugby contributed to the constitution of rugby as a technology of domination. Rugby, for example, was no longer just a 'dividing practice' (Foucault, 1983a: 208) between males and females, but it also acted to divide and objectify males, subsequently producing particular relations of power that helped 'determine the conduct of individuals' (Foucault, 1988a: 18). The men's accounts revealed, however, that these power relations were not neatly or simply divided between rugby players and non-players but were dense and entangled: power was 'exercised from innumerable points, in the interplay of nonegalitarian and mobile relations' (Foucault, 1978: 94). Those who chose not to play rugby, for example, were not all positioned in one particular social group nor as one type of masculinity. Similarly, not all of the rugby players gained equal social advantage through participating in rugby. They were also subject to dominant understandings of masculinity. Darryl as a school First XV player, for example, reported that he enjoyed playing the piano, writing poetry and the academic side of secondary school life but he kept these pleasures secret. He was concerned that his esteemed subject position as a 'rugby man' could be threatened if his peers, particularly his rugby friends, had knowledge he enjoyed activities which were typically perceived as feminine.

The dividing practices associated with rugby, nevertheless, helped constitute some notable trends. The teenage males who did not play rugby were, for example, characteristically envious of the attention and status granted to the rugby players. Edgar reported: 'the rugby boys were a very high status group, and I wouldn't have minded being in that social group'. The 'non-rugby players' were also aware that they did not necessarily have the same ability to use specific discursive resources to help construct respectful teenage masculine subjectivities. They found it more difficult, for example, to construct a sense of self around the well-worn masculine traits of competitiveness, strength and toughness. In addition, these men reported that, at times, they were positioned adversely through their participation in different leisure activities, given that some of these activities were objectified, in their teenage years, as feminine and/or homosexual. Derek, for example, was aware that as a soccer and chess player he was typically regarded as 'less of a man'; in fact, he knew that these activities were regarded as 'poof's games'. Relatedly, these men's teenage stories of self were not always comforting. Sebastian, for instance, defined his teenage self by stating: 'I was just one of the small, weak, skinny kids that hung around with the loser crowd'. In a similar self-derogatory manner, Lionel reported that he avoided the rough games of rugby at lunchtimes and 'hung out in the library':

> I didn't know what else to do at lunchtimes, but there was enough of us so it didn't really matter. There were four or five of us as a close

group that frequented the library and that number was enough to have validation that you weren't entirely screwed up.

(Lionel)

To negotiate respectful masculine subjectivities these men typically used a variety of techniques with varying degrees of success. Sebastian in his late teens, for example, re-shaped his body through a weight-training programme in an attempt to help constitute an alternative mode of being. He reported: 'I just wanted to get bigger and bigger, because it gave me respect. And I got respect from the rugby players – the people that I had always been intimidated by. I admit that that was important for me'. Sebastian explained this significance:

Because growing up in New Zealand you cannot help but feel a failure if you are not accepted into that rugby culture. And I guess my initial strategy was to think, 'Oh I don't care; I don't want to be like them'. But *secretly* I was weight training to get as big as I could. And I guess I had a desire to be admired by them and I guess that is what I achieved in the end.

(Sebastian)

Sebastian's new sense of self was produced through drawing upon discursive resources associated with the linkage between a dominant form of masculinity and displays of strength and power. His account helped reveal, indirectly, that alternative ways of performing a respected style of masculinity were limited. In contrast, Finn, Edgar, and George transformed their senses of self by drawing on 'reverse discourses' of rugby to position rugby players, in part, as shallow, insecure, weak in character and foolish for risking injury. A reverse discourse often uses 'the same vocabulary' (Foucault, 1978: 101) as a dominating discourse but produces an opposing strategy or social effect. Finn, for example, suggested that rugby players, rather than being tough men, 'were uncritical thinkers and followers of the crowd. ... I saw the rugby players as clones who didn't have the confidence to act independently. They were always in a group and rugby was their security blanket to keep them accepted'. He stated further:

There were players at school that I knew had had serious injuries, one had had a series of concussions and carried on playing. I felt that was a bit reckless, a bit cavalier and a bit foolish. To be honest I thought that that whole 'go hard and ignore the pain' attitude was rather stupid. I never respected that.

(Finn)

George, in similar tone, stated: 'I could never relate to the mentality of the rugby players, that kind of aggressive talk and the language they used, the whole culture seemed very primitive, and how they associated with each other, it was a bit like cavemen'. Through developing reverse discourses about the rugby players, George, Finn and Edgar were able to position themselves as somewhat courageous, independent and intelligent for not playing rugby: while simultaneously positioning rugby-masculinity as less worthy. This rudimentary use of a technology of self acted to transform their senses of self to help 'attain a certain state of happiness' (Foucault, 1988a, 18). Yet, in this process of differentiating themselves from the rugby players, they still clearly drew on dominating understandings of masculinity; they still thought of themselves as courageous and independent. This finding, in a somewhat ironic manner, illustrates the dominance of these discursive resources for constituting masculine identities.

The dominance of rugby, nevertheless, can be regarded from a Fou-cauldian perspective, as providing 'a point of resistance and a starting point for an opposing strategy' (Foucault, 1978: 101) against rugby and its links to dominant understandings of masculinity. Edgar, for instance, with a bitter taste still in his mouth, reported: 'I ended up resenting all the attention that the rugby players got. I think the school had its values around the wrong way – they gave little respect or attention to those who did well academically'. And George bluntly stated: 'for a period of time I considered that rugby players were thugs, basically ma-cho violent types ... that had a really poor attitude towards women. ... I remember being pissed off and anti towards them'. These types of concerns about rugby and rugby players were not exclusively lim-ited to those who felt marginalised by rugby's prominence. Seamus, for example, became highly critical of rugby after he broke a wrist bone in a tackle:

> I realised that a lot of people were getting injured from the game and ... I thought that they would pay for it in later life. I realised that if you had a broken bone that you were more prone to get rheumatism or arthritis. I concluded that from a health perspective the game wasn't worth it.
>
> (Seamus)

Discourses of health provided Seamus with the resources necessary to consciously critique rugby. His discursive re-positioning of rugby was also linked to a changed view of rugby players: 'Amongst my new friends we would make fun of the rugby players ... we would say that they were completely brainless to be able to put up with the injuries and that they had nothing between their ears'. In this respect, Seamus's concern that rugby players would continue to subject themselves to the *pain principle* (Sabo,

1986), encouraged him to view the rugby players disrespectfully. These critical views of rugby, as displayed by Seamus, Edgar, Finn and George, were not typically revealed in public, and as such, they did little to dampen the social significance of rugby within their secondary schools: the dominance of rugby acted to silence their concerns. These reverse discourses of rugby were, nevertheless, reflective of Foucault's contention of the instability and complex relational character of power within relative contexts of freedom:

> One must observe ... that there cannot be relations of power unless the subjects are free. .... That means that within relations of power, there is necessarily the possibility of resistance, for if there were no possibilities of resistance – of violent resistance, of escape, of ruse, of strategies that reverse the situation – there would be no relations of power.
>
> (Foucault, 1987: 12)

This is not to suggest that the cultural dominance of rugby mechanistically or simplistically resulted in critical concerns about rugby; such a belief would undermine the complexities of the interview participants' experiences of rugby pain and fear, and the multiple relations of power that they were enmeshed within. Yet at the same time it is important to reflect that if rugby had not been so dominant and linked to prevailing understandings of masculinity, the concerns against rugby and rugby players would not likely have developed such prominence for Seamus, Edgar, Finn and George.

The adult years: no pain is sane after all

The discourse that constituted rugby as New Zealand's national sport acted to ensure that rugby remained relatively prominent within the interview participants' lives as adults. The majority of these men, for example, had a keen interest in viewing televised professional rugby, and rugby knowledge, particularly of the men's national team, provided a topic of conversation that still helped mark the men as normal. However, in the transition from the teenage years, where the rugby players were often respected as exemplars of a dominant type of masculinity, to the cultural pastiche of adult life, a variety of other ways of performing masculinity gained in status. In this process, the interview participants found that physical involvement in rugby was no longer a prime means of gaining masculine status. Correlatively, the social importance of *participating* in rugby decreased and fewer men continued to play.

The decreased status of rugby was not of concern for the five men in this study who played as adults. These men typically reported that they were not playing with any conscious desire to gain masculine status, but simply enjoyed rugby and its associated social life. They were also aware that adult rugby was played with a greater intensity and likelihood of sustaining significant injury. Yet these men had long been *disciplined* to accept that injury and pain were normal aspects of rugby. This injury normalisation process (see Curry, 1993) appeared so entrenched that many believed they had been lucky to escape permanent disability from rugby:

> I actually had a pretty good run with injuries. You know I got winded and bruised at times, and the odd groin strain – those types of things, but nothing really major ... oh yes I did get concussed once. I ended up banging my head into someone's knee in the tackle. A knee came up and just got me in the side of the head. I don't think I went completely out, just a bit dazed, and didn't know where I was for a bit and I needed some help to get off the field. ... My Dad took me to the hospital after the game and I stayed overnight, just for observation. But I was fine ... so I guess I was quite lucky on the injury front.
>
> (James)

Despite the players' apparent acceptance of pain and injury as relatively normal, the men's relationships with rugby were typically subject to ongoing negotiation; and the fear of future pain and/or disability played a significant role in these negotiations. Willy, who was still playing rugby at the time of his interview, reported: 'Every season since my last year in high school I have thought about quitting. I get sick of putting up with the pain. But I like the game too much to quit'. Even Colin, as a professional player in his tenth season of lucrative rugby, stated that he was thinking seriously of retiring due to injuries:

> I probably won't play next year because I'm sick of dealing with all this shit, I'm sick of icing my legs and wondering if I'm going to wake up today and be able to walk okay or if it's going to give me a bit of stick. I mean you're always going to have problems with joints and muscles if you've damaged them. I'm sort of getting to the end of my rugby career.
>
> (Colin)

Although the adult players appeared to accept pain and injury as relatively normal, they were not necessarily naïve or uncritical about corporeal damage: in fact, the men simultaneously normalised and problematised injury. Moreover, as they aged, many retired from rugby citing concern with injuries, pain and health. James, for example, reported that a 'dirty tackle' that produced a 'compound fracture of the tibia and fibula' helped end his rugby playing days: 'At the senior level there was always the possibility of getting seriously hurt. ... I was concerned about that. So I was already thinking that it would be my last season before I broke my leg'. In contrast to Young *et al.* (1994) who found that *elite* male athletes were 'generally *unreflexive* ... to past disablement' and held 'a relatively unquestioning posture toward the possibility of future injury' (191), the interview participants in this study were clearly concerned with bodily well-being and the threat of future injury. These concerns influenced their withdrawal from rugby.

The complex social processes associated with aging, as noted by de Garis (2000), appeared to be a prime factor influencing the interviewees' understandings of masculinities and rugby. As the men aged, for example, the performances of masculinity that dominated in the teenage years – that celebrated aggression, toughness and pain tolerance – lost their exalted status and were no longer typically thought of as masculinising. These discursive changes impacted on the adult men's relationships with rugby. Darryl for example reflected:

> Rugby for me had been about meeting those [physical] challenges that were put in front of you. But I'm quite willing to now walk away from a challenge like that, but I wasn't when I was a kid or a young man. Now I'm quite happy to say look, you know, that's beyond me, or that's not worth it. I'm no longer interested in trying to prove myself in that manner.
>
> (Darryl)

Darryl suggested that as an adult he no longer had the desire to *prove* his masculinity through meeting the physical and often painful challenges of rugby, in fact, he implied that he had outgrown this particular mode of masculinity. In association with the rugby players' more complex understandings of masculinities, rugby was discursively repositioned from a 'man's sport' to a 'young man's/boy's sport'. This repositioning was reflected in the men's knowledge that participation in rugby was less suitable for *adult* men. James, for example, reported: 'It is a good sport for boys and teenagers, but as men get bigger and stronger and faster the risk of injury increases and some serious damage can be done'. The interview participants who had quit playing rugby during or before teenage years, also typically suggested that rugby was a 'boy's sport', yet this sentiment was often asserted with a degree of disdain. Sebastian, for example, reported: 'I've had friends that have told me about what they got up to on tour in rugby teams and they're pretty horrendous stories, you know, lots of drinking, having fights and stuff, it's pretty boyish'. In a similar derogatory manner Edgar reported: 'The rugby players at university acted in an immature way, it seemed a bit like a boy's club, a boy's thing'. Some of these men, however, suggested that rugby culture was not just the culture of young males but also the product of an older and more problematic time:

> The culture that helped fuel the rugby of the 1950s and the 1960s has softened. They were times where men were impressed with the 'physical'

and the toughness, although I'm not sure that we're completely out of it yet ... it has definitely changed. The old idea of 'she'll be right' and ignoring pain, that's the old macho stupid image which was much more typical of the Kiwi male twenty years ago than it is today. The Kiwi image of men being non-emotional, humble, big, strong, tough that's all changed.

(Derek)

The critical comments about 'boyish' and/or 'old-fashioned' masculinities were reflected within the interview participants' *select* concerns about rugby violence. Lionel, for example, stated: 'Punching on the field is never warranted. The mongrel stuff in rugby, where someone can charge into you in a maul and knock you out, that sort of stuff needs to be removed from the game – it's never acceptable'. Tom added: 'I don't like the idea of people going and rucking the crap out of someone, because I've experienced that and it hurts, it's stupid'. Yet not all of the men were particularly concerned with displays of violence in rugby. George, for example, somewhat reluctantly confessed: 'I don't mind seeing the fights in rugby. Yes, it is gladiatorial stuff, seeing these big men slug it out – of course there is a problem with it – but it's also strangely entertaining'. George was reluctant to admit he gained a certain masochistic pleasure in watching men fight, which further suggested that the once supportive discursive link between masculinity and violence was under threat.

The interview participants were, however, relatively united that the denial of pain when seriously injured was problematic. This sentiment was revealed through comments about a professional player, Norm Hewitt, who had played with a broken bone: 'he's a bloody idiot' (Lionel), 'he's stupid and irresponsible' (Edgar) and 'he's downright foolish' (Finn). Only Willy (aged 21), the youngest of the interviewees, viewed Hewitt's actions favourably: 'He's the man! That's what you have to do in rugby, suck it in. It only hurts when you stop anyhow'.

Although many of the men were critical of select aspects of rugby, they rarely discussed their rugby concerns. The men's reluctance to publicly voice rugby concerns related, in part, to their recognition of the social dominance of rugby. Seamus, for example, informed: 'Rugby is very much in our culture; New Zealanders are still very involved with it. It's almost bred into us. And it's hard to ignore or rebel against'. The dominating discourses that celebrated rugby as 'our' national sport and as a male sport helped silence public concerns about rugby. Rugby's articulations with discourses of nationalism and masculinism, therefore, made resistance against rugby a formidable task: the male critic of rugby, given the workings of these rugby discourses, risks being positioned as unpatriotic and feminine. Hence, although these adult men, in comparison to their boyhood and teenage years, appeared considerably less subject to the technologies of domination associated with rugby, they could not escape rugby's socio-cultural influence. The state of domination of rugby limited the men's margins of liberty to express discontent towards rugby and dominant masculinities. Yet aspects of this discontent typically existed.

Despite the general silencing of public criticism of rugby, many of the interview participants did exercise some power against rugby's social cultural dominance, primarily through discouraging their sons (and daughters) to participate in rugby and/or through actively encouraging them to participate in sports that presented less risk of injury. These micro-level forms of resistance, although clearly not revolutionary or tactically organised, have possibly contributed to the decreased male participation rates in rugby in recent years. More speculatively, these actions may signal that the transformations that have occurred in dominating understandings of masculinity over the last three or four decades are now impacting on the cultural dominance of rugby within New Zealand.

In the same time period, however, greater changes appear to have occurred with respect to understandings of femininities. These changes are reflected, in part, in the small but increasing number of females who participate in the ruggedness of rugby: a sporting activity that females were once actively prohibited from enjoying. To further our understanding of the discursive connections between sport and gender we, correspondingly, wanted to examine our interviewees' experiences of women's participation in rugby. Moreover, we were interested in understanding how female athletic identities were (re)produced by men 'making sense' of women's participation in rugby.

The stronger women get, the more men get confused

The clear majority of the interviewees did not seem threatened or challenged by women's rugby, as one might have speculated from reading Sheard and Dunning (1973), Messner (2002) or Nelson (1994). In contrast, the interviewees' statements about female rugby were typically supportive. George, for example, simply remarked: 'I think it is fine'. Sebastian, in a similarly nonchalant manner, commented: 'It's fine, yeah, it's great'. Although the interviewees were generally supportive it was clear that they were also typically confused about female rugby. This confusion permeated their understandings of women's rugby and acted to nullify or constrain their support. This confusion was related to the workings of multiple and, at times, competing discourses associated with rugby, female bodies, liberalism and feminism. In this section we tease out the workings of these various discourses to illustrate the complex, discontinuous and contingent workings of power associated with sport and gender.

The interviewees' statements of support for female rugby, although seemingly nonchalant, were not offered unconditionally but rather were framed by particular requirements or concerns. One relatively subtle 'requirement' that governed many of the interviewees' statements related to the female participant's *desires* to play rugby. George, for instance, suggested that female participation is 'fine, *if they want to play rugby*, it's cool' and Sebastian similarly remarked: 'I think, *if that's what they want to do*, it's fine'. These interviewees, in other words, were supportive of female rugby on the condition that the female participants 'really wanted' to play rugby. This framing condition was absent with respect to how the interviewees talked about male participation. They did not state, for example, 'if men want to play rugby, then I support that decision'. Male participation in rugby was discursively understood as normal and the interviewees were not typically concerned about male participants' motivations or desires.

Yet the interviewees were concerned about *why* females would want to participate in rugby. More to the point, the interviewees were somewhat confused about women's participation. Derek overtly revealed his confusion by stating: 'I think if they (females) *want* to play, then ok. But why they would want to is sort of beyond me really'. Kahu, who had previously coached a women's rugby team, similarly reported: 'I think it's good (that females are playing rugby) but I don't know why they're doing it, maybe because they enjoy it or something'. Kahu knew that the women he had coached enjoyed playing rugby yet he still felt compelled to suggest that he didn't 'know why they're doing it'.

We argue that the dominating discourse that defined rugby as a *male* social practice made it difficult for the interviewees to understand why females would want to play. This discourse of rugby, therefore, circulated in a manner to prohibit or constrain the interviewees' understandings about female desire to participate. This example helps support Foucault's somewhat dramatic contention that: 'we must conceive discourse as a violence that we do to things' (Foucault, 1972: 229). Indeed, the discourse that positions rugby as a male sport 'blinded' the interviewees' understandings of female rugby enjoyment.

The interviewees' confusions about female rugby were also related to a discourse of femininity that constructs female bodies as physically weaker than those of males. C.L. Cole (1993) argued that this discursive understanding, as produced within certain historical and cultural contexts, relates to technologies of femininity that 'sculpt, fashion, and secure bodily shapes, gestures, and adornments that are recognizably female' (87) and subsequently produce the female body 'as more docile, malleable, and impressionable than the masculine body' (87). The use of these technologies, Cole argued further, 'requires individual labor (desire and time) and is dependent on various industries (workout clubs, video programmes, diet industry, active wear, and science)' (87). Although the discriminatory myths associated with women's bodies and sport participation have been 'scientifically' debunked (Dyer, 1982), the discourse that constitutes female bodies as relatively weak has continued to circulate. Many of the interviewees, for example, expressed concern that females would be more susceptible to rugby injuries in comparison to men: this concern correspondingly acted to limit their support of female rugby. George, for example, stated:

> Well I've watched women play rugby and they do play hard and not being a woman I don't know how much it hurts but it must hurt when you fall over – especially the breasts. I don't know but obviously they like playing, so it can't be too bad. So yeah, if they want to play, give it a go, why not?
>
> (George)

Although optimistic, George is not fully convinced that female bodies are tough enough for participation in what he considers to be a 'rough male-sport'. His *support* of female rugby is, accordingly, constrained. The interviewees, as George illustrated, often singled out the anatomically distinct parts of the female body, with respect to expressing concerns about female participation in rugby. Kahu, for example, stated: 'Yes, I am a little worried about women getting hurt. For example, their bodily functions, their breasts and that, you know, there's a high risk of injury'. Edgar, as a research scientist at a medical school, conveyed a more clinical but nevertheless similar sentiment:

> I don't know the evidence whether women [who play rugby] are at risk of damaging their ability to have children and whether they are aware of that, if that is the case. That would be my major concern, is that they are unaware, because they are different anatomies they're not males, they have to carry a pregnancy for nine months and males don't. So I would be concerned about that … there has to be a realisation that men and women are different and to accept differences rather than to pretend that there aren't differences when there really are, I think that's a lie. … But *if they want to*, if it's acceptable for males, if there is no injury that can come to them, other than ones that already exist, then I'm happy for women's rugby.
>
> (Edgar)

Edgar's last sentence helps reveal how multiple discourses act to constrain his support of female participation: he is only 'happy for women's rugby' if females have appropriate desire to play a *man's sport*, if they will not get overly injured given their *different anatomies* and, in a liberal stance, if it is 'acceptable for males' to play a *rough sport*. Edgar's last point alludes to the fact that he was also concerned about males playing a potentially injurious sport. Indeed, he was critical of the 'violence' of rugby and, irrespective of gender, believed that it was somewhat 'stupid' to play a dangerous sport.

Edgar, accordingly, was not fully supportive of male *or* female rugby: 'If they [male rugby players] chose to have their bodies bashed around by guys who weigh eighteen stone and who run at them at full speed, that's not smart, and it's a shame that they end up encouraging others to take risks'. A minority of the interviewees had similar concerns. Finn, for example, reported that he 'wouldn't choose to play tackle rugby, even socially, because of the risk of injury and would view [female rugby] in the same light as men choosing to play'. And Sebastian commented: 'Yeah I would be worried if my son was in a rugby game, I would be holding my breath until it was over'. The interviewees who were concerned about rugby injury and pain, irrespective of gender, suggested that they would, at the least, not typically encourage anyone into rugby.

Somewhat ironically not one of the interviewees who were concerned about male injuries cited concern about injury to the penis. The male body was an unsexed body, whereas the female body was sexed: a body with breasts and capacity for childbirth. Yet the external genitalia of males in comparison to the relatively protected female genitalia (uterus) are undoubtedly at greater risk of rugby injury. This risk was graphically demonstrated by ex-All Black captain Wayne 'Buck' Shelford when his scrotum was ripped open through rucking in a 1986 match against France, and a testicle was left hanging out. Shelford, apparently not overly daunted, left the field to have his scrotum stitched and then returned to 'play'. Despite the anatomical weakness that exposes males to greater risk of genital injury, the interviewees were, nevertheless, more concerned about the female body's susceptibility to rugby injury. This discriminatory understanding further acted to constrain the interviewees' support of female rugby.

Despite the interviewees' concerns about the supposed susceptibility of female bodies to rugby injury, it was also apparent that the phenomenon of female rugby participation had helped challenge understandings about female bodies. James, for example, stated that when females first started playing rugby he was concerned that players would get hurt. Yet having witnessed the toughness of female rugby players he is no longer concerned about female injury and pain: 'I mean initially it didn't seem a thing that girls would do or should do, I thought their breasts would get hurt ... but it ... seems a lot more acceptable now and clearly their bodies are up to the challenge'. Colin, as a professional rugby player even admired the fitness and strength displayed by the Black Ferns (the New Zealand Women's rugby team): 'I mean Farah Palmer [Black Fern's captain] is an absolute legend as far as I'm concerned in terms of physicality'. And Kahu suggested that women might even play a smarter game of rugby in comparison to men:

> I was at the Maori Rugby Tournament on the weekend and I watched a few of the women's games and they were quite good ... the skill level and the passing were really good. It wasn't all that hard-out stuff like

the men ... but I think its better to let the ball do the work than bang it up all day and get yourself knocked back all the time. ... Yeah, they played it smart.

(Kahu)

The growth of female rugby participation has appeared to help challenge restrictive understandings about female athletic skill, competitiveness and ability to endure pain and injury. This finding lends support to David Howe's (2003) assertion that 'women who play rugby and other confrontational sports are a minority but they can be agents in the resistance against hegemonic masculinity and offer an active, female physicality that can challenge the gender order' (235). However, our findings suggest that, although female rugby players can be understood as 'resistive agents that challenge the gender order', women's rugby can also act to entrench problematic beliefs about females. Kahu, for example, was impressed with the skill of the female players but still reported, 'of course they're not as fast as men or as strong as men'. George similarly reported that women rugby players 'do play hard', but that they should not be allowed to play against men, as the men 'would just physically squash them'. The *skilled* female rugby players were, accordingly, positioned as weaker and slower than males. In essence, the belief was that female rugby players were not as good as their male counterparts.

Coakley and White (1992) argued that comparison between sportswomen and sportsmen results in the production of a fallacious 'gender logic' that works to position women as biologically inferior to men. Paul Willis similarly theorised that when female and male sporting performances are compared this acts to entrench problematic understandings of femininities:

So no matter how the actual physical gap is closed, there is an equal and opposite reaction which expands the cultural and ideological resonance of that gap. It creates anew the frame of reference in which, and by which, the gap was measured in the first place. By accepting the terms of ideological definition, the attempt to approach male performance levels, in fact strengthens popular prejudice about femininity. It creates an expanding bank of the obvious examples of female 'inferiority'.

(Willis, 1982: 132)

We suggest, in contradistinction to Howe (2003) and Willis (1982), that female rugby participation does not transform understandings of femininities in a unidirectional manner, such as by either resisting *or* entrenching masculine hegemony, but that female rugby can be understood as a 'shaky' discursive phenomenon: a phenomenon that has multiple and somewhat unpredictable power effects. Foucault (1978), for example, advised:

We must make allowance for the complex and unstable process whereby discourse can be both an instrument and an effect of power, but also a hindrance, a stumbling-block and a starting point for an opposing strategy. Discourse transmits and produces power; it reinforces it, but also undermines and exposes it, renders it fragile and makes it possible to thwart it.

(Foucault, 1978: 101)

A Foucauldian-informed understanding of power is, therefore, helpful for encouraging recognition that 'sport cannot be understood purely as conformity or rebellion' (Lenskyj, 1994: 358). Drawing from our analysis of the interviews and as informed by Foucault, we understand that female rugby, as an unstable discursive phenomenon, can undermine, challenge, expose but also simultaneously reinforce and bolster sexist beliefs. Female sport, as similar to male sport, is a 'sport without guarantees' (Andrews and Loy, 1993: 270).

One of many potential power effects that female rugby can promote, as Messner (1992) and Nelson (1994) illustrated, is a backlash against feminism and/or stronger women. This gender backlash is assumed to occur in relation to an individual's resentment or feelings of insecurity in the face of social change. Although our interviewees revealed little evidence of a strong backlash, Colin's account proved to be an exception. He appeared aggrieved and even threatened by women's rugby. He stated for example: 'it's just that it's a man's game, you know, there's nothing that we've (men) got left anymore to have as our own'. Colin, as a professional rugby player, was possibly concerned that female rugby players could indirectly threaten his hard-won status as a 'rugby man'. He was particularly adamant that females should not play. In response to a question about how he would feel if his daughter played rugby, he reported:

She wants to play because I play, she loves rugby ... she knows most of the All Blacks. ... She's pumped up, she's constantly wanting me to come out and show her how to pass: she's nearly eight and she can spiral pass. But I wouldn't want her to play. ... Well here we go, I'm gonna speak my mind. Rugby's a man's game. I don't care what anyone says. Chicks who are dykes and butch and all that sort of shit can play it, they can do whatever they like ... but I don't want my girl playing rugby. It's a man's game, I know that sounds terrible, but that's truly how I feel and I think that physically they [females] may be up to it, but I don't want my girl putting herself into situations where she's going to get dusted ... like I've been dusted and I don't want her to do that.

(Colin)

Colin in a paternal manner wanted to protect his daughter from the violence of rugby despite her desires to play. He did not want to see her 'dusted' (e.g. rucked, punched or eye-gouged) or doing the 'dustings' as he believed there are 'better things available for her: she doesn't need to go through that shit'. In a seemingly contradictory manner, however, Colin reported that if he had a son he would encourage his participation at an early age: 'Yeah he'd be turning 18 months and out on the field'. Colin's discursive understanding of rugby as a male sport governed his sexist belief that his daughter and other females should not play. Yet, of more concern, it also appeared to govern his homophobic belief that female rugby players are 'dykes and butch'.

The questioning of a sportswomen's sexuality, when they participate in male dominated sport, is not unusual (Caudwell, 1999; Cox and Thompson, 2000). Indeed, many sportswomen are aware of this homophobic understanding (Caudwell, 1999, 2002). We were, accordingly, a little surprised that only 4 of our 14 interviewees positioned female rugby players as somehow different or 'abnormal' from other females or made reference to them as butch or lesbians. Derek, as an example, stated:

> There are some sports where I think it is natural that women will play them – softball, basketball, hockey – and the game can be just as interesting and exciting and thrilling as the men who play them. And there are some sports where it is not natural, and I don't really think it is natural or normal for women to want to play rugby. ... You know I've seen them [female rugby players] scoring tries and so on, I've seen them running and I think: 'Yep, that's great.' And I see them tackling and I think: 'Oh that's awful'.
>
> (Derek)

Derek's observations of women's rugby, particularly the roughness of tackling, helped confirm his belief that women were *not* naturally suited for rugby. His observations also encouraged him to question the 'nature' of the women participating: He briefly mused that female rugby players were 'possibly gender misfits, maybe' but then recanted. Kahu, in contrast, openly positioned female rugby players as 'queer'. When asked, for example, to explain why he thought females might enjoy playing rugby he blurted out: 'Oh well, I suppose, maybe because half of them are butch'. We assume that the gender (il)logic behind Kahu's statement reflected his knowledge of rugby as a man's game and, correspondingly, he assumed that female players must be manly (e.g. butch). Yet, in reality, Kahu knew that sexuality had little to do with the female rugby players he had coached. He subsequently reported: 'Actually, I think only two in the team were butch, the rest of them had husbands and boyfriends'. Kahu would not have coached the women's team if had not been a supporter of women's rugby, yet he still cast slurs on his players' sexualities. We assumed that his contradictory actions were governed, in part, by a discourse that positions female rugby players as lesbians. The circulation of this discourse, as evidenced by Kahu and Colin, is of concern for several reasons.

The use of a homophobic discourse to position female rugby players can be regarded as an attempt to coerce the workings of power at the micro-level. The positioning of female players as 'dykes', for example, acts to trivialise their sporting achievements by directing attention away from understanding them as strong, competitive and skilled athletes. The circulation of this discourse also constructs a barrier that acts to limit female rugby participation. The tactical employment of this homophobic discourse can, accordingly, be considered as a technology of sexism employed by individuals to constrain or 'normalise' the actions of females. Foucault (1991a) stressed that 'the judges of normality are everywhere ... and it is on them that the universal reign of the normative is based' (304). In this sense, we suggest that individuals who continue to promote and circulate a discourse that positions female rugby players as 'dykes' are acting as judges and police of female normality: they are passing sentences in attempts to discipline, control and regulate female bodies. The power effect of this discourse is likely to help entrench what has been called 'compulsory heterosexuality'.

The disciplinary power of feminism and liberalism

The interviewees were subject to multiple discourses that typically worked to limit their support of women's rugby. They typically 'knew', rightly or wrongly, that rugby was a male sport and female bodies were at greater risk from injury in comparison to male bodies. Four of the interviewees also knew that it was not normal females who played but possibly 'gender misfits' or dykes. Nevertheless, nearly all of the interviewees approved of female participation in rugby, suggesting that if females wanted to play, then they supported that decision. So what were the 'competing discourses' that produced the interviewees' support?

One of the prime influences that shaped the interviewees' understandings of women's rugby was feminism. Moreover, many of the interviewees appeared to be in general agreement with the prime tenets of feminism. Finn, for example, asserted:

> The rise of feminism in the 1970s was a necessity. The New Zealand female needed and deserved more respect and had to fight for it. The 'rugby, racing and beer' culture, where the women's place was in the home and barefoot and pregnant, had to change. And why women put up with it for so long is beyond me.
>
> (Finn)

In part response to the circulation of feminist ideals, we assume that the interviewees found it difficult to argue that females should not play rugby simply because they were females. Such an argument would have positioned an interviewee as a 'sexist male': an apparently untenable subject position. The only exception was Colin. Yet he was, nevertheless, aware that his sexism sounded problematic:

> I know that my stereotyping and ... my chauvinistic stuff is not going to stop the game going ahead for women but ... it's a man's game. I know that sounds terrible but that's truly how I feel ... I can hear myself, I know what it sounds like ... and I can sit here and say 'Oh that's not how I feel', but I know I'm being totally honest with you.
>
> (Colin)

Although the discourse of feminism did not silence Colin's voice of concern about women's rugby he was aware that his 'chauvinistic stuff' positioned him in a problematic manner. Feminist ideals also worked to encourage the interviewees to be careful about how they talked about women's rugby. George, for example, self-policed his own words when he realised that they might be interpreted as sexist:

> If they [females] want to play rugby it's cool. I think if they're trying to play like men – no I'll put it a different way without getting myself in deep trouble – I think if they try to play it with the traditional attitude of hard playing rugby punch ups, that sort of stuff, then that's pathetic ... if they play a smart game of rugby then, yeah, I'm for it.
>
> (George)

Feminism regulated the interviewees' statements in a manner that made it difficult to oppose female rugby participation; but it also worked to confuse many of the interviewees. Seamus was particularly bewildered about female rugby:

> I've got nothing against it at all. I feel that if they want to play rugby that's fine, *but* sure it's not my type of girl ... *but* I've got no problems with it. It's an opportunity for them to play it, that's really good. *But* ... there's no fun in watching it. I don't enjoy it *but* that's fine. And to me it's not very appealing for a woman to do that type of sport *but* that's not to say that I don't think they should have the opportunity. *But* ... it's the roughness of the game that I think just doesn't become them ... as they should. I think there's other things that they could do. It's, you know, my own personal belief and that's not to stop them and I would never, you know, it's whatever you do in life you're fine, that's cool, right?
>
> (Seamus)

Despite claiming he's 'got nothing against it at all', Seamus clearly did have problems with women's rugby. He believed that the roughness of the game was inappropriate for females or, at least, his 'type of girl'. Yet given the workings of feminism he felt compelled to state that the opportunity for women to play was 'really good'. In essence, given the multiple and competing discourses that surrounded women's rugby, Seamus was confused. His statements vacillated between support and rejection. And although he suggested that female rugby was 'fine' we suggest that the power effect of his confusion would not result in any material support or celebration of female rugby. Indeed, he reported that he had no interest in watching televised female rugby.

Another doctrine that governed the interviewees' statements of support for women's rugby was liberalism. The power effect of liberalism was such that even if an interviewee disliked rugby, he did not believe he was in a position to actively discourage others from playing. Sebastian, for example, stated that women's rugby participation is 'fine, it's like great . . . I mean I've got qualms about anyone [males or females] playing rugby, you know, but it's anyone's choice; they can do whatever they like'. Although Sebastian was critical of aspects of rugby culture, irrespective of gender, he did not want to appear intolerant of an individual's choice to participate: He wanted to appear liberal. Derek, similarly, reported, 'Well, you know, I guess I'm a bit of a libertarian in some respects, what people want to do, go ahead and do it . . . so if they [females] want to play, then ok'. This statement was of some surprise given that Derek had previously acknowledged: 'I don't really think it's natural for women to want to play rugby'. Yet he did not want to appear intolerant or prejudiced so he hesitantly supported women's rugby.

The discourses of liberalism and feminism merged in a manner to govern the interviewees' statements of support for female participation in rugby, yet this confused support was not likely to counter the marginalised status of women's rugby.

Tentative conclusions concerning sport and gendered bodies

Our Foucauldian study concerning men's experiences of rugby revealed that the clear majority of the interviewees did not appear threatened by the advent and subsequent growth of women's rugby. In contrast, many were supportive although in a generally confused manner. This confusion was linked to the multiplicity of discourses that helped constitute the interviewees' understandings of women's rugby. These discourses were primarily concerned with female bodies, rugby, liberalism and feminism. Each of these discursive objects or concepts, however, was also subject to multiple and potentially competing truths. Women's bodies, for example, were known as susceptible to injury and pain, yet could also be known as strong, fit and athletic. The multiple and, at times, competing discourses that helped constitute the phenomenon of women's rugby did not, therefore, coalesce in a simple manner to produce a coherent and logical understanding. In contrast, we suggest that women's rugby could be understood as an unstable discursive phenomenon with multiple and, at times, competing power effects.

Although the majority of the interviewees' suggested that female rugby was 'ok' or 'cool' or 'fine', this support was typically subject to a variety of conditions and, although not insincere, we propose that it is not likely to result in material encouragement that would fuel the growth of the sport. Many of the interviewees, for example, suggested that they would not proactively encourage females to participate in rugby – as they might for gymnastics, tennis or swimming – and they would not be specifically keen to watch mediated coverage of women's rugby (if available).

The likely end-result of this 'confused support' is that males will continue, in the foreseeable future, to dominate participation in rugby and rugby is likely to remain known as a male sport. Yet we also recognise that the discursive positioning of rugby as a 'man's game' is unstable, contested and subject to change. Indeed, our research findings offer relatively different readings of the relationships between sport and masculinities in comparison to previous research of sportsmen's experiences in culturally dominant, aggressive and highly institutionalised team sports (e.g. Light and Kirk, 2000; Messner, 1992; Sabo and Panepinto, 1990; Schacht, 1996; Young et al., 1994). This previous research, which has typically examined elite sportsmen's experiences through a lens filtered by hegemony theory, has predominantly concluded that although the sport/hegemonic masculinity relationships are not produced simplistically, the cultural dominance of heavy-contact sports primarily encourages males to relationally distance themselves from practices deemed feminine and to believe in the values of toughness, competition, pain tolerance and physical dominance.

Our research findings, in contrast, support the judgement that sport does not unambiguously produce culturally dominant conceptions of masculinities, but 'acts as a contradictory and complex medium for masculinity making' (Fitzclarence and Hickey, 2001: 118). Thus, although rugby provided an influential context in which the interview participants negotiated formative understandings of masculinities and self, these negotiations did not result in the clear affirmation and reproduction of a dominant form of masculinity. In contrast, these negotiation processes were often undertaken with varying degrees of tension, particularly in relation to the fear of injury and an amalgam of multiple and, at times, competing discourses; including discourses of ethics, health, violence and feminism. These complex negotiation processes resulted in the constitution of diverse, complex and at times seemingly paradoxical understandings of masculinities and rugby. Many of the interview participants, for example, performed an inconsistent range of practices in relation to rugby that simultaneously disturbed and supported dominating understandings of masculinity.

A somewhat general trend, nevertheless, was evident. This trend suggested that as the interviewee participants aged into adulthood their understandings of what it meant to be manly developed in complexity and tended, for want of less value-laden adjectives, to 'soften' or 'mature'. These men subsequently questioned the appropriateness of links between masculinities and performances of risk, pain tolerance and violence and were, relatedly, cautiously critical of select aspects of rugby culture, such as cavalier attitudes about bodily well-being.

Our results question whether popular heavy-contact sports played predominantly by males, such as rugby, should *primarily* be represented as producers of dominant and problematic masculinities. Although this finding could be regarded as a more optimistic reading of sport/masculinity relationships, the interview accounts suggest that concern about rugby's position of social significance is still clearly warranted. The state of domination of rugby and its discursive links to masculinities indirectly acted to limit material support for female rugby players and alternative resources for the construction of respected masculine subjectivities, while also limiting margins of liberty to express discontent towards rugby and dominant masculinities. Moreover, although rugby's position of cultural importance resulted in numerous points of resistance, these micro-level forms of resistance appear unlikely to support a reversal, within the near future, of the current states of dominance: the games of truth surrounding rugby and masculinities were not played with a 'minimum of domination' (Foucault, 1987: 18).

Rather than end this chapter on a 'pessimistic' note we, however, suggest that our study also reveals signs of hope for those with socially transformative intentions. The discourses of feminism and liberalism, for example, each have their own genealogies but can be linked, in part, to the deliberate actions of people over many years. These discourses, as points of resistance 'spread over time and space at varying densities' (Foucault, 1978: 96) now appear to circulate in a manner to encourage support for female participation in sports previously dominated by males. Nevertheless, a political challenge clearly remains as the omnipresent 'judges of normality' are still actively policing the gendered performances of sportswomen and sportsmen.

In such states of domination, where resistance is evident but unlikely to alter problematic relations of power, Foucault suggested: 'the problem is in fact to find out where resistance is going to organise' (Foucault, 1987: 12). In light of this viewpoint, we suggest that rugby or rugby players should not be reductively considered as *the* social problem, but critical concern should be directed towards the discursive articulations that help constitute rugby's current state of dominance, particular masculinities and gendered relations of power. The social problems associated with rugby, for example, primarily stem from the discourses that position rugby as New Zealand's national sport and as a sport specifically for males. These dominating discourses indirectly help rugby to act as a technology of dominance that encourages males into a set of normalising practices: practices that many males may be critical of but, nevertheless, find difficult to publicly resist and disentangle themselves from.

We suggest, more specifically, that a potential strategy to 'organise' the existing concern and/or resistance towards rugby, could stem from Foucault's contention 'that there is no power relation without the correlative constitution of a field of knowledge, nor any knowledge that does not presuppose and constitute at the same time power relations' (Foucault, 1991a: 27). Therefore, to lessen the effects of problematic social practices it is desirable to change our field of knowledge or ways of knowing, our means of communicating and ultimately ourselves. Although such a political task is formidable and fraught with potential risks, in the next section of our book we draw on Foucault's ideas to examine how larger scale social transformation might eventuate from individuals' actions. In Chapter 10, more specifically, we examine how Foucault's theory can inform a pedagogical strategy to promote alternative ways of knowing heavy-contact sport and gendered bodies.

Part 3

Aesthetics of ethical self-stylisation

Chapter 7

The technologies of the self

> I would like to say, first of all, what has been the goal of my work during the last twenty years? It has not been to analyze the phenomena of power, not to elaborate the foundations of such an analysis. My objective, instead, has been to create a history of the different modes by which, in our culture, human beings are made subjects.
>
> (Foucault, 1983a: 208)

In Chapter 2 we examined Foucault's 'modes of objectivation': the sciences (e.g. economics, education, biology, psychiatry, medicine or penology) that, through the discursive construction of the truth, objectify individuals; and dividing practices that divide an individual inside him/herself or separate him/her from others by creating categories such as mad and sane, criminals and law-abiding citizens, or healthy and diseased. These modes of objectivation constitute the technologies of power as they 'determine the conduct of individuals'. This chapter deals with Foucault's third interest: 'the way a human being turns him- or herself into a subject' (Foucault, 1983a: 208). This is what Foucault termed the technologies of the self. Foucault's two later volumes on sexuality – *The History of Sexuality, Volume 2: The Use of Pleasure* and *The History of Sexuality, Volume 3: The Care of the Self* – elaborate on the techniques of the self that were used in classical Greek culture of the fourth century BC and in Greek and Roman culture of the first two centuries AD respectively.

To fully conceptualise Foucault's understanding of the individual within his theoretical framework, we will first briefly revisit his theoretical assumption of an individual as subjected to power, but also as an active subject within power relations. We will then detail more closely the concept of the technologies of the self and finally, examine when the technologies of the self might act as practices of freedom.

Governed subjects: Foucault and subjectivation

As we detailed in Chapter 2, Foucault's understanding of power as relational enabled him to think of ways in which individuals can use power. He regarded power as a series of relations within which an individual interacts with others. It is an interplay of nonegalitarian and mobile relations that are in constant transformation due to the acts of individuals who can be located anywhere within these relations. Each individual is, therefore, caught in a network of historical power relations through which s/he constitutes her/himself as a subject acting on others: s/he is subjected to control but also has some freedom to use power to control others. However, while individuals can influence these relations, they are also influenced by them: power relations simultaneously make the individual an object and produce her/him as a subject. In other words, an individual becomes a subject within such power relations.

Throughout his work Foucault had been interested in this process of subjectivation: how an individual acquires an identity within power relations that both 'subjugate and make subject to' (Foucault, 1983a: 212). This process is two-fold: first, it makes the individual a subject to someone else by control and dependence, and second it ties him/her in his/her own identity by a conscience or self-knowledge. Foucault demonstrated that the confessional mode of western society has particularly locked individuals into specific categories (see Chapter 4), categories that are produced by the discursive construction of certain types of knowledge. In *History of Sexuality, Volume 1* (1978) Foucault argued that such an apparatus of subjectivation was possible when the sovereign power of kings transformed into 'bio-power' that used the bio-politics of population to control the individual. This form of power governs the individual through a set of governmental institutions and a production of knowledge that supports the existence of such an apparatus. Identities are produced through sets of such forces that require the individual to continually reflect and confess his/her troubles. Foucault labelled this incessant engagement in self-interpretation the 'hermeneutics of the self'. Therefore, the process of subjectivation as produced through governmentality (that enables the use of bio-power through knowledge production) and the hermeneutics of the self locks individuals into a particular identity. In addition, this mechanism is extremely effective as thoroughly naturalised (O'Leary, 2002). Therefore, a huge amount of effort is required to dismantle this system. As Foucault believed that identities produced within such forces were constraining, after demonstrating the mechanism for their construction, he embarked upon a search for other forms of subjectivation. This journey took him to Ancient Greece where he could identify different ways of constructing identities that were not subjected to the controlling apparatus of governmentality. Foucault labelled these as the technologies of the self.

The technologies of the self

> Perhaps I've insisted too much on the technology of domination and power. I am more and more interested in the interaction between one-self and others and in the technologies of individual domination, the history of how an individual acts upon himself in the technology of self.
>
> (Foucault, 1988b: 19)

In his later work, Foucault was interested in exploring the slow formation of self experience; how we begin to understand ourselves as subjects within power relations. Tracking such a formation does not assume a humanist self as we discussed in Chapter 2. As a matter of fact, Foucault was very sceptical of the humanist assumption of a 'sovereign, founding subject, a universal form of subject' and professed even to be 'very hostile to it'. Instead, he believed 'that the subject is constituted through practices of subjection, or, in a more autonomous way, through practices of liberation, of liberty . . . on the basis of a number of rules, styles, inventions to be found in the cultural environment' (Foucault, 1988i: 50–51). He understood the subject as a 'form' (instead of a fixed 'substance') that can be modified under different cultural conditions. Consequently, it is possible for an individual to choose to transform his/her identity by engaging in a process that Foucault labelled the technologies of the self.

One of Foucault's latest and probably most often used definitions for these technologies is that they

> permit individuals to effect by their own means or with the help of others a certain number of operations on their own bodies and souls, thoughts, conduct, and way of being, so as to transform themselves in order to attain a certain state of happiness, purity, wisdom, perfection, or immortality.
>
> (Foucault, 1988b: 18)

Foucault's use of the verb 'transform' is often translated to mean that the technologies of the self materialise in 'resistant' practices that an individual uses to change the dominant discourses. However, Foucault's work does not indicate that an engagement in the technologies of the self necessarily leads to a transformation of power relations. Foucault's focal point in his analysis of sexuality, for example, was to examine how individuals in power relations learned to recognise the discourses or knowledges of sexuality, how they acted upon this knowledge, and how they came to understand and recognise themselves as humans through this particular discourse. This provides an investigation of the individual both as the object and the subject of power relations. For example, in our examinations of sport we would ask how an individual operates within the power relations of sport to understand him/herself as a human being. This is an analysis of the technologies of the self: to identify the actions of an individual within discursive power relations and then map how these actions have moulded discourses and the individual's identity alike. Foucault further elaborated on the technologies of the self in his *The Use of Pleasure* (1985).

In *The Use of Pleasure* (1985) Foucault refers to the technologies of the self as practices that individuals, intentionally and voluntarily, use to set rules of conduct and transform themselves, 'to change themselves in their singular being, and to make their life into an oeuvre that carries certain aesthetic values and meets certain stylistic criteria' (Foucault, 1985: 10–11). This definition embeds a couple of important points. First, the technologies of the self are not devoid of rules or codes of conduct. They do not necessarily reverse discourses. On the contrary, these practices of the self refer to the forming of oneself as a subject within the truth games of sexuality. Second, however, in order to engage in such practices an individual must actively problematise the codes that govern her actions. Consequently, Foucault analysed 'not behaviors or ideas, nor societies and their "ideologies," but the *problematizations* through which being offers itself to be, necessarily, thought – and the *practices* on the basis of which these problematizations are formed' (Foucault, 1985: 11, italics in original). For example, as sport researchers, instead of using the 'ideologies' that govern sport as a starting point for our examinations, we ought to focus on how individual athletes, coaches or managers might problematise the codes of sport and then identify what specific practices develop based on the initial problematisation. As a first step, then, it was important for Foucault to 'locate the areas of experience and the forms in which sexual behavior was problematized, becoming an object of concern, an element for reflection, and a material for stylization' (Foucault, 1985: 23–24). Foucault began by an analysis of 'morality'.

Foucault referred to morality as 'a set of values and rules of action that are recommended to individuals through the intermediary of various prescriptive agencies' (Foucault, 1985: 25). Any such morality can be seen to consist of two aspects: the moral code which denotes the prescriptions for 'good' conduct, and moral acts which denote the way individuals actually behave based on the prescription (i.e. how carefully they follow the code). Foucault further distinguished three aspects of the moral code: it determines first which acts are forbidden, second, which behaviours have positive or negative value and, third, 'how the individual is supposed to constitute himself as a moral subject of his own actions' (Foucault, 1983a: 238). It is this third aspect that Foucault calls ethics. Foucault observed that the first two aspects of the moral code have not changed very much over the centuries. For example, similar to Ancient Greece our moral code asserts that, if one is married, one should engage in sexual relations only with one's spouse. The changes take place in the area of ethics: 'the manner in which one ought to form oneself as an ethical subject' (Foucault, 1985: 26) in relation to the prescriptive elements of the code. Consequently, the individual, while obeying its general principles, can respond to the code in different ways by choosing from a variety of ways to 'conduct oneself morally' (Foucault, 1985: 26). Foucault referred to the process of 'individualising' the code as the mode of subjectivation. Foucault divided the mode of subjectivation, or self-constitution, into four 'aspects': the ethical substance, mode of subjection, ethical work and telos. These concepts will further aid an analysis of how an individual might engage in the technologies of the self.

The *ethical substance* refers to the actual part of one's self that one chooses as the prime material of moral conduct: 'Which is the aspect or the part of myself or my behavior which is concerned with moral conduct' (Foucault, 1983b: 238). These aspects can be acts, desires or feelings, but also one's body shape or health that serve as the material that, for some reason, needs to be problematised. In other words, one asks: What part of oneself should be subject to a work on the self? For example, Foucault noted that the Greeks were concerned about the link between pleasure and desire (aphrodisia) in individual's sexual conduct. In the Christian era the problem was more to do with the flesh: the desires of the flesh needed to be worked over by the ethics. Today, Foucault noted, the part that appears to be most relevant for sexual ethics are individual's feelings (Foucault, 1983b).

Depending on the chosen substance, there are different ways through which individuals are 'invited or incited to recognize their moral obligations' (Foucault, 1983b: 239). In other words, these are the ways of adhering to what is considered ethical. It is important, therefore, that 'one establishes his relation to specific rules and then obliges himself to put these into practice' (Foucault, 1985: 27). This is what Foucault labelled the *mode of subjection*. For example, in Greek society one practised fidelity to seek a life of brilliance, nobility or perfection – to live a beautiful life. In Christian times, sexual ethics were governed by divine law and in today's society, where the rule of religion has weakened, we are probably invited to observe proper sexual ethics by municipal law (heterosexual marriage) or by scientific reasoning (e.g. avoiding AIDS). The mode of subjection, thus, refers to why one should engage in ethical work.

The *ethical work* refers to the work that 'one performs on oneself, not only in order to bring one's conduct into compliance with a given rule, but to attempt to transform oneself into the ethical subject of one's behavior' (Foucault, 1985: 27). These are the means by which an individual changes him/herself in order to become an ethical subject. This is what Foucault labelled 'the self-forming activities' or asceticism (Foucault, 1983b: 239). They are, then, the various conceptual and practical tools that allow one to create one's self in a new way. Such ethical work assumes certain attitudes that facilitate continuous critical self-transformation and then manifests in diverse practices. Ethical work, therefore, consists of the forms of elaboration of the self: the techniques which are used in the work of constituting oneself as an ethical subject. These are the tools or techniques that one has at one's disposal to engage in self-transformation.

Finally, there needs to be a goal for this ethical work. The *telos*, therefore, refers to the kind of being to 'which we aspire when we behave in a moral way. For instance, shall we become pure, or immortal, or free, or masters of ourselves' (Foucault, 1983b: 239). Telos is the mode of being towards which one aims in the ethical work which one carries out on oneself.

Thus far Foucault established that while the prescriptive aspects of the moral code (what is forbidden, what is good and what is bad behaviour) have not significantly changed over the centuries, the ethics – how an individual relates to these rules – have been subject to constant modifications. Greek ethics centred on a problem of personal choice. A free-born Greek male was not obliged or forced to follow any ethics, but chose to do so to have a beautiful existence, to have a good reputation or to obtain a responsible position in the city. Therefore, the reason for making the choice of living ethically, to 'restrain' oneself and master one's own behaviour, was the aesthetics of existence. Today, naturally, we have different ethics based on different concerns. Foucault (1983b), however, considered the current ethics deeply problematic:

> our problem nowadays ... since most of us no longer believe that ethics is founded in religion, nor do we want a legal system to intervene in our moral, personal, private life ... [we] cannot find any other ethics than an ethics founded on so-called scientific knowledge of what the self is, what desire is.
>
> (Foucault, 1983b: 231)

What we can learn from the Greeks is that we can follow 'guidelines' other than science to create an ethical life.

Based on the Greek ethics of personal choice of living a beautiful life, 'moral' actions or behaviours should not be considered always as only conforming to a rule, scientific knowledge, law or as deriving only from a moral code. Rather, they are actions of self-transformation that allow an individual to construct him/herself as an 'ethical subject'. This is a process of subjectivation where

> the individual delimits that part of himself that will form the object of his moral practice, defines his position relative to the precept he will follow, and decides on a certain mode of being that will serve as his moral goal. And this requires him to act upon himself, to monitor, test, improve, and transform himself.
>
> (Foucault, 1985: 28)

Consequently, ethical substance depends on the moral code available in the individual's culture. There can be 'no forming of the ethical subject without "modes of subjectivation" and an "ascetics" or "practices of the self" that support them' (Foucault, 1985: 28). Therefore, an important aspect in an analysis of the techniques of the self is first to acknowledge that while there are rules, codes of conduct, refined within power relations that an individual must take note of, s/he has a certain choice within such codes to make these rules their own. However, such choice must be taken through self-reflection, which entails problematisation of one's behaviour and an awareness of turning into an ethical subject. This is possible through modes of subjectivation, a process through which one refines one's choices. These choices then manifest in practices of self through which an individual becomes an object of their desire to transform into a more ethical being. Therefore, the focus is on transforming one's self, not the code of conduct, into an ethical subject through self-reflection and self-examination.

Such a focus on individual choice based on ability for self-reflection might denote a return to the humanist self to some readers. It is important to keep in mind, however, that Foucault was deeply anti-humanist and emphasised time after time that an individual 'with his identity and characteristics, is the product of a relations of power exercised over bodies, multiplicities, movements, desires, forces' (Foucault, 1980i: 74). Therefore, it is not possible to conceptualise an individual outside of power relations exercising an entirely free choice to act as s/he pleases. An important aspect of Foucault's technologies of the self is to recognise the moral code of conduct according to which the individual develops his/her ethical reflections. In addition, it is equally important to recognise that Foucault (1980i: 74) opposed the Marxist idea of 'pre-given identity which is seized on by the exercise of power'; an identity that needs to be liberated by exposing the ideologies upholding this power. Foucault's idea of the technologies of the self does not liberate such a 'true' self, but rather refers to attempts to build a certain type of identity within the relations of power by using one's own power ethically. Again, it is important to keep in mind that Foucault did not advocate that all power relations were equal (see Chapter 2). Therefore, not all individuals have an equal opportunity to manoeuvre within power relations. But as a function of existing in relationship to other human beings, each individual, Foucault demonstrated, will by necessity assume some power. Consequently, 'since each individual has at his disposal a certain power, and for that very reason can also act as the vehicle for transmitting a wider power' (Foucault, 1980i: 72). In this sense, Foucault's theoretical stance of power as relational and his anti-humanism coincide in his examination of the technologies of the self. While Foucault analysed the technologies of the self through the sexual ethics of Greek and Roman times, his 'teleology of the subject' is relevant for today's individual who is to re-create an identity within the fixtures of today's apparatuses of domination.

According to Timothy O'Leary (2002), Foucault's discussion of the modes of subjectivation enables us to problematise and then refuse the way the self is constructed today. Therefore, instead of conforming to a fixed identity, we can critically reconstruct the way our identities have been formed within the intersection of the governmental power apparatus/discursive knowledge production/true self and consequently, to live our lives well. While 'a well-lived life' is not a clearly defined concept, we aim to illustrate how one could approach the mode of subjection, its ethical substance, particular tools and techniques and its goal through an analysis of a sporting identity.

As a first step, it is important to note that an athlete who hypothetically engages in the technologies of the self, does so within the existing moral code of sport. S/he, however, can engage in ethical behaviour in several different ways depending on her/his goal. To do this s/he needs to ask first: what part of my sporting self should I address (*the ethical substance*)? This means problematising a part/parts of one's athletic identity. For example, an athlete can begin to question the violence that is assigned to an athletic identity. After identifying violence as a problematic aspect of his/her self, the athlete needs to ask: why should I engage in problematising violence (*the mode of subjection*)? S/he might, for example, conclude that violence and the resulting 'send offs' and bad reputation hampers her/his success in sport. After this reasoning, the athlete needs to ask what tools (*the ascetics*) are available for her/him to change the violent behaviour. These can vary depending on sport and the individual, but are actions toward less violent behaviour. While in contact sports some physical violence takes place due to the required contact, an athlete can consciously reduce other types of violence: shouting, yelling or offensive gesturing. In addition, the athlete might aim to increase her/his technical skills to be able to respond to demanding situations with improved ability rather than violent behaviour. Finally, the athlete must determine her/his goal to think what kind of person does s/he want to be or what kind of life does s/he want to lead (*the telos*). In our example here, the athlete might have decided to reduce her/his violent behaviour to become more successful in his/her career. Alternatively, the athlete might want a better life in terms of having fewer injuries, a prolonged sport career, more lucrative sponsorship deals or desires to be a 'better' person, as according to the prescription of our cultural moral code, violent behaviour has negative value.

At this point, some readers might ask: how do the technologies of the self relate to power relations and discursive knowledge production? Isn't the individual supposed to problematise the codes that govern his/her actions? In other words, aren't technologies of the self 'resistant' practices? At this point of his examination, Foucault did not analyse how individuals' actions actually changed the moral code. For example, he did not analyse if the Greeks engaged in the technologies of the self to oppose the dominant idea of self-mastery as a goal for ethical life. On the contrary, Foucault examined how individuals reacted and made sense of 'moral' codes around them, not necessarily changed them. As a matter of fact, Foucault noted that the moral codes have not changed very much over the centuries, yet how individuals make sense of them has varied a great deal. As a result, some sport researchers have understood the technologies of the self as coping strategies that athletes use to succeed within the often contradictory, discursive requirements of their sports. For example, in their study of women's gymnastics, David Johns and Jennifer Johns (2000) argued that a successful gymnast applied a technology of the self, which in this study was dieting, to cope with the judges' requirement for a thin and small body. In a similar vein, Gwen Chapman (1997) examined how women light-weight rowers coped with weight management practices required for competing in their sport. Chapman pointed out that each rower could choose the specific foods and degree of restrictions in her food intake, refuse regular team weigh-ins or drop the sport if she didn't agree with the weight management required for the high performance level. Chapman interpreted these choices as the technology of the self, because they revealed that dieting is not 'a totally dominating discipline that controlled rowers' every action' (Chapman, 1997: 216). Foucault, however, identified an active problemisation of one's identity as a first step in the analysis of the technologies of the self. Johns and Johns or Chapman did not interrogate athletes' critical attitude to their sporting identities. It was not evident that athletes, after critical questioning of such identity, used the dieting techniques to think what kind of persons they desired to become or what kind of life they liked to lead. On the contrary, Chapman for example, noted that the rowers left both their athletic identities and feminine identities unproblematised. For Foucault, then, the technologies of the self were more than an individual's ways of coping with the dominating discourses. The technologies did involve a problematisation of one's identity and only after such questioning could one engage in ethical conduct.

Foucault examined how the ethical conduct of sexuality based on the ethical substance, mode of subjection, ethical work and telos changed over several centuries from Ancient Greece, to early Christianity, to the sixteenth century, to modern society. In Greek society the ethics were based on the ideal of an aesthetics of existence: how to live a beautiful life, and an individual's behaviour was then based on this mode. Adherence to the ethics, however, was an individual's choice. In modern society, on the other hand, Foucault believed that we have no such choice. Our ethics are singularly grounded in science: we embrace 'an ethics founded on so-called scientific knowledge of what the self is, what desire is, what the unconscious is, and so on' (Foucault, 1983b: 231). We are, therefore, locked into one identity, the true self, that we, paradoxically, never appear to find even with the help of scientific knowledge. However, if analysing the technologies of the self does not free us from the scientifically constructed, singular 'modern' self, what is the meaning of examining these technologies?

Foucault did not advocate a direct application of the Greek ethical practices into contemporary society – on the contrary, he believed that practices from a different era and from a different context could not be applied to today's context as such. His aim, however, was to demonstrate that there are different ways of thinking about one's relationship to one's self from today's psychoanalytic, humanist or medical science orientation to self-examination. In this sense, the Greek example can aid us to think critically of our own practices, and this process can provide further possibilities for reversing today's dominant scientific discourses that limit the construction of modern identities. Foucault was, however, reluctant to offer programmes for future liberation and did not engage in solutions for finding new ethics to replace the current focus on the endless, humanist quest for the true self – he actually considered it very difficult to find a new ethics for our era. To be true to his anti-humanist, non-universal and contextual understanding of the self, Foucault maintained: 'All my analyses are against the ideal of universal necessities in human existence. They show the arbitrariness of institutions and show which space of freedom we can still enjoy and how many changes can still be made' (Foucault, 1988a: 11). Therefore, changes can and will happen, but they actualise against a particular cultural and historical context. The Greek technology of the self, based on the conduct of a beautiful life through the maintenance of aesthetics of existence, is not the solution for our era, but can help us problematise the present ethical substance. The technologies of the self, however, are ultimately about the role of the self within power relations – how an individual makes sense of the limitations set for him/her within the power relations and the truth games s/he is involved in. Therefore, we can further inquire how an individual might alter the discourses after problematising or adjusting his/her behaviour to them. Foucault himself was reluctant to talk about 'resistance', but discusses in several interviews the practices of freedom, practices that actually might create change in the discourses.

Technologies of the self as practices of freedom

Foucault's reluctance to talk about 'resistance' to power stems directly from his understanding of power as productive, something embedded in all human relations. As we noted in Chapter 2, there can be no individuals who, entirely outside of power relations, engage in interaction to resist and transform dominance: interaction always installs the individual as part of the power relations and as a user of power. As Foucault observed: 'It seems to me that power *is* "always already there", that one is never "outside" it, that there are no "margins" for those who break with the system to gambol it' (Foucault, 1980f: 141, italics in original). While he did not advocate an equal distribution of power, there are no 'innocent' powerless against 'selfish' powerful when power is understood as a product of force relations. Therefore, it is not possible to resist from outside of power relations: 'resistance is never in a position of exteriority in relations to power ... one is always "inside" power, there is no escaping it, there is no absolute outside of it' (Foucault, 1978: 95). Instead of 'refusal' or revolution that rids an individual or groups of individuals of power, there are multiple points for resistance that modify and change the course of power relations. Therefore, it is possible to engage in practices that free the subject from dominating power relations and as far as an individual is part of the power relations there is possibility for freedom.

To clarify his understanding of freedom Foucault (1987) distinguished between liberation and the practices of liberty. Although there are definitely attempts at liberation from dominance, such as 'colonial people' seeking liberation, that does not, according to Foucault, necessarily translate into practices of liberty, because liberation opens up new relationships of power, which have to be played with a minimum of domination (Foucault, 1987). The problem of freedom, Foucault insisted, is not solved by liberating one's self, but rather it constitutes a moral problem: how will one practice one's liberty? How can one practice freedom? Therefore, he argued, practices of freedom refer to deliberate practice of liberty. In Antiquity, ethics, as a deliberate practice of liberty, was manifested in the care for oneself. One took care of one's self to discover the ethical dimension of freedom – to learn how to practise freedom ethically. Greek ethical self-care implied a relationship with others: the care for the self was always aimed at the good of others, because it was designed for administering one's power in a non-dominant manner. In this sense, the ethical care of the self can be understood as a conversion of power, because 'it is the power over self which will regulate the power over others' (Foucault, 1987: 8). Consequently, the care for the self can assist today's individuals to play the games of power with a minimum of domination and replace the search for self-fulfilment with some other ethical substance, possibly similar to the Greek ethical substance of a beautiful life. The key for the practices of liberty, Foucault reminded us, is the problematisation of one's freedom. What does it mean to be free in today's society? What does it mean to be free within the power relations of sport? How does one practice one's power ethically, for the minimum of domination, within the field of sporting relations?

To summarise, Foucault argued that individuals try to control others by using several kinds of techniques in their relationships. These relationships can be between athletes in a team, a coach and an athlete, team managers and the performance personnel, but also extend to the construction of knowledge around the practice of sport. Within power relations of sport, it is determined what knowledge and what ethics counts as valuable and individuals at different levels of sport aim to influence these formations and thus, control others. They retain, therefore, a certain amount of liberty in the relations of power within sport. Therefore, free individuals have a certain amount of control over their relationship to their own selves and over their relationships to others. In Ancient Greece, the dominant use of power was kept to a minimum through an ethical conduct of the care of the self that meant caring for others. It remains to be investigated what constitutes freedom in today's world, including the sporting world. However, because practices of freedom always take place within (not outside) power relations, it is perhaps clearer to focus on changes in power relations and the discursive formation of sport rather than resistance to or transformation of power. Foucault did indicate a direction for practices of freedom for today's world in his essay on 'What is Enlightenment' (Foucault, 1984a).

Foucault (1984a) discussed the theme of 'freedom' by arguing for a direction for today's philosophy as a critical 'attitude' (rather than universalising doctrine). The task of philosophy, Foucault contended, is to critically examine the limits for our practices and through awareness of such constrains we should develop 'a practical critique that takes the form of a possible transgression' (Foucault, 1984a: 45). Philosophy, for Foucault, was 'work carried out by ourselves upon ourselves as free beings' (Foucault, 1984a: 47) and thus, its task is to give impetus 'to the undefined work of freedom' (Foucault, 1984a: 46). We elaborate on 'philosophy' as a work of freedom for sport research in Chapter 9. While not every individual is a practising philosopher, everyone can engage in a critical testing of the societal limits. The possibility to 'widen' such limitations opens up space for practices of freedom. As a matter of fact, Foucault began his essay with Baudelaire's analysis of the French painters, not philosophers. Baudelaire 'made fun' of artists who idealised Antiquity in favour of their own present culture and used Constantin Guys as an example of an artist who was able to actively construct the present, 'the reality' in his paintings. He was a painter who exemplified 'extreme attention to what is real' but confronted it 'with the practice of a liberty that simultaneously respects this reality and violates it' (Foucault, 1984a: 41). What is important in this discussion is the same philosophical attitude that Foucault advocated: a critical interplay between what is real or 'true' and the simultaneous exercise of freedom to make the reality into one's own. Baudelaire also identified so-called 'dandyism' as an exemplary attitude that constantly stretches the boundaries of reality by creating an individual as a particular type of art. For Baudelaire, a dandy 'is a man who tries to invent himself': a man who is facing 'the task of producing himself' (Foucault, 1984a: 42). Baudelaire located the possibilities for active self-invention within art. This idea of continually creating one's self as a piece of art that stretches societal limitations fascinated Foucault.

According to Foucault, thinking of art as a grounding for an ethical self could provide possibilities for self-formation that are currently obscured in our society:

What strikes me is the fact that in our society, art has become something which is related only to objects and not to individuals, or to life. That art is something which is specialized or which is done by experts who are artists. But couldn't everyone's life become a work of art? Why should the lamp or the house be an art object, but not our life?

(Foucault, 1983b: 236)

He was also fascinated by the Greek practice of thinking of one's self, including the body (or bios) as a piece of art: an individual recreates him/herself as a work of art. Here physical activity can intersect with Foucault's notion of practices of freedom. Sport and exercise can offer the continual creation of one's self as a piece of art through possibilities for recreating one's body. Foucault (1983b) suggested, thus, an individual's relationship to one's self was more like a creative activity, a constant process of invention. His idea was that art has the capacity to give birth to new life-forms directly; if we think of our lives as works of art, we regain the ability to think creatively and challenge the limitations of the 'natural' identities formed through the games of truth. Aesthetic stylisation of the self denotes a self that is open to re-creation alongside constantly changing conditions in society.

Foucault's 'aesthetic self' and particularly his example of Baudelaire's dandy has also received severe criticism. Critics claim that Foucault's aesthetic self uncritically celebrates the attitude of dandyism and by doing so normalises a particular gendered set of practices that, rather than refashioning, create an oppressive identity. Lois McNay (1994), for example, argued that from a feminist perspective, the heroisation of Baudelairean male avant-garde literature promotes virile self-mastery that implies a derogation of the 'feminine'. From her point of view, the aesthetic element in the ethics of the self is not problematic per se, yet when elaborated through uncritical heroisation of the masculine virtues, 'the transgressive force of the theory of ethics is undercut, appearing as it does to rely on an unexamined and nostalgic fantasy of masculine agency' (McNay, 1994: 153). McNay argues that Foucault fetishises the (male) aesthetic practice. Therefore, he fails to acknowledge that his notion of aesthetic existence is embedded in gendered social relations.

Other readings of Foucault, however, emphasise a definite difference between an artistic aesthetic and Foucault's notion of aesthetics as a mode of giving a new form to the self. O'Leary (2002), for example found Foucault's suggestion of speaking of the individual as an artist of his/her own life, not superficial dandyism, but denoting fundamental re-constitution of the subject in and through certain techniques of life. It is about giving one's life a certain style without following a pre-determined code or attempting to surface one's true subjectivity. Therefore, aesthetics as an ethical practice is primarily a matter of giving a form to one's life through the use of certain techniques. One would, nevertheless, need to invent the principles and rules according to which these techniques would be developed. By thinking in aesthetic terms, however, we can develop techniques which will allow us to think differently, to think of the self as a continual work-in-progress rather than for ever searching for a 'ready-made', true self. O'Leary concluded:

> The critical task, and therefore artistic task ... requires a constant work on, and surpassing of, the limits of our subjectivity ... it is a question of continually breaking the limits of the rigid, object-like forms of subjectivity which are given to us by our culture – even when these forms are self-imposed. The result of such a work ... is an ephemeral, never to be completed work-in-progress.
>
> (O'Leary, 2002: 133)

Foucault's 'aesthetic of existence', therefore, calls us not so much to make ourselves beautiful, but to imagine ourselves and our lives as a material that can be formed and transformed (O'Leary, 2002). It is clear, for example, that simply building a perfectly proportioned fit body does not stretch the limitations of one's identity. A beautiful body does not necessarily assist us to think of our lives as work of art. Foucault himself was reluctant to offer clear guidelines on how to think of one's self as a piece of art that challenges the limitations of existing identity formation, but other scholars have read his work with a 'liberational' intent.[1] For example, several authors have examined the use of Foucault's theory for feminist politics.

Many feminist scholars have turned to Foucault to understand the discursive construction of femininity in today' s society (e.g. Bartky, 1988; Bordo, 1993; Butler, 1993; Hekman, 1996; McNay, 1994; McRobbie, 1997; Morris, 1990; Probyn, 1993). Moya Lloyd (1996) suggested a reading of the technologies of the self, particularly, for the feminist analysis of transgressive practices for women. Lloyd contended that while Foucault's own contestation of individual practices as practices of freedom with potential to change the discursive dominance were 'only vaguely suggested' (Lloyd, 1996: 243), nevertheless, a two-pronged strategy for such an action can be traced in his later writings. Lloyd (1996) interpreted Foucault as suggesting first 'a politics of refusal' (243): we can form a new kind of subjectivity by rejecting the individuality imposed on us by the discourses. For example, a woman can reject the narrowly defined, thin and toned feminine body ideal imposed on her by the dominant fitness discourse. Refusal of a given identity necessitates a critical attitude: without problematising one's present condition, there is no refusal. Therefore, from a Foucauldian perspective refusal cannot be 'purely reactive politics: an uncritical (maybe unconscious) resistance to power, a spontaneous politics' (Lloyd, 1996: 244). This means that an exerciser, through a conscious, active critique, finds the body ideal problematic. A woman, however, who is involved in bodybuilding creates a body that is different from the ideal feminine body but, without an active problematisation of such an ideal, she is engaged in reactive politics, not in practices of freedom in the Foucauldian sense. In her study of women's bodybuilding Jennifer Wesely (2001) appeared to misinterpret such reactive politics as Foucault's practices of freedom.

Wesely (2001) examined how the heavily built bodybuilder's body can create a site for the technologies of the self, because through bodybuilding 'individuals can and do reify dominant constructions of gender identity' (Wesely, 2001: 168). She concluded however, that bodybuilding is an activity that neither reinforced nor challenged gender identity but provided a body continuum on which the participants continually negotiated their identity. Wesely did not, however, report women bodybuilders' active problematisation of feminine identity or the competitive bodybuilder's identity, but seemed to assign bodybuilding as a 'resistant' activity simply because it created a body shape different from the ideal feminine body in America. Unlike Wesely, from a Foucaudian perspective, it is not feasible to picture in advance which feminine practices 'reflect the internalization of hegemonic norms of femininity' and which 'are stages of self-aestheticization' (Lloyd, 1996: 251). For example, practices that seem to co-operate with the current construction of femininity such as dieting, wearing fashionable clothes, shopping, exercising or undergoing cosmetic surgery are not in themselves oppressive. Similarly, practices that seem to openly challenge this identity, such as rigorous weight training – as demonstrated in Wesely's study above – or playing contact team sports, are not necessarily 'liberating'.

However, mere critical thinking is not enough to create a deep transformation in the discursive construction of the fitness or sport truth games. As a second step in her strategy, Lloyd focused on how this critique works in practice: we need to 'test the reality' in order to 'grasp the points where change is possible and desirable, and to determine the precise form this change should take' (Lloyd, 1996: 245). The care of the self through which the individual engages in ethical work to re-invent herself determines the form for change.

According to Lloyd (1996), such Greek ascetic practices as writing the self, dietetics, interpretation of dreams, or the production of the self as works of art in the manner of Baudelaire's dandy can be used as active self-(re)invention, stylistics of existence, or new modes of self-subjectivation. Lloyd reminded us, however, that these practices of self-transformation are not acts of liberation – they appear within certain parameters and 'are always in some way imbricated within or modulated by contemporary practices or existing (though not necessarily dominant) patterns of behavior' (Lloyd, 1996: 246). From a feminist perspective, then, Lloyd read Foucault's conceptualisation of emancipation as an individual's 'freedom to invent a self' (Lloyd, 1996: 252): through self-awareness individuals create new types of experiences that can lead to transgressive practices. At the same time, instead of the humanist quest to 'liberate man in his own being' (Foucault, 1984a: 42) an individual is facing the task of actively producing him/herself in art. These practices further establish a chance for public impact by provoking confusion about the discursive construction of the present feminine identity, out of which grows 'a problematization – a questioning, critical thought' (Lloyd, 1996: 258).

Lloyd argued that feminists should find such a chance to bend, disrupt or undermine gender norms very seductive. However, there are a multitude of self-aestheticisation practices – wearing the latest fashion, make-up, hair-style, or building a new body in yoga classes – that individual women use to produce a self in contemporary society. Any practice of femininity has 'the potential to operate transgressively' (Lloyd, 1996: 250) when embedded in the double act of critical self-stylisation. Therefore, wearing the latest fashion does not serve as a practice of freedom from the limitations of the current feminine identity, but if an individual woman's conscious, critical efforts to make a political statement through dress can provoke 'a critical, querying reaction' (Lloyd, 1996: 258), she has potentially problematised women's present cultural condition and can have an impact on power relations. Accordingly, Lloyd (1996) reiterated:

> In the case of the production of gender, therefore, individuals are subject to a range of practices, some of which are capable of inversion, subversion, perversion, while others operate more or less rigidly. My argument is that it is the activity of critique that makes possible the differentiation between them. This, I contend, is what offers a radical edge to the stylistics of existence. It is not the activity of self-fashioning in itself that is crucial. It is the ways in which that self-fashioning, *when allied to critique*, can produce sites of contestation over the meanings and contours of identity, and over the ways in which certain practices are mobilized.
>
> (Lloyd, 1996: 250, italics in original)

In sum, Lloyd maintained that the technologies of the self when invested in a doubled trajectory of critique and self-aestheticisation, can motivate political activity and transgress women's condition and thus, act as practices of freedom. Therefore, building a new body in a fitness centre does not, in itself, serve as a practice of freedom. If an individual woman consciously engages in critical efforts to make a political statement through, for example, her improved 'core' strength, she can provoke 'a critical, querying reaction' (Lloyd, 1996: 258) about the ways the fit feminine body is constructed. By doing this, she has potentially problematised women's present cultural condition and can have an impact on power relations. Chapter 8 elaborates further on how women might consciously make a political statement through their exercising bodies.

Conclusion

The technologies of the self are practices that an individual can use to transform him/herself. They are not necessarily practices that transform the discourses – they do not necessarily free an individual from the domination of disciplinary discourses and create change in societal conditions. They can, however, act as practices of freedom, but certain conditions apply. An individual must problematise the limitations of his/her current identity; s/he must think critically about being an athlete, a physically (in)active woman, a sports fan, a coach or a health professional advocating physical activity. Only after such problematisation, can an individual engage in practices of freedom. For Foucault, such practices necessitate an ethical care of the self that actualises in self-aesthetisation: an individual, critically aware of the disciplinary impact of dominating discourses of sport on his/her identity, actively decides to change him/herself and, by building a more aesthetic self, promotes ethical practices that use power with the minimum of domination.

In this book we aim to provide further examples of how Foucault's practices of freedom can inform studies of physically active bodies. This final section of our book focuses particularly on this concept and aims to expand upon the previous interpretations of sport as the technologies of the self. More specifically, in Chapter 8 we examine how exercise practices might be turned into practices of freedom. Furthermore, in Chapters 9 and 10 we trace the role of the sport researcher in producing practices of freedom through his/her engagement in research writing and teaching.

Chapter 8

Aesthetic self-stylisation

Mindful fitness as practice of freedom

In the previous chapter, we introduced the main principles of Foucault's technologies of the self. These are the techniques through which an individual can engage in active self-fashioning. Furthermore we explained that through the practices of freedom it is possible to extend the limitations of one's existing identity, or in Foucault's words, to change the current process of subjectivation by governmentality. Such active shaping of the self by the self is possible because Foucault conceptualised the subject, not as a substance, but a form that one is, under certain conditions, free to choose to modify. Foucault understood self-transformation as a continual artistic process of creation. Individuals, however, constitute themselves as subjects of the moral code of their culture that simultaneously provides a field where it is possible to recreate oneself. In this chapter, we aim to examine how we could approach the artistic process of recreating ourselves in today's cultural field. We ask, more specifically, how fitness practices might work as practices of elaborating an ethical self and thus, what potential do they have in the recreation of existing identities?

In Chapter 3, we demonstrated how health-related fitness forms intersect with the apparatus of governmentality through their link to today's biopolitics of disease control. In Chapter 4, we discussed how commercial fitness forms act as disciplinary techniques to produce docile bodies through the discursive construction of the ideal body in fitness. Consequently, fitness seems to exist as a space for the techniques of domination and control. However, as new fitness forms evolve continually, we became interested in how the currently popular 'mindful' fitness forms might serve as the practices of freedom for their participants. Our intention is not to claim that no other fitness form can assume such a role. In terms of the practices of freedom, it is important to determine how an individual engages in the ethics of self-care through aestheticisation practices. Therefore, a similar analysis to ours could be conducted regarding any sporting or exercise practice as long as the focus is on the aesthetic stylisation of an ethical self that can lead to a re-creation of one's identity by disengaging the process of subjectivation from the intersection of power/knowledge/true self. To interrogate possible techniques of ethical self-care, we first explain what constitutes mindful fitness in today's fitness industry. After creating the context for our discussion, we aim to locate ethical 'self-constitution' through an interview study of mindful fitness instructors.

Mindful fitness

The so-called mindful fitness practices have now become increasingly popular in the fitness industry. The *Yoga Journal* reported that in 2005, 7.5 per cent (16.5 million) people in America practised yoga. The Pilates Method Alliance estimated that more than nine million Americans attend Pilates classes (Davis and Davis, 2005). IDEA Health and Fitness Association, the largest association for fitness industry professionals in the USA, has published information regarding mindful fitness since the early 1990s and even held a special convention of mindful fitness in 1994. In its annual industry trends survey in 2004, IDEA indicated that Pilates and yoga were the most rapidly growing fitness programmes (only personal training was estimated to have a higher growth rate) (Ryan, 2004). In 2005 the same survey reported that 66 per cent of IDEA business members offered Pilates or yoga and in addition, merging yoga or Pilates with other programmes such as personal training has become increasingly popular (Ryan, 2005).

Due to this growing popularity, the IDEA *Fitness Journal* started a new special section on mind–body fitness forms in 2004. As these forms have become more common in the industry, IDEA has established a specific mind–body fitness committee to create an industry wide definition for activities that can be offered under the umbrella term mindful fitness. In 1998, it defined mindful exercise as physical exercise executed with a profound, inwardly directed awareness or focus (Monroe, 1998).[1] Participants concentrate on observing their own movement patterns through proprioceptive awareness (proprioceptors are small organs that sense where the body or individual body parts are located in space). This process is aided by a focus on breathing, proper bodily alignment and the use of intrinsic energy. In these classes, both mind and body work together to create a holistic sense of self. Consequently, a number of diverse activities can be classed as mindful fitness. While all of the mindful fitness practices embed such important features as 'being present' during the activity, process orientation, slowness, and embracing the activity itself, the most common practices classified as mindful fitness are yoga, Tai Chi and Pilates.

As generally acknowledged, yoga originated in India where it evolved as part of the Hindu religious tradition.[2] Tai Chi is also an 'eastern' movement form that is based on the Taoist idea of health as a balance or harmony of the mind and body.[3] While their movement qualities are quite different, yoga and Tai Chi both consist of pre-designed exercise routines which are carefully followed. Both also emphasise an internal focus and awareness during the movement and proper breathing that aids in the concentration. While both movement practices derive from 'eastern' forms of spiritual and religious knowledge, they are often adapted to 'western' cultural needs. These movement forms have become a part of the global system that provides for the needs of a transnational community of practitioners (Strauss, 2005). For example, there are several variations of yoga that are modified to the safety precautions required in the 'western' fitness industry. They have become what Edward Bruner (1996) called transplanted traditions and often aim to combine the best of both worlds as western scientific knowledge is fused with eastern spirituality. A western movement form that derives from the eastern tradition, but without a religious connection, is Pilates.[4]

From the eastern tradition Pilates assumes the idea of calmness, the importance of the body's centre (so-called 'Powerhouse') and the idea of limberness of the entire body. From the western tradition, Pilates includes strength training and a set of exercises to be performed on the floor or with different equipment. Like yoga and Tai Chi, Pilates movements are performed with concentration, control, precision, slowness, proper breathing and relaxation (Gallagher and Kryzanowska, 1999). The goal of the exercise routine is to train the mind to master the body and thus increase self-confidence and courage (Gallagher and Kryzanowska, 1999).

In addition to yoga, Tai Chi and Pilates there are a number of hybrid or incorporated mind–body forms. For example, Ralph La Forge (1998) estimated that there were about 1,700 mind–body exercise forms offered in the USA. A hybrid form can consist of a combination of two or more mindful fitness forms, such as yogalates that includes exercises from yoga and Pilates. Alternatively, hydrid forms add mindful exercise components – attention to the movement process, correct physical form and focus on breathing – to other exercise forms. Step aerobics can turn into mind–body step, toning class can become yoga sculpt and aerobics yogaerobics.

While such classes can ride on the hype of mindful fitness fashion, they also potentially transform the disciplinary exercise routines discussed in Chapter 4. However, anyone who has ever attended these classes has also observed a strict adherence to traditional, 'authentic' ways of performing asanas, the correct order of the original Tai Chi movements or claims for 'original' Pilates exercises. Therefore, at first sight such regimented activities, deeply embedded in traditional rules, resemble the military disciplinary routines producing docile bodies discussed by Foucault (1991a). Sarah Strauss (2005), however, discussed how yoga practitioners restructure their bodies and their selves: yoga improves health through stress reduction and provides freedom from the demands of everyday life of the commercialised modern society. Such an approach to yoga seems to resemble a pursuit for the technologies of the self: it is an attempt to seek freedom from one's identity as a 'good' consumer. Strauss's yoga practitioners regarded yoga as a universal spiritual system for both health and morality maintenance and used yoga as a tool in the quest for a good life. They appeared, however, to engage in a quest for finding their 'true' selves that needed to be liberated from the superficiality of the commercial, modern living: 'an authentic Self – a self which is at ease, relaxed, able to express itself without being buffeted about by external pressures' (Strauss, 2005: 58). This observation requires a closer analysis of how the technologies of self might differ from the modernist, disciplinary quest for discovering one's true identity. In other words, when does a search for practices of freedom turn into masked governance through bio-power and the endless quest for the 'true' self? Therefore, while mindful fitness instructors can create new experiences for their participants, the discursive construction of fitness might not have changed.

Mindful fitness forms and the discourses of fitness

Mindful fitness forms operate in the same discursive context as other western fitness forms. They are governed by the health apparatus as well as the apparatus of the beauty industry with which commercial fitness practices tend to connect. It is at the intersections of these that the 'mindful fitness identity' is constituted. To analyse mindful fitness as a practice of freedom it is necessary to first mirror the premise of these fitness forms against western discourses of health and the body beautiful to locate possible conceptual fracturing in these discourses.

One of the foundations of mindful fitness forms is the notion of 'eastern spirituality' or rather what is made of this concept in the western fitness context. As a westerner reading western fitness texts on yoga and Tai Chi, it is not immediately obvious that 'eastern spirituality' refers to what we mean by mind–body integration. It seems rather that these fitness forms advocate control of the mind that is achieved when the body is controlled (Tai Chi) or evolution of the soul freed from the body (yoga). Pilates promotes a similar principle: exercises (and the body) are to be performed under strict control of the will.[5] Apparently, the promise of the mindful fitness is a discovery of the strong, confident and controlled 'true' self; a notion not dissimilar to the idea that within each ugly, fat body a confident beauty is screaming to be let out – it only requires body discipline and hard work. Is the practice of creating a controlled, willed self creating a subject different from the discursively constructed self? We assume that it can be, and it is definitely positive to focus on one's moving self in the mindful fitness classes, to relax and concentrate, but this by itself is not a sufficient premise for a subjectivisation process divorced from the discursive logic of the self. The mindful fitness forms, similar to health-related fitness (see Chapter 3), can serve as discursive devices of bio-power when linked with the scientific health research.

The link between physical activity and health is so central to the fitness industry that the promotion of mindful fitness activities is also justified by their ability to improve health. We discussed the definitional connection between physical fitness and illness prevention earlier in Chapter 3. However, when attached to mindful fitness the definition of health is now expanded. For example, Mary Monroe defined health as 'physical, mental, emotional and spiritual – true health of each client may be a blend of all four' (Monroe, 1994: 35). Knowledge on the physical body is no longer sufficient when we talk about health, rather health is a relationship between mind and body. Strauss (2005) found yoga practitioners to be following a similar logic of health; they defined health as a balance between physical, mental, spiritual and social well-being that can be best achieved through moderation. Health in this sense ensures self-reliance and provides the individual with a freedom to pursue one's own goals independent of the desires of others. While such an expanded notion of health might appear to stretch the boundaries of scientific knowledge on health, it is not a guarantee for freedom from the limitations of discursively constructed identity as an illness free, and thus, obedient and useful citizen. Monroe, for example, drew a parallel between mindful fitness and alternative medicine united with their focus on preventative practice: 'We are not in the business of exercise. We are in the business of preventive medicine' (Monroe, 1994: 37). Mind–body exercise potentially prevents or cures diseases connected to the mind (psychosomatic conditions), for example, stress, anxiety, depression, fatigue, eating disorders, substance abuse problems, cardiac rehabilitation, hypertension, blood lipid disorders, coronary disease, insulin resistance, immune system deficiencies, gastrointestinal disorders and chronic pain (Monroe, 1994). Despite a call for a broader understanding of health, mindful fitness, like the health-related physical fitness, becomes a means for illness prevention. La Forge yearned for more scientific research to clearly establish the link between illness prevention and mindful fitness exercise:

> Despite all the interest in and apparent benefits of mind–body exercise there is a lack of peer-reviewed, controlled research trials investigating its effects on physiology, behavior and health. Most existing research on mind–body exercise is statistically underpowered and/or lacks valid comparison with research on more popular exercise programs.
>
> (La Forge, 1994: 58)

The IDEA *Fitness Journal* continues to promote 'peer-reviewed empirical data supporting the positive effects of mind–body methods' (Davis and Davis, 2005: 11) in its mind–body section. Therefore, there is a similar need for an acceptance from the medical community that underlines the discourse of illness prevention and physical activity in general. In this sense, mindful exercise forms need the same verification from bio-scientific knowledge as other exercise forms in order to be taken seriously. Apparently, science and medicine are such strong discourses in our society that it is nearly impossible to exist without their acknowledgement. It is more beneficial to align mindful exercise with these discourses than challenge the premise of medical knowledge as disembodied and unsuitable to judge the benefits of mind–body forms. Obviously, it is also crucial to the American fitness industry to be closely allied with the medical establishment to create a firm connection with insurance companies. By advertising its medically proven capacity to prevent illness, similar to alternative medicine, some of the health insurance money will be directed to the fitness industry as clients now can, at least potentially, get their exercise classes reimbursed by their insurance companies. Therefore, the mindful fitness industry operates within the same discursive climate as the rest of the fitness industry: the medical discourse underlines the mindful fitness knowledge in the professional literature, but the popular literature has, as usual, taken a slightly different approach.

We discussed earlier how popular knowledge defined exercise as a body shaper (see Chapter 4). It is now well publicised that celebrities such as Madonna or Christy Turlington are yoga devotees and the former Spice Girl, Geri Halliwell, has her own yoga video series. In the popular media, mindful fitness interfaces with the discursive construction of the perfect body. For example, the cover of a recent issue of the British *Health and Fitness* (October, 2005) markets Slim and Sexy Ultimate Pilates Shape-Up. The actual article is presented by a well-qualified Pilates instructor who also demonstrates the exercises, and the text makes no connection with building an ideal, toned body (Trahan, 2005). However, the cover slogan indicates that we still aim for that perfect body, but instead of toning exercises and aerobics, the readers are told to perform Pilates and yoga to obtain that sexy, perfect body. According to these media texts, we still feel good only if we look good.

Obviously, mindful fitness forms exist in a contemporary discursive societal context and consequently, one way of knowing about the mindful fitness forms is through mediated texts. However, to examine the technologies of the self means deciphering what individuals make out these discourses: how do they create a self through mindful fitness practices in the western fitness industry? The technologies of the self denote an individual practice of freedom; an individual's attempt to live ethically. Therefore, to understand mindful fitness forms as the technologies of the self, it is imperative to learn how individual practitioners engage in these practices, how they might use mindful fitness to problematise aspects of their identities. We will next delve into a European modification of mindfulness to examine how individual mindful fitness instructors might problematise the current fitness identities. This discussion is based on an ethnographic research project in an English fitness club and interviews with the club's mindful fitness instructors.

Exercise instruction as a practice of freedom: the research setting

The purpose of this ethnographic project was to analyse how fitness practices might act as practices of freedom and thus, how individuals in the field of fitness might generate change by reconstructing an identity formed through the main discourses of contemporary fitness. The ethnographic field work was based in a London health club that is a member of a mid-priced chain in the United Kingdom. The club offered a variety of group exercise classes such as aerobics and step, but also mindful fitness classes such as Pilates, yoga and a hybrid class combining Pilates, yoga and Tai Chi.

The field work began with participation in all types of mindful fitness practices, but soon concentrated on examining the class that combined several 'pure' mindful forms. This was a new group exercise 'format'. As it was officially 'trademarked' for this fitness club chain, we will refer to this class with a pseudonym Hybrisise in this chapter. Hybrisise was a very successful product for the club as it was popular among its members (significantly more popular than yoga or Pilates) and thus, we explore how Hybrisise, particularly, could provide a setting for practices of self-transformation. After informing the club's management about the research, the participant-observation phase consisted of attending four classes weekly over the course of one year. The club had four Hybrisise instructors and to get a broad understanding of the meaning of Hybrisise it was necessary to participate in sessions taught by all the different instructors. Detailed field notes regarding the format of the class, the instructors' teaching styles and the participants' reactions to the class were written. Moreover, as often as possible, informal discussions with the participants and the instructors took place before and after the class.

In addition to participation in the classes, semi-structured, in-depth interviews with the Hybrisise instructors in the club (three females and one male) were conducted. The participant-observation phase was integral to defining the structure of the interview guide. Before conducting the interviews each interviewee was approached separately to inquire about her/his willingness to take part in this study. During these interviews, the instructors also advised the researchers to contact the female creator of Hybrisise who would be able to tell them everything there was to know about Hybrisise. Following their recommendation, we initiated contact through email as she was placed in the head office of this fitness chain in central London. She was interviewed there to deepen the information gained from the Hybrisise instructors. All the interviewees were white and between their mid-twenties to mid-thirties. Having worked within the fitness industry between three to ten years, all the instructors had fitness industry qualifications. In addition, two of them had university degrees in sport sciences. To protect their anonymity we identify them by pseudonyms in this chapter. In this study, we chose to focus on the instructors', not the participants', views of the activity, and we now briefly return to Foucault's understanding of power to explain the choice of subjects further.

In every relationship, Foucault (1987) insisted, all parties have a certain amount of power and therefore, there is always a possibility for 'resistance' that arises from the ethical use of power by the individuals involved. However, he added that certain power relations are more asymmetrical than others and consequently the margin for resistance varies depending on each individual's situation. Foucault related his principle directly to women's situation:

> in the traditional conjugal relation in the society of the eighteenth and nineteen centuries, we cannot say that there was only male power; the woman herself could do a lot of things: be unfaithful to him, extract money from him, refuse him sexually. She was, however, subject to a state of domination, in the measure where all that was finally no more than a certain number of tricks which never brought about a reversal of the situation.
>
> (Foucault, 1987: 12)

For example, while all exercisers are part of creating fitness discourses, participants in group exercise classes are not necessarily the key creators of change because they have only a limited freedom and knowledge to shape the actual classes and consequently, their margin of 'resistance' is rather small (see also Chapter 7). Therefore, this study examined how instructors or programme developers might practise their freedom ethically through an engagement in the technologies of the self. Before analysing how Hybrisise might act as a practice of freedom, we explain briefly what characterises this exercise class.

Exercise instruction as a practice of freedom: Hybrisise as an exercise form

As its name indicates, a Hybrisise class is a mixture of different exercise forms. Its creator Lydia described the premise of the class: 'Briefly ... it is a mixture of the principles of yoga for flexibility, the principles of Pilates for posture alignment, and the principles of western strength training for muscle strength, and the principles of Tai Chi for relaxation and clarity of mind'. The instructors in the club aligned Hybrisise with other commercially viable products such as Body Balance by Bodyworks, Equilibrium by Nike or Natural Stretch by Reebok, which are also modifications of the three mindful fitness forms. The interviewees further described Hybrisise as an infusion of popular fitness practices, but attributed its success to its combination of the best of 'western' and 'eastern' training principles.

The main characteristic that distinguishes Hybrisise from western resistance training is the slow, controlled manner in which each movement is performed. Breathing becomes an integral part of the execution of the exercises as it facilitates control and sets the pace for each movement. This allows the participants to concentrate on the actual exercises which, combined with the physical effort, create the distinctive mind–body element of the class: 'That's why they call it a mind–body class: if you can incorporate your mind into the way you are working, you do it perfectly. But as soon as your mind wanders off, you mess up your movement completely' (Pauline). As in a yoga class, the actual movements are pre-choreographed into sets of combinations titled 'salutations'. Hybrisise instructors play background music, but the salutations are not performed to the beat of the music as this would disrupt the actual execution of the movement.

Each session contains about five to six salutations that target different muscle groups in the body (e.g. upper body, lower body, core). All the salutations are performed on a mat and thus, unlike an aerobics class, there is not much movement in space. The focus is on flexibility, stability, balance, muscle strength and endurance rather than cardiovascular conditioning. All the instructors also mention that in a Hybrisise class it is possible to 'modify' the salutations to suit participants with different fitness and experience levels. This is an advantage that Hybrisise offers over other group fitness classes they teach:

> You can work at different levels, so it's quite easy to modify these exercises. I think Hybrisise is so popular, because it can be easy or you can make it incredibly hard ... you can basically modify to any level of participant, fit or unfit.
>
> (Larry)

A Hybrisise class contains, therefore, a built-in progression: one can begin with the easier options and then progress to a harder version of the same movement.

In sum, Hybrisise is an infusion of mindful fitness with western resistance training principles that can accommodate a wide variety of exercisers with an easily modifiable movement vocabulary. Mary provided a fitting summary of a Hybrisise class by focusing on its differences from other mainstream group exercise classes:

> What makes Hybrisise different is that it is the only type of class which is slow and focuses on stretching; focuses on thinking about oneself rather than focusing on what the instructor is doing or the class around you is doing, or how high one can get one's knees. ... It's a personal

development type of class, [the participants] tune into themselves, [and work at] their own level.

(Mary)

Based on Mary's summary, it is possible to conclude that a Hybrisise class provides a substantial alternative to other group fitness classes, but does this fitness practice provide possibilities for the technologies of the self through which an individual actively problemises her/his identity? Does it provide additional possibilities to change the existing discursive construction of fitness and, thus, act as practice of freedom?

Exercise instruction as a practice of freedom: reconstructing fitness identity?

Foucault's concept of the technologies of the self is grounded in an individual practice of the ethics of self-care. This involves first a process of active self-reflection on how one could live a well-lived life in today's society. As we pointed out in Chapter 7 Foucault observed that ethics, as a subset of morality, consisted of four aspects: ethical substance, mode of subjectivation, ethical practice and telos. Therefore, an ethical life addressed all these aspects. To do this, one has to begin by refusing, by problematising the way the self is constructed. This constitutes the ethical substance for today's individual and we were interested, therefore, whether the interviewees engaged with ethical substance by problematising an aspect of their identities. A fitness instructor might witness a continual struggle to obtain the ideal body through exercise and diet. From previous studies we already know that the ideal fit feminine body is an ever elusive goal (e.g. Markula, 1995 and 2001). The discrepancy between the ideal image body and one's own body has been argued to cause such strong body dissatisfaction that it can lead to eating disorders (e.g. Bordo, 1993; Davies, 1998; Eckermann, 1997; Malson, 1998; Spitzack, 1993). On these grounds one could argue that the feminine identity when attached to the ideal fit body is limiting women's lives and should, indeed, be problematised by fitness professionals.

After identifying the ethical substance, one will necessarily ask why one should engage with such work of change? This is the mode of subjectivation because through questioning arises a realisation for a need to create one's self in a new way. Foucault suggested that one is to create one's self as a work of art: it is possible to give a new form to one's self through aesthetics that challenges the disciplinary body practices determined by an external code. Consequently, we ask how Hybrisise practices can, according to the instructors, promote aesthetic self-stylisation? In this context, the Hybrisise exercises can be understood as tools for creating a new type of fit individual.

The final question is what kind of individual, what kind of identity should replace the current fitness identity? This is the telos, the goal for ethical life. Through this ethical dimension practices of self-care can change the discursive, disciplinary power relations and 'free' one's identity from the governmentality of bio-power/knowledge/true self. For example, by refusing the current fitness identity that is based on constructing an ideal body, an instructor can care for him/her self, but at the same time care for others by actively demolishing the myths behind the construction of such a body. This constitutes the practices of freedom through which an individual can, as Lloyd (1996) suggested, make a conscious political statement through his/her body and have an impact on power relations.

To examine if Hybrisise instructors consciously engaged in practices of freedom by leading this type of mindful fitness activity, we asked them to discuss the actual practices of Hybrisise (the ethical practice): what are its benefits? After identifying what possible tools for body aesthetics Hybrisise provided, we proceeded to examine the instructors' critical awareness of Hybrisise to create potential change (the ethical substance and the mode of subjectivation). Finally, we hoped to conclude with what, according to the instructors, was the ultimate goal of mindful fitness practice (the telos) and whether they understood Hybrisise as a practice of freedom from discursively constructed fitness identity(ies).

Practising Hybrisise: aesthetic self-stylisation?

Any everyday fitness practice has the potential to become 'a practice of freedom' through which an individual, with increased self-understanding, can transform him/herself. In addition, most fitness practices can be seen as practices of aesthetic self-stylisation as they constantly shape, create and modify exercisers' body shapes. Indeed, when asked about the benefits of this particular class, the instructors indicated that Hybrisise had changed their body shapes. The body benefits, however, are not necessarily at the top of everybody's list of fitness benefits from Hybrisise.

All the instructors referred to the Hybrisise class as a place to relax and calm down from their otherwise hectic work lives. For example, Larry found that Hybrisise class is 'chill out time' because teaching it provides him with an hour to relax and 'de-stress'. Similarly Mary remarked: 'you do it [the Hybrisise class] so slowly that you can actually do your own stretching. It's calming after a really hectic day. You can do an hour ... of Hybrisise and you come out feeling wonderfully stretched, nice and tall and in peace'. In addition, both Larry and Mary mentioned that teaching a Hybrisise class had particularly improved their flexibility. Based on their comments the Hybrisise body aesthetics emphasised body alignment (feeling tall), flexibility and a calmer, relaxed mind. In this sense, Hybrisise appeared similar to yoga: the participants in Strauss's (2005) study defined it as releasing stress and improving flexibility both literally and figuratively.

Other instructors talked about how Hybrisise had actually changed their body shapes. Interestingly, Lydia who created this product, found her body taking significantly and visibly different shape after her involvement with this activity:

> When I was teaching aerobics and step classes and doing a lot of personal training, I felt very tired, very heavy all the time, although I was super fit. Probably cardiovascularly more fit than I am now, but although I was happy and strong, I wasn't quite the shape I wanted to be. I wanted to be lithe, I wanted to run but found running very difficult because I had too much muscle. As soon as I started to teach Hybrisise. . . . I lost weight immediately, because I learned to lengthen my muscles with the movement and I learned to work without weight. . . . I felt so much stronger, but I looked leaner and taller and people commented how I lost weight.
>
> (Lydia)

Some instructors emphasised the toning benefits provided by their involvement in Hybrisise. Pauline had actually replaced her weight training with Hybrisise because she gained strength more effectively but without muscle tightness:

> I used to weight train . . . but now I don't do any weight training . . . because in Hybrisise you get more toned and defined and faster. In Hybrisise you've got all your weight on your arms or legs. It also helps with everyday living like keeping good posture . . . if you loosen your muscles, like in Hybrisise, you lengthen them, so you get more toned and defined.
>
> (Pauline)

Pauline's comment is interesting as she did not favour Hybrisise to obtain leaner looking muscles, but to gain strength in a more functional manner that utilised her own body mass. Larry believed that, in addition to relaxation and de-stressing, Hybrisise helped to tone his midsection:

> [the benefit] to me personally, is core stability. I'm quite weak in that area, so I feel that I'm helping myself, toning myself, getting stronger in the core. I like to challenge myself, so I enjoy doing that even if that part of the exercise is hard.
>
> (Larry)

It was obvious that Hybrisise could help build an ideal body: the toned and thin feminine body and the tightly packed mid-section of the masculine body. Could this type of body, then, be considered as an innovative manifestation of a recreated self?

To a certain extent the Hybrisise aesthetics shifted the emphasis from the looks of the body to other, less visible exercise benefits such as relaxation and better alignment. This decreased the disciplinary gaze directed at the exerciser's body shape. On the other hand, Hybrisise effectively reproduced the disciplinary thin and toned feminine ideal. As we discussed in Chapter 7, it is not feasible, however, to picture in advance which feminine practices reflect the internalisation of discursive femininity and which are stages of self-aestheticisation. What makes a difference here is Foucault's insistence on critical awareness: for what purpose has the individual engaged in a particular practice (the ethical substance and mode of subjectivation). Did Hybrisise simply build a fashionable body or did it evoke a political statement toward changing the fitness discourse as advocated by Lloyd (1996) in Chapter 7? To answer this question, it was imperative to understand the instructors' awareness of the underlying meaning or philosophy of Hybrisise.

Critical awareness: problematising the current fitness identity

Lydia, Hybrisise's creator, was clear about her concept behind it: while its immediate benefits were flexibility, posture re-alignment, strength, relaxation and clarity of mind, Hybrisise's ultimate purpose was to prepare us to react to everyday life situations:

> [Hybrisise] make[s] us to reflect on habitual movement patterns or habitual thought [patterns]. When we are in our offices, we don't think how we move, how we walk, how we breathe. It's making people aware of how they live their lives.
>
> (Lydia)

This awareness was then needed to improve how we function in everyday situations and in a Hybrisise class muscles were trained based on functional goals in mind. Lydia explained:

> One of the goals of Hybrisise is to train the real life muscle function of every single muscle. You don't see sit-ups in a Hybrisise class, purely because [sit-ups] just work the Rectus Abdominis and there is no function in everyday life that works the Rectus. . . . This is what we are trying to teach people . . . real life muscle strength, and the ability to react to life.
>
> (Lydia)

Lydia quite categorically dismissed the role of the Rectus Abdominis in our everyday movement patterns, but did not openly state why it is so relentlessly trained in most other fitness sessions (the Rectus Abdominis is the most superficial of the abdominal muscles and is often referred to as the 'six pack'. It is usually trained for better 'looks' rather than for functional purposes.). She was similarly critical of weight training machinery that, according to her, did not improve everyday functionality: 'all the machines we have, that multi-million pound industry, that's all in straight lines, but when do you ever walk through a door like that? You don't; you are in an angle, you walk through diagonally'. Obviously, she advocated a change to current practices, but did not clearly articulate why a switch to 'functionality' from resistance training was needed. Consequently, she did not comment on why resistance training machines are so popular and why many people prefer to isolate specific muscle groups to train them 'in straight lines' rather than adopting the more 'multi-dimensional' movement patterns she advocated in Hybrisise training.

Lydia consistently talked about the functional rather than body-shaping benefits of Hybrisise. With the improved functionality, people could also become 'healthier' and were able to prevent painful conditions created by habitual tensions and previous injuries. Lydia cited one of her clients who asserted that Hybrisise had significantly reduced the pain caused by her fused lower vertebrae. Similarly, Lydia believed, Hybrisise was a very useful exercise form for the aging population: 'our older clients absolutely love Hybrisise, because it's balance work and helps prevent falls and accidents'. The everyday functionality, however, was not limited to the workings of the body, but incorporated the mind.

In Hybrisise, a balanced everyday functionality was achieved through exercises that train both the neurological and muscular systems: the synergy of the mind with the body. Interestingly, Lydia looked for support for the integrated self from the physiological, scientific research:

> It's not just a muscular programme ... but also works the synergy of the neuro-muscular system and messages from the brain to the muscles. For example, if you seek to perform a basic lunge and balance ... they [the clients] wobble all over the place because they've not done that movement before ... the brain is not firing the right muscle fibres at the right time to do that movement smoothly.
>
> (Lydia)

Based on these principles of the integrated self, Lydia choreographed all the Hybrisise sessions used within the entire fitness chain.

To ensure the quality of each session, she then tested her choreography in her own classes before releasing it to the other instructors. To educate the instructors about the functional philosophy behind Hybrisise, Lydia had devised a training system to qualify Hybrisise instructors. Once the instructor was qualified s/he received a new Hybrisise choreography every three months. Based on her carefully planned programme and thoroughly executed training, Lydia was confident that the instructors understood the principles of each salutation in the Hybrisise sessions.

All the interviewed instructors were familiar with the training structure and had either obtained qualifications or were in the process of training. Despite Lydia's detailed information about the functional principles of each salutation, however, the meanings of these exercises were not necessarily internalised by the instructors. Pauline, for example, stated that no one in her club knew exactly what each salutation was for or what was the exact idea behind Hybrisise:

> I'm just putting everything together ... I think you are supposed to [have a structure] ... but I keep mixing it, I get bored and annoyed doing the same thing over and over. So, I keep adding stuff ... but you stick to some of the choreography and nobody in this club knows ... what it is supposed to be like. As long as you do your Hybrisise some way ... then they are happy with it.
>
> (Pauline)

Becky suspected that the entire Hybrisise concept was based on commercialism:

> Because everyone loves yoga, everyone has heard of or tried Pilates, it's the in thing to do. ... They [the club's management] came up with it basically to save in budget, because they couldn't afford yoga and Pilates teachers. It sounds terrible, but that's basically the gist of it.
>
> (Becky)

Similarly to Becky, Mary thought that Hybrisise was yet another fashionable industry trend that a fitness club had to adopt to survive: 'it's just following the fashion with Geri Halliwell doing "ballet Ashtanga" ... it's following a trend but I think it's a good trend'. Interestingly, Mary did find Hybrisise a positive 'fad', but nonetheless a fad, and when asked about the actual principles behind Hybrisise, she instructed us to ask Lydia directly. It seemed that the instructors did not necessarily promote Hybrisise as an alternative exercise form and had not entirely internalised Lydia's functional Hybrisise philosophy. Did they, then, refer to the possibility of obtaining a beautiful body when teaching Hybrisise?

The instructors were reluctant to talk about Hybrisise as a class for improved body shape. For example, Larry recommended Hybrisise for 'anyone who wanted to get stronger, more stable, pretty much anyone really'. Becky suggested that it was better to attend other types of classes for toning benefits whereas Hybrisise was 'a little bit broader'. She was, however, unsure how Hybrisise differed from such toning classes as Legs, Tums and Bums other than being slower and not done to music:

> You don't have to work with beats of music. Hybrisise is a lot more floor work whereas in the other type of classes, like aerobics and toning classes, you spend a lot of time standing up, maybe you use some equipment, weights, barbells, whereas in Hybrisise you rarely use any kind of equipment.
>
> (Becky)

While the instructors were aware that Hybrisise, as a combination of yoga, Pilates and Tai Chi, improved flexibility, core stability and the ability to relax, they operated at the level of execution of the particular movements. They did not emphasise the functional philosophy behind having to perform moves in a particular way. While some of them mentioned improved quality of everyday life, none of the instructors used the term functionality when addressing the outcomes from Hybrisise. From the instructors' point of view, Hybrisise was a persuasive way of making people work harder when they were first seduced to the class by media created fads.

Interestingly, the instructors believed that the participants sought the same old body benefits from Hybrisise. Larry, for example, had discovered that 'strengthening up the back and stomach, that's usually the selling point of Hybrisise. People always want to have a nice strong, flat tummy', and Becky added that 'people like it because it [Hybrisise] gets you toning . . . definitely our members here wanna work on that more than anything else'. All the interviewees also felt that the media exposure of the celebrities practising yoga, such as Madonna and Geri Halliwell, were the major incentives for clients' interest in yoga, Pilates and Hybrisise. A discussion with Larry illustrated the instructors' conviction that the participants were there to obtain the toned celebrity look.

QUESTION: Why do you think these types of classes are so popular now?

LARRY: People see all these pop stars, Geri Halliwell, Madonna, do all these types of classes, and think 'Oh, maybe if I do that I'm gonna look like them' . . . people actually believe they are going to turn into these [famous] people if they do these classes, it's not really going to happen, or may well happen . . .

QUESTION: Do they refer to Geri Halliwell . . . ?

LARRY: Yeah, but I just say, that's dedication, very, very hard work, very, very strict eating patterns, hard weight training, as well as doing this style of exercise. She actually does yoga, but I'm sure she does a hell of a lot of other exercise as well to get looking like that. I can't believe that's all she did. People refer to the great physique of Madonna, she is now 40, what ever she is, has great figure, has done a lot of yoga, or so we know. We don't really have an idea, do we. Again, I can only suggest that if it works for them, it can work for anyone, but you have to put a lot of hard work and dedication into it to get there. You can't just come to one Hybrisise class once a week and then all of the sudden you turn into a Madonna lookalike or Geri lookalike.

Larry was reluctant to use the improved body shape as the main selling point for Hybrisise, but was unable to offer other reasons (e.g. functionality) for obtaining core strength or feeling better. Instead of openly challenging the pursuit for the ideal body, he normalised it by reverting to the disciplined body work required for obtaining such an ideal.

While the instructors themselves did not want to sell Hybrisise as a means for a better body, they claimed that for the participants, at least initially, that provided the main attraction. The participants, then, appeared to have the least critical awareness of the problematic discourse of the ideal body. They, therefore, might have used Hybrisise, not so much as a technology of self, but as a variation of other disciplinary body practices. At this point, we question to what extent can we expect ordinary fitness consumers to obtain critical awareness of the disciplinary impact of their exercise practices? How and where would they have gained such an ability to question the premise of these practices? As demonstrated earlier in this chapter, the media seem to promote mindful fitness through the promise of the ideal body and therefore, the popular discourse that reaches the average consumer reinforces the search for the body beautiful as the dominant fitness discourse. Foucault (1983a, 1988i) didn't believe in the humanist premise of each individual possessing an innate ability to resist (as implied in the term 'agency') and therefore, the individuals have to gain an ability to problematise their identities and to develop practices to change it. Foucault's own work didn't demonstrate how such an articulation materialised. In this study we observed that as one's knowledge and experience of the fitness industry increased, so did the critical awareness of discursive practices and the need to engage in alternative practices. Consequently, we could assume that obtaining education might be one of the key factors in developing practices of freedom. We must, however, keep in mind that knowledge, particularly scientific knowledge, serves also as a discursive tool used to dominate and discipline individual bodies. At the same time, Foucault (1987) insisted that knowledge, similar to power, is not in itself evil or bad, but what matters is how it is used. In our study, we could conclude positively that individuals like Lydia, made definite attempts to use their knowledge ethically to create change. We will return to this question of ethical use of knowledge in Chapters 9 and 10 where we discuss how academics with a knowledge base that is usually considered significantly larger than that of fitness instructors or consumers, might use their power ethically. In this chapter, however, we continue by asking: What was, then, the exact goal for Hybrisise practices? Did fitness instructors use aesthetic self-stylisation practices and critical awareness to free their identities from the disciplinary process of subjectivation?

The telos: self-transformation?

At first sight, Hybrisise body aesthetic resembled the oppressive thin and toned body ideal. However, like knowledge, no body shape itself is in itself oppressive, rather what matters is how this shape has been used to discipline individual exercisers. Therefore, it is important to identify how a particular body shape becomes part of a dominating discourse. Every body shape has the potential to create a reconstructed self as long as the body practices needed for its creation are embedded in a critical awareness of the discursive conditions surrounding us. Therefore, the Hybrisise body, if it is based on conscious effort to challenge the discursive domination of the body ideal, could act as an innovative, political statement. This way, Hybrisise could become a practice of freedom. Active care of the self allows for a responsible use of power and consequently, we can escape 'a domination of truth, not by playing a game that was a complete stranger to the game of truth, but in playing it otherwise' (Foucault, 1987: 15). This could mean that a fitness instructor should use her/his power position ethically by, for example, carefully delivering fitness practices that, instead of exposing the participants to the dominating, disciplinary discourse, would foster critical awareness, self-reflection and self-transformation. However, the instructors, who operated at the level of teaching practice, did not seem to have a deep critical awareness of the discursiveness of their exercise practices.

Because the instructors were unaware of the exact functional meaning of each detail, they did not follow Lydia's advice too literally. As superfit people, they did not actively seek alternative fitness practices such as Hybrisise. As a matter of fact, given a choice, they would not choose to participate in such a class. For example, Larry noted:

> I must admit . . . I'm more of a fast, more energetic style instructor. I do like the step classes and spinning classes . . . just to get in cold and do a Hybrisise class, I probably wouldn't enjoy so much as doing another form of class.
>
> (Larry)

None of the interviewed instructors turned to Hybrisise because they thought it was a more beneficial class to participants than other group exercise classes. They became Hybrisise instructors because of vacancies left by previous instructors or Hybrisise classes being added to the timetable by the club's management. For example, when asked how she came to teach Hybrisise classes, Pauline explained:

> I was forced to do it. Remember Andrea? She used to teach the class and was off abroad and they [the management] told me I need to do it. And I didn't know what it was and so, I said: 'Give me the file and I'll read it and learn what I'm supposed to do'.
>
> (Pauline)

In this sense, the instructors did not actively seek alternative practices to the traditional fitness modes. Unquestionably, however, the instructors cared about the quality of their instruction. For example, Pauline described: 'Fitness is my passion, so I put everything into it. I try to make it interesting plus give you the workout that you want'.

In conclusion, teaching a Hybrisise class did not significantly increase the instructors' awareness of the discursive fitness practices and thus, they did not particularly reflect on their selves or their practices to create themselves as more ethical users of their power. Parallel to our earlier discussion of participants' critical awareness of discursive body practices, we ponder if we were expecting too much from the fitness instructors: where would have they gained an ability to critically evaluate the fitness industry and their own identities within it? To answer this question, it might be fruitful to examine fitness instructor training courses to identify if critical thinking is part of an average fitness instructor's education. In addition, it is difficult to assess the extent to which the instructors were aware of their power to influence fitness practices on a larger scale. While they all assumed a position to modify the content of their classes and thus, challenged the fitness practices at some level, they were not necessarily aware of their power to expand the limits of the identity based on the ideal fit body. In many ways they did not consider Hybrisise embedded in a deeply grounded transformation in fitness, but rather assumed that practices such as Hybrisise were media-hyped creations for a new way of getting an ideal body. Therefore, their own identities as instructors were largely unproblematised in the current, body shape oriented fitness industry. Neither did they advocate practices that would free the participants from the 'conventional' fitness identity. Lydia, the creator of the Hybrisise programme and the most experienced instructor, offered quite a different story.

Lydia indicated that she came 'from a traditional fitness background' and had a degree in movement studies. Like the interviewed instructors, she had taught a wide range of group exercise classes such as aerobics, step and spinning. At the time of the interview, Lydia was a Reebok master trainer and worked for the fitness chain as a fitness consultant for new trends. She recalled that after about six years within the fitness industry, she became 'bored' with 'the traditional stuff' and thought that 'there is nothing in this, this isn't new. There's got to be more to a studio than a grapevine, there's got to be more to a bike than just pedalling as hard as you can and sweating and being very uncomfortable'. She began to seek alternative ways of fitness and qualified as a Pilates instructor and an Ashtanga yoga instructor. While she embraced the principles of each form, she learned that Pilates and yoga in their pure forms did not attract participants:

> I thought maybe there is a way of marketing something that takes the principles of Pilates and principles from yoga and the principles of strength training and put a little bit Tai Chi in there for relaxation and clarity of mind and then people don't associate it against Pilates or against yoga . . . they are coming to Hybrisise.
>
> (Lydia)

While Lydia's rationale for Hybrisise was partly driven by the commercial realities of the fitness industry, she was actively seeking new practices that would give the participants 'what they need before they know that they need it'. In this sense, Lydia more than the other instructors, was aware of a need for change in the fitness industry and was also in a position of power to make such changes happen. Although Lydia readily acknowledged having an impact, she felt her influence extended mainly to individual instructors and participants with whom she had direct contact in a class setting:

QUESTION: Don't you think you have a big impact on what people do?
LYDIA: Oh yeah, definitely, that's why I always went into what I do because I train staff . . . when you are training in a class setting, you get 30 or more participants and that to me is a bigger impact [than doing personal training].

Lydia defined herself as being 'in the forefront of the industry' (presenting in conferences, travelling internationally) but more to obtain new ideas for practice rather than actively seeking a position as an advocate for mindful fitness forms. However, unlike the other instructors, Lydia had actively reflected on the meaning of the fitness practices she was involved in and strongly believed that Hybrisise as a fitness form provided a viable alternative to other group fitness forms. Her practice of self-care then translated into her creating an exercise class that emphasised the functional benefits of fitness and therefore, she did use her power to initiate change in her fitness chain. However, in the larger scale of global fitness Lydia, as the instructors stated, was following a fashionable trend. To expect her to function on such a scale was perhaps unreasonable, particularly considering that Foucault understood the technologies of the self as localised practices of freedom. In this sense, Lydia had managed to create a successful change in her operating field, yet she might not have been able to divorce Hybrisise entirely from the influence of the dominating discourse of the ideal body and commercial fitness world.

Conclusion

It is obvious that Foucault's concept of the technologies of the self is complex and it is difficult to determine what practices of freedom might mean for a critically aware, self-stylised fitness leader for whom ethical care of the self translates to ethical care of others. According to Foucault, the technologies of the self permit an individual to transform him/herself by becoming recuperated, rather than disciplined, by power relations and relations of knowledge. Hybrisise appeared to offer that possibility, but only if its practice was accompanied by critical awareness. For example, a possibility for alternative fitness practices emerged when knowledge was used critically toward ethical self care. It is interesting to note, however, that the ultimate decisions about the fitness forms offered in this health club chain are made by the marketing department, not necessarily the fitness experts. Lydia explained that while she 'brainstorms' new ideas for fitness classes, these ideas are discussed by 'a panel' consisting of the fitness chain's chief executive, 'marketing brand director' and 'a few other people in marketing'. This panel decided which of Lydia's ideas were viable products for the company. Their ethics of care or their critical awareness of the discursive construction of fitness would be an interesting topic for a future examination of the fitness industry.

The exercises in Hybrisise classes could easily turn to service the dominant body ideal and for many participants, no doubt, this was the major incentive to exercise. However, the focus on functionality can provide a more multi-dimensional goal that allows for a practice of the ethics of self-care. Therefore, Hybrisise can act as a practice of freedom for the individuals, instructors and participants alike, who embed their practices in critical awareness. The problem arising from our research was the construction of such critical awareness. How are individuals to obtain critical awareness of the limitations of their identities in this society where identity is pre-defined by the scientific construction of the true self? How do we learn to question our subjection to such an identity instead of obediently looking for it? It is important to emphasise that Hybrisise, or any other fitness practice can serve as a practice of freedom if it creates the self as a piece of art; a self that is continually recuperated by the ethics of self-care. Any fitness form, sport or physical activity can act as a practice of freedom by expanding the limitations of the discursive identity. However, the practitioners – the fitness leaders and managers, coaches, physical education teachers and the participants – need to engage in ongoing critical practice of ethics of self-care in order to transgress disciplinary bodily practices. The ethical practice of one's freedom does not need to derive from practices that emphasise everyday functionality, but such a refocus can offer a way to play the fitness truth game differently. Any fitness form through which the participants can problematise the dominant discursive construction of (gendered) identity and re-create their selves can transgress the limitations of the 'natural' (gendered) identity. This means a return to our question of how to evoke critical awareness in fitness consumers at all levels of the fitness industry. This question points to our roles as researchers of fitness.

Based on this study, knowledge and experience seem to allow for the critical thought required for practices of freedom and, thus, create the foundation for individual transformation in the discursive condition of the fitness industry. As researchers in this field, we actually possess significant knowledge of and experience in fitness. What was our ethics of care; our responsibility for changing the fitness practices? How did we use our critical awareness to initiate localised practices of freedom? How did we engage in the technologies of the self? Should we problematise our own identities as researchers to create change? We examine these questions and the ethics of the researcher's care of the self in the next chapter.

Chapter 9

The ethics of self-care
The academic self as a work of art

In this book we have discussed how Foucault understood the formation of power relations in today's society and how he saw knowledge as inevitably tangled with such power relations to create certain types of subjects. In addition, we have dedicated this section of our book to the third axis of Foucault's work: how an individual creates a self in connection with the other two axes. This dimension of his work centres around 'the technologies of the self': the slow formation of the self through practices of the self upon the self. In Chapter 8, we examined how individual fitness instructors might use their instructional practices to create a self that potentially frees the modern identity from the docility of the discursive power relations. In this chapter we continue to identify how the technologies of the self can transgress the unified identity created within the discursive knowledge/power axis, but this time tracing the technologies of the self for an academic self: what are the possibilities for a sport scholar to use the technologies of the self to transform his/her identity and through that process transform sport studies and sport in general?

We begin with Foucault's discussion of the role of philosophy, or any area of academic study such as sport studies, in creating change in current society. Due to his premature death Foucault did not have a chance to formulate the technologies of the self for today's context. However, there are several interpretations on how to 'liberate the "modern self"' from discursive power relations, some of which we have already introduced in this book (e.g. Lloyd, 1996; O'Leary, 2002). In this chapter, we draw on Gilles Deleuze's (1988) work that appears to illuminate specifically how an academic can engage with the technologies of the self and by forming a 'new' self affect the way we know about sport and sporting people. Finally, we discuss the practice of writing as a part of the technologies of the academic self.

The role of the philosopher: transformation by 'liberating' thought

On several occasions Foucault discussed the role of the academic as an active social critic. Foucault saw his own work as

> following lines of fragility in the present – in managing to graph why and how that which is might no longer be that which is. In this sense, any description must always be made in accordance with these kinds of virtual fracture which open up the space of freedom understood as a space of concrete freedom, that is, of possible transformation.
>
> (Foucault, 1994: 449–450)

The intellectual[1] is situated along these fractures, tracing spaces for freedom. The ultimate purpose of intellectual work, then, is to engage in social transformation.

Foucault himself was involved in several social activist groups among them the Information Group on Prisons (GIP) in France (see also Chapter 1). In this sense, he advocated practical engagement in social affairs. At the same time, he distinguished between 'reforming' others and social transformation. Reforms, for Foucault (1977b), were totalising programmes developed to change other people's conditions or to correct what seemed to be 'wrong' in their lives from an outsider's perspective. While at first glance this appears to be an honourable goal, Foucault asserted that instead of reforms we need 'revolutionary action'. Such action goes beyond creating prescriptive programmes that he described as embedded either in reformist thinking of changing 'the institution without touching the ideological system' or in the humanist 'desire to change the ideological systems without altering institutions' (Foucault, 1977b: 228). An intellectual should disrupt the underlying principles of the formation of certain power relations: to 'attack the relationships of power through the notions and institutions that function as their instruments, armature, and armour' (Foucault, 1977b: 228). Foucault used his own involvement in GIP as an example:

> The ultimate goal of its [GIP's] interventions was not to extend the visiting rights of prisoners to thirty minutes or to procure flush toilets for the cells, but to question the social and moral distinction between the innocent and the guilty. And if this goal was to be more than a philosophical statement or a humanist desire, it had to be pursued at the level of gestures, practical actions, and in relation to specific situations.
>
> (Foucault, 1977b: 227–228)

To engage in revolutionary action an intellectual cannot imagine him/herself 'somewhat ahead and to the side' of the 'collectivity' (Foucault, 1977a: 208) as someone, who rather arrogantly, visions shaping others' political will from the distance of an academic ivory tower. An intellectual is not to tell others what to do – 'By what right would he do so?' – but rather to question, reveal and struggle against power 'where it is most invisible and insidious' (Foucault, 1977a: 208). An intellectual or an academic questions underlying power relations and aims to disrupt them through theorising, by thinking critically. This does not mean offering merely theoretical philosophical statements as solutions to problems. Theory itself should be seen as practice, not expressing, translating, serving or applying practice. 'It is an activity', Foucault asserted, 'conducted alongside those who struggle for power, and not their illumination from a safe distance. A '"theory" is the regional system of this struggle' (Foucault, 1977a: 208). Theory, in short, facilitates critical thinking that then translates into concrete action. Foucault summarised:

> The work of an intellectual is not to shape others' political will; it is, through the analyses that he carries out in his own field, to question over and over again what is postulated as self-evident, to disturb people's mental habits, the way they do and think things, to dissipate what is familiar and accepted, to reexamine rules and institutions and on the basis of this reproblematization (in which he carries out his specific task as an intellectual) to participate in the formation of a political will (in which he has his role as citizen to play).
>
> (Foucault, 1988g: 265)

To think critically about society at large, one must be able to, first, think critically of one's own environment. The role of an academic is primarily 'to struggle against the forms of power that transform him into its object and instrument in the sphere of "knowledge," "truth," "consciousness," and "discourse"' (Foucault, 1977a: 208). One is to begin the transformation of social conditions by engaging in a struggle that concerns one's own interests, one's own objectives and one's own methods of knowledge production. Therefore, it is imperative to continually question the formation of an academic field and how academic selves are moulded within power relations as certain types of producers of knowledge. It is important to acknowledge that academics also exercise power as knowledge producers and thus, should take an interest in how they execute their power.

In sum, Foucault maintained that the work of an intellectual should be embedded in a desire to disrupt the underlying principles for the formation of certain power relations. The aim is to create change, but it is imperative to begin transformation from one's own realm, a societal arena that one understands well. Academics understand best their own context of academia where their role is to think critically. According to Foucault, only critical thought can lead to changes in society. He emphasised, however, that intellectuals should aim beyond superficial reform to 'real' transformation. Instead of stating 'that things are not right as they are' (Foucault, 1988f: 155), we should challenge the familiar modes of thought for '[a] transformation that remains within the same mode of thought, a transformation that is only a way of adjusting the same thought more closely to the reality of things can merely be a superficial transformation' (Foucault, 1988f: 55). In this sense, the role of an intellectual is to 'liberate thought' and 'see how far the liberation of thought can make those transformations urgent enough for people to want to carry them out' (Foucault, 1988f: 155).

If the intellectual's pursuit is to liberate thought, it means turning to academic research practices and thinking critically of them. It requires an engagement in the technologies of the self: actively creating a self that, divorced enough from the discursive construction of knowledge, can think critically. As Foucault noted: 'For me intellectual work is related to what you could call aestheticism, meaning transforming yourself. ... This transformation of one's self by one's own knowledge is, I think, something rather close to the aesthetic experience' (Foucault, 1988c: 14). The profound question for academics, as intellectuals, is how to think differently. How can we transform ourselves by our knowledge? Gilles Deleuze's (1988) interpretation of Foucault's technologies of the self can help answer this question.

Gilles Deleuze: Foucault's fold

> If at the base there has not been the work of thought upon itself and if, in fact, modes of thought, that is to say modes of action, have not been altered, whatever the project for reform, we know that it will be swamped, digested by modes of behavior and institutions that will always be the same.
>
> (Foucault, 1988f: 155–156)

Because Foucault asserted that critical thought is an imperative prerequisite for all transformation, we have to establish how to develop into critical thinkers within the power relations of discursive knowledge production: i.e. the academy. Taking critical thinking seriously means considering the role of the academic self within Foucault's power/knowledge axis. Deleuze's interpretation of Foucault's technologies of self relates the concept of critical thought to the technologies of power.

As we have concluded earlier, the technologies of the self expresses the third and final dimension in Foucault's work. Deleuze (1988) titles the first two, power and knowledge, as the outside. The third dimension he labels the inside and notes that Foucault was interested in how that is caught up with the other two axes. Similar to several other interpretations of Foucault's work, Deleuze (1988: 96) claimed that Foucault's mission became an examination of 'how to get free of oneself', the self formed through subjection to the power/knowledge nexus of the present society. Consequently, the academic self is formed through a process of subjectivation and should be freed from itself and the domination of the current power/knowledge axis.

Deleuze (1988) departed from the concept of 'liberation' of the self to emphasise Foucault's concern with the ethical use of power: forming a different 'modern' self does not mean an outright rupture of the power relations, but rather involves harnessing the existing power relations and knowledge to disrupt the current process of subjectivation. This is possible if we conceptualise the inside and outside as relational where the inside turns into a source of power by using the power of the outside. Deleuze (1988) used the terms folding and doubling to describe this process as he visualised the inside folding the outside into itself. This doubling allows for a conceptualisation of a self that is a separate dimension from power relations and knowledge formation, yet exists concurrently with them. There is, therefore, a perpetual communication between the three dimensions. Within this composition of forces, subjectivation – the relation to oneself – continually transforms: 'Recuperated by power-relations and relations of knowledge, the relation to oneself is continually reborn, elsewhere and otherwise' (Deleuze 1988: 104). Obviously, then, it is possible to recuperate one's identity in today's cultural context by folding the outside within the inside. But what are those folds? How do we reshape the unified modern, academic identity?

Deleuze (1988: 105) reminded us that the struggle for subjectivity required resisting first the 'individualising' constraints of power and second, the 'known and recognized identity, fixed once and for all'. A contemporary struggle for subjectivity, according to him, 'presents itself, therefore, as the right to difference, variation and metamorphosis' (Deleuze, 1988: 105–106). We can exercise this right by folding the power relations and the knowledge that form our selves and bodies, the outside forces, into ourselves to seek freedom from the unified construction of identity. Foucault already offered some possibilities for doubling the outside forces: academics can fold by practising criticism, by creating new forms of thought, to continually challenge what we know and consequently, create new selves recuperated by new critical ways of thinking. Therefore, an academic should aim to become 'a thinking being who problematizes himself, as an ethical subject' (Deleuze, 1988: 118). As this process has to begin with altering one's own thought, the 'elaboration of self by self' is a fundamental aspect of an intellectual's work: 'This work of altering one's own thought and that of others seems to me to be the intellectual's raison d'être. ... I would like it to be an elaboration of self by self, a studious transformation, a slow, arduous process of change' (Foucault, 1988g: 264). The technologies of the self should, therefore, comprise an important aspect of the everyday ethics of an academic: how an academic begins to understand her/himself.

The practices of freedom that implied a responsible use of power – to use one's power with a minimum of domination – means not merely pointing out that 'things are going wrong' but challenging the power relations and knowledge production that create unified subjects. As academics exist within those power relations, the idea is to use their power as knowledge producers to fold the outside forces to create transformation through critical thought. For Foucault, this is an exciting prospect that should be full of creativity and imagination:

> I can't help but dream about a kind of criticism that would not try to judge, but to bring an oeuvre, a book, a sentence, an ideal to life; it would light fires, watch the grass grow, listen to wind, and catch the sea-foam in the breeze and scatter. It would multiply, not judgments, but signs of existence; it would summon them, drag them from their sleep. Perhaps it would invent them sometimes – all the better. ... I'd like a criticism of scintillating leaps of the imagination. ... It would bear the lightning of possible storms.
>
> (Foucault, 1988h: 326)

Such inventiveness, according to Foucault, requires continuous curiosity by the academic, something that is largely lost in today's world of competitive social science knowledge production. To actualise the attitude of curiosity, to tap into critical thought, to use the past to fold the present to create a future thought, academics usually write. To detach from one's current identity to be able to think critically, a researcher needs to write. Therefore, writing constitutes an integral element of the technologies of the self for an academic.

Writing as a technology of the self: hypomnemata

In his examination of the Greek's 'culture of the self' Foucault (1986) pinpointed writing as an important practice of the self. Such practices, titled as askesis, were an important aspect of Greek arts of existence and thus constituted a part of the techniques of the self for an Ancient Greek, free male. However, taking care of oneself implied knowledge, attention, and technique, not just being interested in oneself. Foucault (1983b: 246) observed that '[n]o technique, no professional skill can be acquired without exercise, neither can one learn the art of living, the *techne tou biou*, without an askesis which must be taken as a raising of oneself by oneself'. This training took various forms such as abstinence, memorisation, examinations of conscience, meditations, silence, and listening to others. An additional technique was writing the so-called hypomnemata. These could be 'account books, public registers, individual notebooks serving as memoranda. . . . Into them one entered quotations, fragments of works, examples, and actions to which one had been witness of' (Foucault, 1983b: 246). Writing intersected with the 'culture of the self' through the understanding that when a person obtains the perfect government of the self, one learns to use one's power ethically, with a minimum of domination. As Foucault (1983b) asserted: through writing one could create and maintain 'a sort of permanent political relationship between self and self' (246). The hypomnemata further

> constituted a material memory of things read, heard, or thought, thus offering these as an accumulated treasure for rereading and later meditation. They also formed a raw material for the writing of more systematic treatises in which were given arguments and means by which to struggle against some defects (such as anger, envy, gossip, flattery) or to overcome some difficult circumstance (a mourning, an exile, downfall, disgrace).
>
> (Foucault, 1983b: 246)

While the hypomnemata were meant for self-reflection, Foucault was careful to make a distinction between them and writing personal diaries in the sense that we know them today:

> As personal as they were, the hypomnemata must nevertheless not be taken for intimate diaries or for those accounts of spiritual experience (temptations, struggles, falls, and victories) which can be found in later Christian literature. They do not constitute an 'account of oneself'; their objective is not to bring the arcane conscientiae to light, the confession of which – be it oral or written – has a purifying value.
>
> (Foucault, 1983b: 247)

The hypomnemata did not aim to reveal the hidden true self as in confessionals for the church or to 'say the non-said' to one's psychoanalyst, but, 'on the contrary, to collect the already said, to reassemble that which one could hear or read, and this to an end which is nothing less than the constitution of oneself' (Foucault, 1983b: 247). The hypomnemata were meant to collect the fragmentary information transmitted by teaching, listening, or reading 'to establish as adequate and as perfect a relationship of oneself to oneself as possible' (Foucault, 1983b: 247). Therefore, writing the hypomnemata was

> an ontological and not psychological form of contemplation . . . . When grasping the mode of being of your soul, there is no need to ask

yourself what you have done, what you are thinking, what the movements of your ideas or your representations are, to what you are
attached.

(Foucault, 1983b: 248–249)

Through writing one was to gain an ontological knowledge of how to
become an ethical human being and through a perfect relationship with
one's self, to learn how to use one's power with a minimum of domination.
In his discussion of Foucault's interpretation of hypomnemata, Pierre Hadot
(1992)[2] added one more rationale for this type of writing. One was to gather
previous 'thoughts' to be able to return to the past. By writing, one could
detach one's soul from being concerned about the future as the past thought
focused one's mind to the present to enjoy it or to act in it. This, according
to Hadot, could be the use of hypomnemata today. We can practise the
same exercise of writing to concentrate on the present while freeing ourselves
from a concern about the future or the past. Whoever 'practices this exercise
sees the world with new eyes, as if he were seeing it for the first time. He
discovers, in the enjoyment of the pure present, the mystery and splendour
of existence' (Hadot, 1992: 231). To experience if one actually could see
the world with new eyes one of the authors of this book, Pirkko Markula,
embarked on an experimental project of writing hypomnemata. In what
follows she accounts for her practice of ethical self-care as a potential
practice of freedom through writing.

Writing hypomnemata: practising the ethics of self-care

In Chapter 8, we examined, through Foucault's technologies of the self,
how instructors in a hybrid form of mindful fitness might have engaged
in a redefinition of the current, unified fitness identity through their fitness
practices. The conclusion was that the instructors did not commonly attempt
to think critically about fitness knowledge as their daily concerns focused on
the proper execution of the movement technique and the correct instruction
of the exercise form. They had to cope with the demands of a constantly
changing industry whose desperate need for new commodities was beyond
an individual instructor's control. When involved in this project, however,
I had to confront my own position in the relations of power that steer
the fitness industry: Where was my own ethics of care that might act as a
practice of freedom? Was my role as a researcher to simply record other
people's actions into academic papers and based on the results suggest
'reformative' actions for the fitness industry professionals? Was it fair to
expect the instructors to think critically of their practices and their identities
when I not once brought my role as a fitness researcher into question?
As we have demonstrated in this chapter, without a critical thought of
how my own identity is formed within the discursive power relations and

how that steers my knowledge production, I can only hope to initiate superficial change instead of transforming the fitness power/knowledge nexus.

According to Foucault, my role as an academic is not to direct other people's political will, but to generate critical thought that establishes a need for change. Once the premise of fitness practices is challenged, it makes sense to change them. To evaluate how a fitness instructor's identity shapes his/her practices, to think critically of it, I had to acquire such an identity myself. I had to leave my academic ivory tower and enter the field to actively search for ethical fitness practice. Consequently, I took part in a Pilates mat instructor training course. This was my attempt to build an aesthetic self by the self: my academic critical self was to create an ethical instructor self. In this sense, I followed Foucault's (1988d) idea of a 'specific intellectual' for whom a critical questioning is an essential element of life. I was to critically examine the values embedded in mindful fitness instruction to then create an ethical fitness practitioner out of myself. At this point, obviously, my academic identity was not the focal point, although I did presume that as a 'professional intellectual' (Foucault, 1988d: 108) I had acquired an ability to focus my critical gaze on the limiting aspects of a fitness instructor's identity – I assumed that I had an ability to fold (Deleuze, 1988) the dominating fitness discourses by critical thought and thus, develop ethical practices. To maintain such a focus, I was to experiment with writing hypomnemata. Furthermore, I wanted not only to highlight the current values of instructor training, but develop into an ethical, academic practitioner of fitness. Because writing is integral for using my power positively, I wanted to explore if I, as Hadot (1992) suggested, could see the fitness industry as if I were seeing it for the first time and discover new aspects of it to initiate positive, imaginative criticism for my own thinking.

As the meaning of writing hypomnemata is to learn how to behave ethically, the first problem I confronted was to think what ethics might mean in today's fitness industry. This meant reflecting on the possibilities of using my power for a minimum of domination in everyday situations. In the previous chapters, we had established that the dominating fitness discourses promoted the 'body beautiful' or assigned ill health solely to the individual's responsibility, both of which resulted in docile bodies. Therefore, I was clearer about what I did not want to promote than what ethical fitness practices should look like. As noted in Chapter 8, any fitness practice can act as a practice of freedom and equally as a technique of domination. I chose, however, to examine Pilates instructor training because, as a mindful fitness practice, it might embed additional possibilities for transforming the body beautiful or the 'illness' free body. But it also might not. Could the experienced Pilates educators provide me with information that I could later reread in my quest for ethical Pilates practice or critical thinking about fitness research? What things could form 'a raw material for the writing of more systematic treatises in which were given arguments and means by which to struggle against' (Foucault, 1983b: 246) the dominating discourses of fitness?

In addition to struggling to think what ethical fitness practices should be, I had to re-orientate my approach to writing. Hypomnemata are not field notes that report events and interactions in the field. They are self-reflective accounts without being confessional diaries. What exactly might such writing entail? My first reaction was to write down my observations in terms of the setting, the participants and the things we did. My second reaction was to reflect on my personal reactions as a learner with academic qualifications in a fitness industry setting. To help dislodge myself from the boundaries of research writing and particularly from confessional writing, I identified as my guiding principle to 'observe what is already written/said about the ethical conduct of a Pilates instructor' in the course. Based on Foucault's description of what constitutes the ethical care of the self I created five categories – interpretation of norms of behaviour; aesthetic practice; critical self-awareness; responsibility of one's own actions that lead to a recognition of moral obligation; and self-transformation – on which to base my writing. I will now discuss separately each category of writing to establish what kinds of issues could be included in hypomnemata of ethical fitness instruction.

In the first category, interpretations of norms of behaviour, I aimed to determine what kind of knowledge was behind the construction of a Pilates exercise class. This, I thought, would help me to establish the norms of behaviour, the ethical principles for Pilates instruction. My notes indicated that the main guidelines promoted working with 'normal, healthy' populations. I further recorded that this meant two things. First, a Pilates instructor should not pretend to be a medical professional and should not give advice on medical conditions, but focus instead on preventative work with healthy populations. Second, a Pilates instructor should not overestimate clients' ability to perform physical skills, but is there for a 'normal' person with limited movement quality and awareness. This led me to write about detailed instructions on correct body positions and not only during the exercises, but also in everyday life. I further recorded instructions for proper wording that did not connote violent contractions, strain or effort, but rather emphasised lengthening, floating or spiralling. According to my notes, then, the instructors were encouraged to focus on improving the clients' everyday lives and be sensitive to each clients' abilities and limitations. It was evident that the discourses of the illness-free body or the body-beautiful were not a foundation for Pilates instruction, but neither were these problematised. For example, my notes include a discussion about the promise of weight loss through Pilates participation at the end of the course. It was concluded that Pilates is not a fat loss technique, but when combined with cardio-vascular work and proper diet it can aid in weight loss. There was, however, no discussion about why and who should loose weight.

In the second category in my hypomnemata, Pilates as an aesthetic practice, I observed that Pilates increases core stability and thus, improves posture. It was not about pain, effort or burn, I wrote, but rather the clients should leave the class energised, feeling more relaxed and more in tune with their bodies. Interestingly, my notes state that a Pilates instructor was not necessarily required to have the ability to do the movements him/herself to teach a beginners' class as the emphasis was on verbal instruction and imagery rather than demonstration. While this 'softer' approach seemed to allow freedom from the dominating discourses of fitness, in my notes I constantly worried about the possible contradiction between the demands of the fitness industry clients and the Pilates philosophy: how does one convince exercisers to come to class when they are not there to change their bodies or work hard to feel the pain?

The third category of my hypomnemata, critical self-reflection, proved a difficult challenge. I was quite unsure about what to report under this heading. As this category was not based on a straightforward recording of the instructions on teaching practice, my notes oscillated between comments of becoming more aware of my own bodily posture and self-criticism of my teaching.

As my fourth category, I analysed what was taught about the instructor's responsibilities. While a Pilates instructor was not responsible for reha-bilitation or curing illnesses, s/he was responsible for teaching safe and appropriate execution of the exercises. Therefore, I concluded, it should be integral to understand how each exercise fulfils the principles of Pilates rather than repeating the correct verbal instruction. The instructor also had to be responsive to participants' needs and be able to provide modifications regarding clients' requirements. I wrote in detail how, in actual practice, this meant a constant negotiation between keeping the participants mov-ing while providing mostly verbal, detailed, individualised instruction. At the basic level, I recorded, the instructors were taught only 15 modified movements from the original vocabulary of 35 Pilates exercises. Therefore, I observed an additional challenge to keep one's class interesting through a repetitive practice of 15 exercises.

My final writing category, self-transformation, proved as problematic as the category of self-awareness. Turning into self-reflection consistently slipped into confessional self-criticism – probably typical of the deeply in-grained need to reveal 'the unsaid' of a modern person. Similar to my category of self-awareness, I reflected in detail on the strategies of be-coming more confident as an instructor or to fit in as a group member in my instructor course. Feeling rather defeated I finally wrote: 'unable to do this [self-transformation]'. As self-transformation into an ethical instructor was the ultimate aim – only this way can an individual use one's power positively – I possibly failed to produce hypomnemata and instead had written detailed notes on the philosophy of Pilates and personal confessions. My initial reaction to this experiment was quite negative: the hympomnemata did not enable me to critically evaluate myself as an instructor or to challenge the values of Pilates instruction in general. Particularly, because my notes on the crucial categories of critical self-reflection and self-transformation were without much substance, not much critical questioning of my practice of Pilates philosophy was included in my writing.

In general, writing the hypomnemata to become an ethical fitness practitioner was more difficult than I had originally thought, despite my status as 'a professional intellectual'. There was a great tendency to switch into the confessional mode of diary writing. In addition, when writing my notes, I had become like any instructor who is mainly concerned with proper instruction rather than reflecting on deeper meanings behind the exercise form or designing transgressive practices. It was clear, however, that an instructor course can create an instructor identity independent from the dominant discourse of promoting the ideally beautiful body. Similarly, a Pilates instructor's identity is not firmly embedded in the discourse of an illness-free self. In addition, the experienced Pilates trainers actively encouraged us trainees to challenge such commonly held fitness notions as 'no pain, no gain'. Pilates as a 'worthwhile' exercise form was, however, justified by a connection to science, particularly to movement analysis derived from physiotherapy research. For example, the entire course kicked off with a two-hour lecture on the working of Transversus Abdominus as based on scientifically verified electromyography (EMG) results. All the recommended course texts were aimed at professional physiotherapists. In my notes, I wrote about this connection rather 'matter-of-factly': it was good for the instructors to know about the basic biomechanics behind the muscle function as I had confronted so many who just repeated 'a mantra' of Pilates benefits without any understanding of the actual muscle work. I, therefore, seemed to celebrate the scientific validation of Pilates exercises and unquestioningly internalised a 'correct' way of instructing them. Simultaneously, I recorded how difficult it was, despite all the knowledge, to actually perform those movements, to feel that one was using the intended muscle to complete an exercise or listen to one's bodily needs to modify the given movements. I wonder now, putting it in Deleuzian terms, did I manage to fold the 'science' of the bodily mechanics without being, uncritically, dependent on the scientific discourse? This critical question was the first positive outcome that I might not have been able to pin point immediately from my hypomnemata, but on which ethics I can continually reflect. Therefore, writing hypomnemata, as Foucault pointed out, serves not as a one-off 'fix', but as a continual and gradual development of the self by the self.

When I now consider my notes, I realise there were a number of further positive outcomes from this writing experiment. For example, I did consciously develop a type of Pilates ethics and felt more strongly about my responsibilities to actually instruct others. During the course, my knowledge of Pilates movements and how to conduct a class transformed. The connection between the practice and Pilates principles emerged much more clearly than through mere participation in a class. The emphasis on 'normal' people's movement abilities, gradual progression and modifications fitted with my idea of ethical fitness practice. As a result, my actual Pilates practice transformed.

Despite my reluctance to step back into the fitness industry, I decided that I would, following my training, teach a beginners' Pilates mat course. I found myself taking my ethical responsibility very seriously as I aimed to offer classes informed by ethics in the commercial world of fitness that is filled with all sorts of offerings under the umbrella term Pilates. The focus on everyday functionality worked well and turned into what the participants named as 'bodily positivity': listening to and feeling one's own bodily needs. I did not once refer to the 'body-beautiful' or the 'illness-free body' to 'sell' my classes. This experience strengthened my belief in the possibilities for change due to practices of freedom by an individual instructor, who, however, must consider using her power ethically in addition to knowing about the practice. I currently continue to practise critically informed Pilates instruction. A continual folding of the forces of the fitness industry requires on-going askesis, both physical exercise and writing exercise. Therefore, hypomnemata are a great device for continual professional practices for fitness instructors, coaches, managers and sport studies researchers alike. Writing such notes is one way to become a 'specific intellectual' who critically assesses everyday situations (what one is doing at the moment) and the values underpinning such practices (Foucault, 1988d). To use hypomnemata constructively requires practice and a long-term commitment, but they can effectively serve as tools of self-care independent from the subjectivation of individual's self by dominant discursive knowledge.

My experiment with writing hypomnemata still implied an idea of reformation: providing progressive programmes for fitness industry professionals to create transformation. Writing about fitness practices did not necessarily help me see research, knowledge and the discursive construction of my researcher's identity with new eyes. Foucault (and Deleuze), however, suggested academic territory as a starting point: critical questioning of how the researcher's identity can be freed from the limitations of the discursive production of knowledge and power. Only by producing critical thought can we develop transformative theory/practice. In this vein, some scholars have promoted writing as a specific practice for ethical self-stylisation for academics.

Writing as a technology of the self: a critical, artistic practice?

O'Leary started from Foucault's understanding of philosophy as a critical, reflective practice to argue for an integral role of writing as the technologies of the self for an academic:

> philosophy ... is a critical, reflective practice which, by calling into question our present modes of subjectivity and their relation to truth, our present modes of thinking and doing, is capable of transforming the way that we relate to ourselves and others, and thus of changing the way that we live.
>
> (O'Leary, 2002: 152)

O'Leary elaborated that such critical practice, according to Foucault, is also an artistic task because creating an ethical self requires constant work if we aim to break the limits of the rigid forms subjectivity imposed on us by our culture. The self, like a piece of art, is a never to be completed work-in-progress. Writing occupies an important place in this task of continual self-transformation. According to O'Leary, literature as a self-forming activity turns into 'autopoesis'. He used Nietzsche's autobiographical work as an example of writing that 'rather than recounting a life, it deliberately creates a life' (O'Leary, 2002: 135). In this text, Nietzsche created a character of himself whose life, experiences, scholarly and literary texts he used to demonstrate how self-creation could be done through writing. Whether O'Leary advocated that all academics take on writing autobiographies is a different matter. However, self-reflexive writing can be seen as one way of transforming one's identity and creating a self capable of critical thought and thus, transformation. O'Leary discussed other forms of academic writing as possible technologies of the self that could allow for critical work of the self upon the self.

As philosophy (or social science) offers a way for an academic to elaborate one's self as an ethical being, it should change one's way of thinking and inevitably, not only one's way of being, but also one's way of life. Academic, philosophical writing should then act as a type of askesis, an exercise of the self through which it is possible to modify one's self. Ultimately, academic writing should also lead the reader to think differently and result, not only in self-transformation, but in the transformation of social conditions. Such writing O'Leary labelled as philosophical essai, that 'is a test, an attempt, an experiment: a technique which forces the subject to a limit and, in this process, transforms and modifies it' (O'Leary, 2002: 143). The role of essai writing is more to seek modification of the knowing, writing subject rather than show off increased 'knowledgeableness' (O'Leary, 2002: 143). He argued further that Foucault imagined the Greek philosophy as a way of life or a spiritual exercise where a critical attitude was part of the aesthetics of the self, a practice of the self. Philosophy, therefore, is not about seeking knowledge but about engaging in the ethics of care, experimental self-formation, an elaboration of the self, an askesis. This is not self-criticism for the sake of it, however, but should ultimately link with political and cultural criticism in the act of writing and reading of the philosophical essai.

It is clear that writing, as the main outlet for academic critical thought, should become an academic askesis, the actual practice of self-care for ethical academic practice. Therefore, following O'Leary, it is important that academic writing also 'implicates the subject of knowledge'. Writing should first and foremost lead to a modification of the author's way of being and acting in the world. This does not necessarily mean that all academics turn to self-reflective, narrative or autoethnographic writing. While such writing, if well executed, can indeed develop into a critical self-forming activity that leads to social transformation, any type of writing through which one has worked on oneself to create more ethical practices can serve as the technologies of the self. An academic writing as askesis does not even necessitate writing in the first person. For example, hypomnemata can serve as records of critical thought. These notes might never be published yet they can serve as guidelines for ethical, academic research practices. It is important to remember, Foucault emphasised, that writing as a practice of ethical self-care implies critical thought and therefore, is not to be confused with confessional tales or simply recording personal experiences. To function as askesis, writing should concern critical transgression of the limitation of the existing identity, not descriptions of one's experiences *per se*. The self is used as a tool to continually bring into question the dependence of subjectivation from the power/knowledge nexus. Foucault himself opposed the genre of 'intellectual biography' and found talking about his own life 'boring' (Foucault, 1988c). Nevertheless, although his work was not explicitly autobiographical, Foucault maintained that his thinking continually evolved in the course of writing it (Foucault, 1988c, 1989b):

> Whenever I have tried to carry out a piece of theoretical work, it has been on the basis of my own experience, always in relation to processes I saw taking place around me. It is because I thought I could recognize in the things I saw, in the institutions with which I dealt, in my relations with others, cracks, silent shocks, malfunctionings ... that I undertook a particular piece of work, a few fragments of autobiography.
>
> (Foucault, 1988f: 56)

The important point is that the academic self is 'implicated'. This does not mean 'confessing' the deep truth about oneself, detailing one's life story or referencing all one's previous texts in every work one produces. It is, rather, a mode, a type of critical thought that grounds one's writing. Foucault was often annoyed with the continual references to the author's own work if it serves no purpose in advancing the 'critical thought':

> There are books for which a knowledge of the author is a key to its intelligibility. But apart from a few great authors, this knowledge, in the case of the most of the others, serves absolutely no purpose. It acts only as a barrier. For someone like me – I am not a great author, but only someone who writes books – it would be better if my books were read for themselves, with whatever faults and qualities they may have.
>
> (Foucault 1988i: 53)

The purpose of ethical self-stylisation through writing is to continually problematise knowledge, power relations and the self by placing them as 'objects' for critical thought.

Conclusion

> I was just saying that philosophy was a way of reflecting on our relationship to truth. It should also be added that it is a way of interrogating ourselves: if this is the relationship that we have with truth, how must we behave?
>
> (Foucault, 1988h: 330)

In this chapter, we have continued to examine Foucault's technologies of the self for contemporary life. As these technologies refer to the relation of one's self to one's self, they have important implications also for academic practices. Foucault understood the life of an academic as a continual transformation of one's self through one's knowledge. Such knowledge is gained by thinking critically. Deleuze (1988) elaborated that critical thought is possible when the subject, the self, is derived from the relations of power and knowledge rather than being dependent on them. It is possible for the self to be continually recuperated by the knowledge/power nexus (rather than being dominated by them) by folding these outside forces into the self. This process reshapes both the inside (the subject) and the outside (discursive formation of the power relations). The ultimate aim of academic work is transformation. This is impossible, however, without the critical thought that first divorces the academic self from being the subject of someone else's control and the prisoner of his/her own identity. If social transformation is not grounded on such critical thought, it can only reach temporary reformation. The academic's role is to interrogate the underlying relations of power and the complexities of their formation.

Because critical thought occupies such an integral role in attempts for transformation, the role of the intellectual is mainly to provide 'theoretical' thought. Theory, however, should never be conceptualised separate from 'practice'. Writing, for example, can form academic 'practice', even better than the production of totalising programmes for others in society to reform themselves. To be embedded in critical thought and thus, to act as askesis, as a practice to create an ethical self, academic writing should 'implicate' the author's self. It should transform the self as it aims to transform outside forces. This does not mean a dip into confessional writing, autobiography or an exhaustive account of one's previous academic achievements. Including the author's voice explicitly in the text can definitely serve as a self-transforming activity, but its purpose should be to fold the outside forces to critically question what is previously thought. Writing about personal experience *per se* does not necessarily double the discursive power relations into the inside to recuperate the self. When done without critical thought, it only deepens the dependence of one's self from the discursive construction of the modern unified identity. The type of writing is less relevant than its intent to continually question whether change and what kind of change is necessary. As Foucault concluded:

> I dream of the intellectual who destroys evidence and generalities, the one who, in the inertias and constraints of the present time, locates and marks the weak points, the openings, the lines of force, who is incessantly on the move, doesn't know exactly where he is heading nor what he will think tomorrow for he is too attentive to the present; who, wherever he moves, contributes to posing the question of knowing whether the revolution is worth the trouble.
>
> (Foucault, 1988e: 124)

Such an intellectual is a 'specific intellectual' who gains a more concrete and more immediate awareness of struggles that are 'non-universal' and problems – 'multinational corporations, the judicial and police apparatuses, the property speculators etc.' (Foucault, 1980d: 126) – which are specific, yet confront all of us in multiple different forms. To continue to investigate how academics can become critically aware of the 'non-universal' yet confront the 'larger' problems by using their power ethically, in the next chapter we examine how teaching can act as a practice of freedom from the power/knowledge nexus.

Chapter 10

Ethical games of truth

Critical pedagogy and collective stories

In Chapter 9 we examined how sporting researchers could draw on Foucauldian ideas to participate 'in the formation of a political will' (Foucault, 1989c: 306) and to transform sport studies and sport practices. In this chapter we continue to illustrate the political practicability of Foucault's work by examining how an academic can adopt Foucault's ideas to teach as a critical, ethical pedagogue. This is an issue of particular relevance because distributing research knowledge through lecturing is a large aspect of the role of most academics, yet it is rarely addressed as a political issue, at least not from a Foucauldian perspective. Moreover, a range of important pedagogical questions arise if one accepts Foucault's assertion that knowledge, as a subjective construction, is intimately tied to the workings of power. In recognising the power-knowledge couplet, for example, one might ask: how does a lecturer decide what knowledges should be presented to tertiary students? How should these knowledges be presented? And how do these knowledges relate to the on-going production of subjectivities and relations of power? These questions are important given that some sport lecturers participate in the circulation of knowledge concerned with contentious topics (e.g. as related to the links between sport and sexuality, violence, gender relations and body image) and with a desire to promote critical thinking and/or social change.

In this chapter, we develop a specific pedagogical strategy designed to encourage the games of truth surrounding sport to be played in a more equitable manner. We begin by examining the concept of critical pedagogy and how different social theories have influenced this concept. We then discuss how Foucault's political ideas can inform ethical use of sport and exercise knowledge in tertiary teaching. To illustrate further how Foucauldian tools could influence pedagogical practices we provide a reflexive case study of a teaching strategy we have used to examine issues surrounding rugby, pain and masculinities. This case study was inspired by the findings from our investigation of the relationships between rugby and masculinities within New Zealand (see Chapters 5 and 6). Finally, we reflect on the 'effect' our teaching strategy had on students' understanding of rugby identities.

Critical pedagogy and Foucault

The concept of critical pedagogy was introduced to sport studies and physical education in the mid-1980s (Kirk, 2004b). It developed in this time period in relation to the popularisation of critical theorising, and a belief that traditional ways of teaching helped promote 'particular epistemological and political views which benefit a few at the expense of many' (Fernandez-Balboa, 1997a: 6). Within school physical education, for example, traditional forms of teaching have typically been believed to benefit able-bodied, competitive male students at the expense of others (Humberstone, 2002). More generally, concerns were expressed that teachers operated from a 'position of privilege and autocracy ... determining what and how students learn and by when. ... .As such, students are dehumanized and rendered empty containers to be filled up' (Fernandez-Balboa, 1997b: 134). Doune Macdonald (2002) reported that during this formative era, discussions concerning critical pedagogy revolved around the ideas of 'hegemonic capitalism, patriarchy, domination, inequality, alienation, democracy and empowerment' (167). In other words, a 'particular dogma' (Giroux, 1994: 27) of neo-Marxism and neo-liberalism shaped the early development of critical sport pedagogy. Schools were accordingly conceptualised as ideological institutions that acted to entrench various hegemonies and reduce the 'freedom' of individuals. The corresponding political aims were to teach in a counter-hegemonic manner to emancipate students, enhance their 'personal autonomy' (Marshall, 1997: 592) and 'alter oppressive structural constraints in a practical way' (Kanapol, 1998: 64).

Underpinning these critical aims was a belief in a binary division between dominators and dominated or between different classes of people. Power was, accordingly, conceived to stem from the ruling groups and work to control subordinate groups. Members of the subordinate groups were viewed as oppressed and alienated from their true selves. The critical pedagogues of the time, correspondingly, believed that counter-hegemonic strategies could be implemented in schools to thwart the oppressive forms of power, break the binary divisions, free the oppressed, and create a more egalitarian society.

Although neo-Marxist and neo-liberal ideas still influence contemporary critical pedagogies, since the early 1990s different theoretical perspectives – such as cultural studies (e.g. Giroux, 1994), postmodernism (e.g. Fernandez-Balboa, 1997a) and feminist poststructuralism (e.g. Wright, 2004) – have produced multiple approaches to performing critical pedagogy. In this academic context, Foucault's theory challenged existing pedagogies and informed alternative teaching practices (e.g. Burrows, 2004;

Kirk, 2004a, 2004b; Marshall, 1996; Wright, 2004). James Marshall (1996), for example, drew on Foucault's contention that all individuals are subject to various truths and the workings of power, to argue that the neo-liberal educational goal of producing morally autonomous individuals was destined to fail. Foucauldian critics, more generally, drew particular attention to the theoretical limitations of the humanist self and the idea that power works repressively within a binary-like division. Their contention stems from Foucault's idea of the positive effects of the ethical use of power.

Foucault's critical ambitions, in brief summary, did not relate to strategising how to overthrow the ruling classes or free people from the exploits of consumer capitalism but, and *perhaps more radically*, aimed to disrupt the knowledge foundations of modernism to change how people know and govern themselves and others. Through aiming to change people, he aimed to change how people interact and to promote less domineering relations of power. It was his belief that the dominant (i.e. scientific) ways of knowing, that divide people into inflexible categories, are closely connected to many contemporary social problems, such as racism, sexism, homophobia and terrorism. Although Foucault did not believe that people could ever be free from power relations, or even that power relations are necessarily bad, he was concerned with promoting new forms of subjectivity as a potential strategy to alleviate current issues in the workings of power. Foucault summarised his political views by stating:

> The thought that there could be a state of communication which would be such that the games of truth could circulate freely, without constraint and without coercive effects, seems to me to be Utopia. It is being blind to the fact that relations of power are not something bad in themselves, from which one must free one's self. I don't believe there can be a society without relations of power, if you understand them as a means by which individuals try to conduct to determine the behavior of others. The problem is not of trying to dissolve them in the utopia of a perfectly transparent communication, but to give one's self the rules of law, the techniques of management, and also the ethics, the *ethos*, the practice of self, which would allow these games of power to be played with a minimum of domination.
>
> (Foucault, 1987: 18)

From a Foucauldian perspective, teachers and students exist in relations of power, and teachers typically have greater opportunity to exercise power than students, but this is not necessarily problematic. Foucault (1987), in reflecting on 'the pedagogical institution' (18), stated that in a situation where a teacher knows more than a student, it is often appropriate for a teacher to transmit this knowledge but one should aim to avoid 'the effects of domination which will make a child subject to the arbitrary and useless authority of a teacher, or put a student under the power of an abusively authoritarian professor' (18). Foucault was, accordingly, concerned that a teacher should not attempt to govern the conduct of the students (i.e. exercise power) in an unethical manner. He stated that the ethical problem relates to how humans interact with respect to 'knowing how one can make allowance for the other's freedom in the mastery that one exercises over oneself' and with a care for others (Foucault, 1985: 252). Foucault was concerned about the ethical use of knowledge which, in a rudimentary summary, related to promoting knowledge in a critically reflexive manner and with a caring respect for one's self and the rights of others. More generally he hoped that this knowledge could be used to problematise issues, rather than simply developed into a formalised set of interdictions and such use of knowledge, Foucault maintained, could produce 'an aesthetics of existence, the purposeful art of freedom perceived as a power game' (Foucault, 1985: 253).

From this brief overview of Foucault's political and ethical concerns we can question: (1) what 'rules of law' or ethics could pedagogues use to circulate knowledge that (2) could potentially promote new forms of subjectivity and (3) help the associated games of power to be played more equitably? To help answer these questions we first examined how Foucauldian tools had been used within sport pedagogy.

Sport pedagogy and Foucault

Within sport pedagogy, Foucauldian tools have typically been used to offer a critical understanding of primary and secondary schools, physical education (PE) practices and the production of various student subjectivities. One of the first sport researchers to draw on Foucault was John Hargreaves (1986), who provided a historical analysis of the relationships between physical education (PE) knowledge/discourse, student bodies and the workings of power. Hargreaves contended that 'PE knowledge orders a field and structures a programme of control over' (163) teachers entering the field. Yet he also suggested that additional sets of power relations – such as between PE teachers, pupils and school administrators – all play a role in shaping how teachers deliver the PE curriculum. In this manner, Hargreaves conceptualised that teachers do not simply exercise power over pupils in a simplistic or unidirectional way. He subsequently argued that if one wants to understand the social effects of PE, it is important to study the broader networks of power within which students, teachers and schools are enmeshed.

In his analysis of PE, Hargreaves (1986) drew closely from Foucault's ideas on disciplinary power. He analysed, for example, the rigid control of space in PE, the close monitoring of bodily movements and the gaze of authority as a technique of control. Yet Hargreaves did not conclude that the outcome of student inculcation in the discipline of PE was the simple production of normalised bodies. In contrast, he reported that it was 'important to bear in mind that the expansion of power afforded by the development of the modern PE programme constitutes both power *over* pupils and also power *for* them' (171, italics in original). He suggested, more specifically, that some of the pupils from 'working class' backgrounds are encouraged through their success in PE/sport to conform more broadly to 'models of behaviour promoted in the PE programme' (175) and the achievement values of the school. Thus, the productive power of PE can change how some pupils conceptualise and practise education, which can have far-reaching social effects.

Reflecting on Hargreaves' findings, Jennifer Smith Maguire (2002) suggested that PE can act as an example 'of the positive exercise of disciplinary power, producing individual responsibility and competence such that the effects far outlast the individual's mundane participation in gym class' (300). Moreover, she reported: 'In connecting PE to broader power networks and political agendas, Hargreaves provides a key insight into the sustainability of the effects of the disciplines: the active involvement of the individual means that disciplines give rise to self-discipline' (300). Yet Hargreaves also concluded that PE not only helps produce disciplined individuals but also contributes to the production of problematic sets of power relations, such as, between different class and ethnic groups. He specifically noted: 'The antagonism of the lower-working class "lads" towards working class boys who conformed with the school's demands ... bordered on hatred, and it exemplifies the power of the fragmenting process which the school and PE help to foster' (Hargreaves 1986: 175). Hargreaves' Foucauldian analysis, accordingly, reveals how a programme of control aimed at disciplining the body has far-reaching and unplanned consequences.

In a similar investigation of Foucault's technologies of domination, David Kirk (2004a) examined how PE in Australian schools since the early 1900s has historically employed various disciplinary technologies that govern students' bodies with the overall aim of producing docile but productive citizens. He argued that the unambiguous use of 'drilling and exercising, school medical inspection and competitive team games' (Kirk 2004a: 55) as forms of corporeal regulation, illustrated that the body 'is not a "natural" phenomenon, despite the hegemony of medical and biological science' (55). Yet Kirk's prime aim was to use his critical historical study of schooling practices to raise questions about contemporary PE. He suggested that since the 1940s a 'looser' form of power over the body has emerged in contexts outside of the school: a more liberal form of power that is not dependent on direct disciplinary techniques but one that requires individuals to self-discipline and self-govern. This liberal form of power, however, appears to be in contrast to the disciplinary techniques still unimaginatively used in PE classes. Kirk subsequently argued: 'School physical education and sport may be in crisis, at least in part because they represent a series of modernist bodily practices concerned with normalising and regulating children's bodies through methods and strategies which are perhaps already culturally obsolete' (2004a: 63).

The studies by Hargreaves (1986) and Kirk (2004a) demonstrated how Foucault's tools can be used to conceptualise PE differently. In addition to examining how school PE can normalise children into docile bodies, researchers have used Foucauldian theory to detect how PE could also potentially 'liberate' such scientifically constructed bodies. Indeed, Kirk (2004b: 203) asserted that the prime aim of a Foucauldian pedagogy is to help construct *new forms* of subjectivities that 'challenge and possibly subvert the institutional imperatives for docility-utility'. To achieve this aim, Jan Wright (2004) advocated that sport pedagogues could use Foucauldian tools to reveal how 'institutional and cultural processes work to produce particular forms of identity or selves, particularly as these relate to the social construction and control of the body, well-being and health' (29). She illustrated, more specifically, how the discourses of health as presented in school physical education textbooks construct a link between health, slender body shape and physical activity in a problematic manner (e.g. some teenagers might develop eating disorders). Wright, accordingly, illustrated how Foucauldian tools are useful for problematising pedagogical discourses that are often taken for granted in PE contexts. Moreover, through this process of problematising knowledge, students can be provided with opportunities to understand their world and themselves differently. In other words, they are offered opportunities to create new subjectivities.

According to the Foucauldian pedagogues, teachers can help students to problematise and interrogate knowledge and then construct new forms of student subjectivities (e.g. Burrows, 2004; Kirk, 2004a; Wright, 2004). Yet this still leaves the question of how a teacher can undertake this critical task in an *ethical* manner? Moreover, what knowledges should a teacher problematise? And how should this knowledge be presented to students? These questions, although important, have not been commonly examined by critical sport pedagogues. Moreover, Foucauldian analyses within critical sport pedagogy typically focus on school physical education. Consequently, little is known about how Foucault's tools could be employed to shape political and ethical teaching practices in tertiary education.

To contribute to this under-examined pedagogical area, we designed a teaching strategy that aimed to modify the games of truth surrounding sport. While any type of sport could have been chosen as an example, we decided to draw from the study of rugby and masculinity that we introduced in Chapters 5 and 6. The results from this study revealed a dominating discourse of rugby-masculinity that limited men's identity construction. Therefore, our aim was to use Foucault's ideas concerning political change and the ethical use of knowledge to possibly expand the boundaries of sporting identities. Foucault's work, in contrast to the critics who have suggested it offers little hope for change or strategies for enabling transformation, is replete with interconnected ideas on how researchers can actively participate in political activities (see Chapters 8 and 9). More generally, he argued that 'ideas' are only valuable if they are practically examined, tested and used. He stated, for example, with respect to his interpretations and adaptations of Nietzsche:

> The only valid tribute to thought such as Nietzsche's is precisely to use it, to deform it, to make it groan and protest. And if commentators then say that I am being faithful or unfaithful to Nietzsche, that is of absolutely no interest.
>
> (Foucault, 1980e: 54)

Foucault, accordingly, encouraged researchers to use and even adjust his ideas to help develop new ways of thinking. In following his suggestion we made his ideas 'groan and protest' (Foucault, 1980e: 54) to develop a pedagogical strategy that aimed to distribute knowledge in a critical and ethical manner. We will first discuss the ethics of using teaching as a political strategy and then note the value of problematising the current identity construction through teaching. We will further argue that it is possible to initiate such problematisation through evoking 'marginalised knowledges'. Finally, we examine how to present such knowledges to students in a constructive manner.

The ethical use of knowledge

Our first task – determining a set of ethical pedagogical guidelines – was complicated by Foucault's refusal to provide policy alternatives or ready-made solutions to complex social problems. If Foucault refrained from such guidelines, how were we to go about defining what ethical pedagogy might mean? Although some commentators have been subsequently disappointed or confused by Foucault's stance, his refusal was not a theoretical weakness or sign of mulishness but a logical consequence of his method and associated analytic focus (Smart, 2002).

In one of his last interviews before his death, Foucault (1989c: 305) explained that: 'The role of the intellectual does not consist in telling others what they must do. By what right would he [sic] do so?' In short, Foucault did not believe that he had the authority, as an intellectual, to use his position to tell others what to do. Moreover, he was critical of other researchers who claimed to know universal truths and who formulated blueprints for social change and encouraged individuals to slot into their revolutionary plans. He urged people to 'remember all the prophecies, promises, injunctions, and plans intellectuals have been able to formulate in the course of the last two centuries and of which we have seen the effects' (Foucault, 1989c: 305). He explained further, that 'even with the best intentions, those programs become a tool, an instrument of oppression' and suggested, as an example, that 'Marx would be horrified by Stalinism and Leninism' (Foucault, 1988a: 10). Foucault (1980d: 132), accordingly, argued that the role of the intellectual was *not* to be 'the bearer of universal values' or the designer of all-inclusive political strategies.

Influenced by Foucault we did not believe we had the ethical right to tell our students 'what to do' with respect to their relationships with rugby. Therefore, our ethical pedagogy had to differ from the critical pedagogies that are governed by grand political narratives, and which attempt to overtly govern student thoughts and fields of action. Henry Giroux (1994) was similarly concerned about pedagogical practices that aim to tell others what to do. He reported that this form of critical pedagogy can be akin to

> [a] form of pedagogical terrorism in which the issue of what is taught, by whom, and under what conditions is determined by a doctrinaire political agenda that refuses to examine its own values, beliefs, and ideological construction. While refusing to recognize the social and historical character of its own claims to history, knowledge, and values, a politicizing education silences in the name of a specious universalism and denounces all transformative practices through an appeal to a timeless notion of truth and beauty.
>
> (Giroux, 1994: 16)

We were also aware that many of our students had crafted comforting stories-of-self based on their rugby exploits and, therefore, had much invested in their current sporting identities. A teaching strategy of positioning rugby or rugby players as social problems would, as promoted by a dogmatic critical pedagogy, be likely to cause resistance and resentment from many of the students: such a strategy would not encourage the games of power to be played with less domination. In drawing on Foucault's anti-essentialist stance we also accepted that rugby should not be conceptualised as *inherently* problematic or, on the other hand, as morally worthy. In contrast, our political concern lay with challenging how rugby and rugby players were typically known or discursively constructed within New Zealand, and the associated power effects that stem from these knowledges or discursive positionings. We were particularly concerned, for example, with how rugby is known as a 'good sport for males' and how this knowledge helps shape understandings of masculinities and gender relations (see Chapters 5 and 6).

Our initial ethical pedagogical aim, correspondingly, was to circulate

knowledge surrounding rugby and masculinities to encourage critical reflection and allow individuals opportunities to problematise the discourses
surrounding the construction of rugby identities. The idea of problematisation relates to the ability to recognise how all knowledge has been
discursively constructed in different contexts, over time, via power struggles
and, most importantly, that one does not have to accept such knowledge as
an unimpeachable truth. Thus, the aim was – not the emancipation of rugby
players from the ideologically constructed, hegemonic masculinity – but to
start a process of expanding the limitations of one's self by questioning
the discursive context for identity construction in rugby. By encouraging
problematisation, Foucault believed, academics can present knowledge that
allows people to critically reflect on social practices, provides innovative
insights, disrupts truths that are taken for granted, and challenges understandings about current social practices. He advocated genealogical analysis
that resurrects and circulates *marginalised knowledges* as a strategy to evoke
the need to problematise the current social condition.

Marginalised knowledges as a tool of ethical pedagogy

Foucault (1980e: 83–85) referred to his genealogies as 'anti-sciences' because
they were based 'on a reactivation of local knowledges ... in opposition to
the scientific hierarchisation of knowledges and the effects intrinsic to their
power'. Foucault, however, did not claim that scientific knowledge was false
or deny that medicine, or even psychiatry, could be of therapeutic value.
Yet he was concerned that the knowledge claims stemming from science
acted to marginalise other ways of knowing: ways of knowing that had once
proven useful and could still be potentially employed in contemporary social
criticism if they were allowed to re-emerge. He referred to these knowledges
in a variety of different ways, such as: 'subjugated', 'disqualified', 'naïve' and
'low-ranking' (Foucault, 1980e: 82). The promotion of this marginalised
knowledge, more specifically, helps circulate a greater range of discursive
resources that allows individuals opportunities to understand themselves
differently and potentially 'liberate' themselves from scientific and judicial
knowledge. Based on Foucault's genealogical aim, we needed to present
our students with marginalised knowledges about rugby and masculinities:
knowledges that would run counter to that circulated in the New Zealand
media, which routinely celebrates male rugby players as tough, patriotic,
skilled and fearless.

Through undertaking an investigation of men's experiences of rugby
(Chapter 6) it was clear that the ability to play rugby revolves, in part,
around a capacity to withstand pain and fear of injury but that many rugby
participants, *eventually*, gain little joy in continuing to demonstrate this
ability. Many of the men interviewed in Chapter 6 who played rugby, for

example, reported that experiences of pain played an important role in encouraging their eventual retirement from rugby. Despite the significance of the interviewees' experiences of pain and injury, all of them remarked that it was difficult to tell others that they were either fearful of playing rugby or disillusioned by repeated injuries. To admit to being fearful of injury or critical of rugby was tantamount to positioning one's self as less manly. Thus, the knowledge of rugby as a potentially dangerous sport that can result in pain, injury and fear, was silenced. This silencing allowed the dominating discourse that positioned rugby as 'good sport for men' to circulate unchallenged and leave the existing power relations between males, and males and females, intact. We decided, therefore, that the men's experiences of pain and injury could be a type of marginalised knowledge that, when circulated to our students, might problematise the way they currently conceptualise rugby. What, however, would be an effective way to present this knowledge to induce critical thought and not resentment or resistance?

Strategising the promotion of marginalised sporting knowledges

Foucault's strategy to present disqualified knowledge to encourage critical thinking allowed the voices or stories of the 'marginalised' to be heard. He adopted this strategy in his attempts, for example, to reform the treatment of French prisoners in the early 1970s by opening up lines of communication so that prisoners could voice, in their own words, their concerns about the appalling prison conditions. In a similar respect, Foucault's (1975) edited text *I, Pierre Rivière*, provided the opportunity for the voice of a Norman peasant, convicted of parricide in 1836, to be publicised in conjunction with other documents surrounding the case. What intrigued Foucault about this case was that Pierre Rivière, the so-called delinquent and mad murderer, had left a detailed, well-crafted and seemingly thoughtful memoir detailing his side of the tragedy: a confession that stood in opposition to how he had been positioned by doctors, court proceedings, and criminological and psychiatric reports. This memoir, therefore, appeared as a challenge to science and juridical understandings by making it difficult for any person of authority to state with certainty what Rivière was in reality. In similar manner, we thought it appropriate to present to our students the 'marginalised' voices of our rugby interviewees to raise the issue of 'what are rugby players in reality?' and correspondingly, 'what are masculinities?'

Foucault refrained from revealing his own views of the crime and from telling other people what to think when he documented Rivière's case. His seemingly neutral stance, however, risked championing the actions of a murderer. Similarly, his focus on the treatment of French prisoners, rather than their so-called *criminal* actions, risked presenting a one-sided set of experiences. Yet Foucault's aim was to open up these marginalised knowledges for critical analysis and to incite greater reflection and debate: particularly with respect to examining how we *know* what constitutes crime, justice and punishment.

Although Foucault's writings on prisons initiated transformations in the French penal system, he was somewhat disappointed that a more widespread discussion and critical analysis of what constitutes crime and justice did not take place. He reported, for example:

> The struggle around the prisons, the penal system and the police-judicial system, because it has developed 'in solitary', among social workers and ex-prisoners, has tended increasingly to separate itself from the forces which would have enabled it to grow. It has allowed itself to be penetrated by a whole naïve, archaic ideology which makes the criminal at once into the innocent victim and the pure rebel – society's scapegoat – and the young wolf of future revolutions.
>
> (Foucault, 1980d: 130)

Foucault recognised that his strategies of promoting marginalised knowledges and of providing conditions that allow the voice of the marginalised to be heard, are political strategies of uncertain outcome. In response he suggested that it was important for academics with political desires to also think about how the promotion of such knowledges might be *used*, that is, their 'tactical productivity ... and their strategical integration' (Foucault, 1978: 102).

Foucault stirred the emotions of his readers by writing provocatively as he hoped to engage them with political issues and, therefore, get them to participate in debate and critique. Foucault argued (1991b: 36): 'what is essential is not found in a series of historically verifiable proofs; it lies rather in the experience which the books permits us to have'. He was, therefore, interested in presenting his critical research in an erudite manner but also with providing his readers with an *experience* that allowed for transformative possibilities. Indeed, he wanted his readers to undergo a 'limit-experience' (Foucault, 1991b: 31): an experience that would push his readers to the edge to induce 'an alteration, a transformation, of the relationship we have with ourselves and our cultural universe: in a word, with our knowledge (*savoir*)' (Foucault, 1991b: 37). To increase the possibilities that his readers would have a limit-experience, Foucault, at times, eschewed the uninspired and objective representational style typical of academic prose and drew on various literary techniques to represent his well-researched arguments in an evocative and provocative manner. This representational style reflected Foucault's passionate concerns regarding social issues and he suggested that an 'experience-book as opposed to a truth-book or a demonstration-book' (Foucault, 1991b: 42) could be an effective tool for generating political interest in a contemporary social issue. To generate students' political interest in the contemporary issues of masculinity, we explored different ways to represent, in an evocative manner, the marginalised voices of men who had played rugby. From this search we eventually drew on Laurel Richardson's (1997) strategy of the collective story: a political strategy she developed in relation to Foucauldian ideas.

A collective story tells the narrative of a group of people who are connected in some way but who may not think of themselves as a group. The sociological task of writing a collective story is to understand the private stories of members of these groups in relation to broader social forces and to represent these stories as a collective, unified, chronological narrative. Through revealing the social and political context within her stories, Richardson (1997) hoped that members of such groups and others could better understand their own experiences so that they could be in an enhanced position to guide their futures. She explained that:

> A collective story tells the experience of a sociologically constructed category of people in the context of larger socio-cultural and historical forces. The sociological protagonist is a collective. I think of similarly situated individuals who may or may not be aware of their life affinities as coparticipants in a collective story. My intent is to help construct a consciousness of kind in the minds of the protagonists, a concrete recognition of sociological bondedness with others, because such consciousness can break down isolation between people, empower them, and lead them to collective action on their behalf.
>
> (Richardson, 1997: 14)

Collective stories, accordingly, aim to give voice to those silenced or marginalised by dominant discourses and help promote transformative possibilities by allowing individuals to develop a sense of community or collective identity; in other words, a new way of viewing themselves.

We were aware that a well-crafted collective story about rugby fears and injuries could engender emotional responses in readers. Indeed, we hoped that such a story might disturb readers and challenge their thinking about rugby and maybe even push them towards a 'limit-experience' (Foucault, 1991b: 31). At the least, however, we hoped that the collective story would provide a forum for promoting naïve, disqualified or marginalised knowledge about rugby: knowledge that could potentially encourage greater critical reflection and debate concerning the links between sport and masculinities, provide discursive resources to promote new forms of subjectivities and help the associated games of power to be played more equitably.

Based on Foucault's theory of marginalised knowledges prompting prob-lematisation, our conclusion was to write an evocative collective story, present it to our students and invite personal reflections to engage in critical problematisation of rugby identities.

The collective story that we will present next, is based on the interviews of 14 New Zealand men whom we have already introduced in Chapters 5 and 6. Unlike these chapters, the rugby story is narrated by one man but his voice represents the collective experiences of the interviewees who played competitive rugby. Richardson (1997) turned to narrative as a representa-tional form because she recognised the social significance of narratives in everyday life. Polkinghorne (1988), for example, reported that narrative is one of the primary ways that humans use to understand lived experiences and to convey those understandings. Narratives can therefore provide an accessible way of distributing knowledge.

Richardson further suggested that a narrative must be well crafted if it is to connect people to the experiences of others. More specifically, a good narrative does not simply describe events but must draw on literary devices to pull readers in. In writing the collective story we aimed to let the interviewees do the speaking, thus we drew directly from their interview quotes with little editing. This allowed the interviewees' voices to be clearly heard and, more specifically, served to highlight their somewhat unique expressions and colloquialisms. Their voices, in this sense, helped give the story a sense of verisimilitude. We also presented the story as a reflexive monologue, which can add a poignant element. Finally, we focused on the five interviewees who played competitive rugby into their adult years because we assumed that many students might conceptualise male adult rugby players as exemplars of manliness: tough, unemotional, strong, resilient and robust. A story that reveals their concerns, and even fears, about injury and pain was designed to disturb this understanding of rugby players.

Once were rugby players: docile bodies revolt

It was very exciting in those days, in the *barefoot days*, at primary school. I'd really look forward to my Saturday morning game of rugby. I'd get quite upset if it rained and I had to stay back on the farm and help milk the cows. The games were exciting and rugby suited me: I was big for my age and when I got my lanky legs pumping I was hard to stop. I'd come from a family that was mad keen on rugby. My Dad used to always knock off work on a Saturday afternoon to watch the big game on TV and my older brother was quite a good player. We would often kick a ball around in the back paddock and practise our sidesteps around the cow-pats and thistles. And at my small country school, all the boys played rugby ... oh I guess there were a few who played soccer but they weren't looked upon very highly at all.

If I got hurt playing rugby I tried not to show that I was in pain, I suppose I wanted to look tough. Yet I remember one cold wet day we played this team from Waimoana – the wrong side of the tracks so to speak – and these kids seemed bigger and rougher than us and for once I was actually scared. I let a kid run past me and I don't think I even attempted to tackle him. We lost the game and afterwards I cried my eyes out because I was so upset. That incident, I think, helped make me become big on tackling as I decided to not let myself get scared again. So from then on I concentrated on tackling and my coach, who was my best mate's old man, told me if I go into the tackle with my shoulder and hit them in the stomach you can't get hurt. I totally took his advice on board and believed it, and after that I just loved nailing kids. So I ended up totally loving tackling.

Of course by the time I was older that advice about not getting hurt in the tackle didn't really apply any more. By the time I was in my secondary school – a boy's boarding school in the city – and was playing for my First XV, I had already been concussed twice: each time going too low in the tackle and getting a knee in the head. I remember one of those times, you know, being not completely there and lying on the ground for a moment and then looking around and thinking, 'Oh, I'm playing rugby' and the game was now down the field. So I ran after the game and when I got there – 'Oh, the game is over there' – and so I'd run over there. The school principal yelled from the sideline whether I was ok and by that time I'd started sort of coming together again. My coach said I should come off but I was 'no, no, I'm fine sort of thing'. I very much wanted to keep playing, so I did. At the end I admit that I thought we had won but I found out we had been thrashed, so I guess I had played in a confused state.

But I actually had a pretty good run with injuries while at school. You know, I got winded and bruised at times, and the odd groin strain but nothing really major. And yes, there was a general soreness after the games; there would be cuts and scrapes from sprigs and boots. And typically on Saturday evenings I would be in some discomfort but

I accepted all that as normal. In fact, I think there was something in the total exhaustion at the end of the game that I enjoyed. I wouldn't have talked about it in terms of enjoying the pain, but I linked the sense of being totally exhausted with a satisfaction that I had played well.

After my last year in the First XV I thought *to myself* that I was not going to play rugby any more, as I was sick of being injured. I was too sore. I was sick of playing 80 minutes and then having four days of where I couldn't do much because I was in pain. But my mates talked me into playing again. Well, I guess, I just liked the game too much.

At the senior level I was suddenly playing with guys who were a lot older and tougher and it was definitely more competitive and serious. Everyone knew what the game was about and they were committed to it. I played with a belief, in the back of my mind, that I could get seriously hurt. It was something that we all knew but didn't talk about. In my first season I admit that it was easy for me to be intimidated and it wasn't because I was small. I was a big unit: six feet three and weighed 15 stone. But I still got scared. Obviously, you know, I was only a kid and these other guys were much more hardened.

I was 18 when I played my first game at the senior level and I played against an All Black and he gave me a hiding – punched me, elbowed me. He talked to me afterwards and just said: 'What I did to you today is how it's going to be every week for you because you're young, people are going to try to intimidate you'. I think that he thought he was giving me a good lesson. But I was shocked by it all. He would punch me when I was bound in the scrum, I was locking and he'd bring his arm out and just go BANG and catch me under the chin. I shat myself when it first happened, I was just like 'what the fuck was that?' And then I'd look up, because he cracked me a beauty, and I was actually quite stunned. I thought 'God, you know, I haven't done anything to him'. And that was how it was. People would punch you and they would kick you in rucks and mauls. It was just every ruck you'd be watching your back as someone would come flying in with a fist, or dropping their elbows or with the boot.

One time after I got kicked in the head and had stitches put in, I came back on the field and my captain said to me: 'It's payback time. If any of those Tech guys are on our side and you're the first one there I want you to dish it out!' And I was like, I don't know if I can do that, because I didn't really know how to and I was a bit scared of jumping on some guy's head or laying my knee into his back. It wasn't about that for me. I was purely trying to do the best that I could. The whole situation made me feel very uneasy.

But I've got no qualms about dusting someone now. Like in my last game, there was this one kid from Te Rapa club who just couldn't keep his hands off the ball and I said to him in the bottom of the ruck: 'Look, get your hands off the ball'. And I went and spoke to the ref I said, 'Look, watch number seven, he's playing the ball in the ruck with his hands all the time, is it ok if we ruck?' And he said, 'Yes, if it's legitimate'. So we clean this young guy out. Clean him out. Clean him out. He still keeps doing it. So one of the props drops his knee into his back, but he still didn't get it, so I just came into the ruck and laid one on him. Broke his nose and he was off. I didn't have a problem with it, he asked for it, and he was warned. He needed a lesson.

I don't like to talk about those sort of things though, as it makes me sound like I'm a thug and I'm not. I mean it's a contact sport, it's a *hard* contact sport and you've got to be aggressive on the field, but I'm not a violent guy. In fact, I'm critical of the stupidity that leads to thuggery and of people who use the game as an inappropriate outlet for their problems. But I wouldn't play the game if I thought it was simply violent.

I'm now 25 years of age and I won't play again next year. I won't play because I'm sick of dealing with all this shit, I'm sick of icing my legs and wondering if I'm going to wake up today and be able to walk okay or if it's going to give me pain. I mean you're always going to have problems with joints and muscles if you've damaged them and I've had that many bloody injuries it's hard to remember them all. The worst was when I fractured my cervical vertebrae and was in hospital with my neck in traction. He was a dirty bastard who did that one: a stiff-arm tackle that knocked me to the ground. I was stretchered off the field but I guess I was lucky, it could have been worse. In fact the neurologist told me that I had to give up the game altogether. And I did for a while, and some thought I was crazy to get back into rugby, especially without a medical clearance, but 18 months later I was playing again.

Anyhow, I'm now too old for the game. My body can't hack it anymore so I'm now retired.

Reflecting on the political effect of the collective story

To understand the political effect of our Foucauldian influenced pedagogical strategy one of us, Richard Pringle, presented the collective story to his New Zealand students. The students were studying towards a degree in sport and leisure studies and were in their third year of study in a qualitative research methods class. He paid careful attention to the discussions and debate that the story provoked in his class and noted any reference to the story that the students made in their assignment work. In what follows, Richard recounts his experiences as an ethical pedagogue.

Before taking the class I had asked my students to carefully read the story and come prepared to discuss their interpretations in class. To encourage reflection on particular themes, the students were also given a range of questions to think about while reading the story. These questions focused, for example, on whether the story had a degree of verisimilitude; how did the character in the story feel about pain, injury, violence and rugby; were there any contradictions in his story; what did the story say about masculinity, and did the story encourage one to think differently about rugby and sporting pain? I used these questions in class to structure a discussion concerning rugby, pain and masculinities.

I followed Foucault's (1989c: 305) guidance to avoid presenting the collective story to tell 'others what they must do' as it was not my role as a teacher to form the political will of others. My modest aim, in contrast, was to modify the games of truth constructing rugby, by problematising rugby masculinities through disqualified or silenced knowledges. More generally, I wanted to promote debate about the links between sport, pain and masculinity. To help present the marginalised knowledge in an ethical manner I did not deny that rugby could be an exciting game to play or watch, and I cautioned the students about positioning rugby or rugby players as inherently good or bad.

As a strategy for generating discussion and debate the collective story worked well. Many of the students engaged in lively dialogue during class and nearly all referenced the collective story in a subsequent assignment. The students suggested that they were interested in reading the story because its representational style was accessible (as perhaps different to some sociological writings), the topic relevant and it was somewhat provocative. Some students, however, questioned the story's authenticity asking: is senior rugby really *that* violent and damaging? Yet the (ex)-rugby players in the class, both male and female, helped support the story's validity. This acknowledgement of rugby's unwritten code of violence contributed to the promotion of a disqualified way of knowing rugby and helped disturb some of the student's understandings of the sport and its players.

It was obvious that one of the prime requirements for a successful rugby career was a capability to endure pain, injury and violence; and that rugby participants, *over time*, become concerned about the cumulative bodily effects of sustaining injury. The collective story, therefore, worked to position rugby as a corporeally risky, possibly violent and potentially unsatisfying sport. Class discussion about this marginalised knowledge provided the opportunity for some of the students to voice *other* concerns about rugby. For example, concerns were expressed about how rugby dominated television sport, the behaviour of some rugby players at a popular student bar and the violent off-field exploits of a recently arrested professional player. Such concerns indicated that 'points of resistance are present everywhere in the power network' (Foucault, 1978: 95) and these points can be revealed within certain discursive spaces. The collective story, accordingly, created the discursive space that legitimated the expression of discontent about rugby. Thus, the story allowed the multiple truths of rugby to be voiced more equitably.

Although one of my aims in presenting the collective story was to generate alternative ways of knowing about sport and masculinities, the students generally found it difficult to make clear links between the collective story and understandings of masculinities. Some suggested, for example, that although the story was about men who played rugby, a similar story could have been written about female rugby players. In other words, the story did not act in an overt manner to problematise masculinities. Others suggested that the story reinforced the idea that one had to be tough, somewhat fearless and aggressive to play senior rugby. Thus the story, they suggested, supported rather than challenged the dominant ways of knowing rugby players. Yet the majority opposed this argument by suggesting that the story tended to critique rather than glorify toughness, fearlessness and violence. They suggested, accordingly, that the story challenged dominant discourses of rugby players. In a similar manner, the students found it hard to definitively *classify* or define the prime character in the story: discussions, for example, circled around questions of whether he was tough, emotional, fearful, violent, caring, confused, duped and/or manly.

The student debate suggested that the story did not didactically tell people *what* to think about rugby. Nor did the story provide a categorical description of 'what the rugby player was in reality'. The story, accordingly, did not work as a disciplinary tool to coerce student thinking. Nevertheless, it was clear that the story did help disrupt taken-for-granted assumptions about the links between rugby and 'being a man', such as the belief that rugby is 'good' for turning boys into men. The story, accordingly, problematised sport and masculinities.

I also hoped that the collective story would circulate a greater range of discursive resources that could allow possibilities for some individuals to understand themselves differently and the potential to practise freedom. Although it is difficult to know within a lecturing situation whether this aim was achieved or not, I have been subsequently informed by a small number of students that they found the collective story 'useful'. One example follows.

Matthew (a pseudonym) was an undergraduate student who at the end of the teaching semester accepted the opportunity to play semi-professional rugby for a club in England. He played well and enjoyed the pre-season matches but in the second match of the competition he re-injured his left knee and needed on-going medical treatment. Midway through the painful season he made the decision to retire from rugby. Upon his arrival back in New Zealand he approached me to talk about undertaking further studies and said that he wanted to explore something about rugby and masculinities. Matthew further reported that he had kept a diary of his English rugby experiences and he then volunteered to read some excerpts. The carefully crafted excerpts revealed his experiences of tension associated with the desire to retire from rugby and the pressure to 'play on'. Through subsequent discussions with Matthew, it was apparent that the collective story (from a year earlier) had played a part in challenging him to think more candidly about the embodied costs of rugby and had subsequently helped make it easier for him to eventually 'practise freedom' by retiring, without undue anxiety, from rugby.

When I reflect on the effect of our pedagogical strategy, I am satisfied that it encouraged debate and critical discussion about sport, pain and masculinities. In addition, it promoted marginalised knowledge of rugby that offered opportunities for opening cracks of resistance and possibilities for (self) transformation. Yet given that 'there can exist different and even contradictory discourses within the same strategy' (Foucault, 1978: 102) I was also aware that the story could be interpreted in multiple ways: as such, I accepted there was no guarantee with respect to the political influence of the collective story.

Conclusion

In sport studies, it is rarely discussed how to distribute knowledge to tertiary students in an ethical but critical manner. In this chapter we contributed to this discussion by reflecting upon a specific pedagogical strategy to problematise the games of truth surrounding sport. Following Foucault's ethical use of power, we aimed to examine how rugby and masculinities could be played in a manner 'more attractive and fascinating' (Foucault, 1987: 20). Foucault did not write expressly on pedagogical issues but his ideas on knowledge/power, social transformation, subjectivity, ethics and the role of the intellectual have proved useful to critical pedagogues (e.g. Burrows, 2004; Kirk, 2004a, 2004b; Marshall, 1996; Wright, 2004). Foucault asserted that it was generally inappropriate for academics to tell others what to do, but suggested it was important for 'specific intellectuals' to problematise the current workings of power and shake up assumptions that are taken for granted. At a broader level, Foucault encouraged the promotion of marginalised knowledge and evocative representational styles as strategies to challenge the knowledge foundations of humanist science and encourage transformations in how people know themselves and others. Moreover, Foucault encouraged academics to use and even transform his ideas to develop innovative thinking in diverse areas of interest. We similarly encourage tertiary educators to think of how they can distribute knowledge in a manner to help future coaches, teachers, fitness trainers, athletes and managers to perform their roles imaginatively and with critical care for themselves and others.

Inspired by Foucault we aimed to illustrate one way that a lecturer could practise critical, ethical pedagogy. Our particular pedagogical strategy promoted marginalised knowledge about rugby by drawing on the voices of rugby players and representing them in an evocative and accessible manner within a collective story. The collective story did not tell the reader what to think about rugby or rugby players but, nevertheless, problematised the taken-for-granted assumption that rugby is 'turning boys into men'. The story encouraged student debate and discussion, and promoted subjugated knowledge of rugby and rugby players. In addition, the collective story worked to create a discursive space that allowed the expression of discontent about rugby to be legitimately voiced. In this manner, we assumed that our pedagogical strategy, at a modest level, allowed the games of truth surrounding rugby and masculinities to be played in a more equitable manner. Indeed, as Foucault (1987: 20) suggested: 'the more that people are free in respect to each other, the greater the temptation on both sides to determine the conduct of others. The more open the game, the more attractive and fascinating it is.' Our specific pedagogical strategy is only one of many possible ways that Foucault's tools could have been used. We, accordingly, encourage others to take up Foucault's challenge and use the context of teaching to distribute knowledge in an ethical and creative manner to 'change something in the minds of people' to show 'that they are much freer than they feel' (Foucault, 1988a: 10).

Conclusion

In this book we have explored the main tenets of Foucault's theory and how it can inform examinations of sport, fitness and physical activity. During this exploration our ideas about Foucault's theoretical contribution have been continually challenged and renegotiated. This is, we suspect, Foucault's intention: he insisted that any investigation should be carried out only step by step and through continual reflection. According to Foucault, such continual critical reflection – thought upon thought – was the main purpose of the philosopher's or social scientist's work, because only by practising criticism, was it possible to repeatedly challenge the political, economic and institutional regime of 'truth' production. Foucault's ideal intellectual, therefore, is 'incessantly on the move' without knowing 'exactly where he [sic] is heading nor what he will think tomorrow for he is too attentive to the present' (Foucault, 1988e: 124). Consequently, we do not intend to present this book as a definitive reading of Foucault's work, but rather as a tool for sport researchers to think differently; to continually challenge the way the sporting self is constructed within the power/knowledge nexus.

Reading Foucault's work is a greatly inspiring, often difficult and confusing process and inevitably, many of our previous conceptions of Foucault's work have gradually changed during the course of writing this book. For example, in the introduction we stated that we both were originally interested in issues of dominance and resistance through sport. Our understanding of these terms, more than anything, has been continually challenged by Foucault. While we were already familiar with his terminology of discursive power relations before engaging with this book, we fully realise its impact now after completing our writing. Foucault's understanding of power as relational, we believe, has helped us to transcend our previous theoretical limitations in a significant manner and we want to, once more, highlight its main principles.

Engaging with Foucault's work has allowed us to conceptually restructure the dualistic framework of oppressive power versus the oppressed, yet resistant individual. This framework of power – that Foucault called a 'law-like' understanding of power and a humanist understanding of the individual – informs examinations that aim to read sport or exercise either as dominant or resistant practices. This framework, Foucault further observed, leads to the idea of power as repressive. Within this logic, power is always seen as negative and facilitating rejection, exclusion or refusal. It is concealed or masked to do its deed: to limit individuals through lack of freedom. It forbids or it permits. Opposite to this power stands the obedient subject who is governed by the law/power. However, the definition of power as law-like governance also opens up space for the idea of disobedience of the law. A disobedient citizen, the resistant individual, deliberately creates transgression. S/he places her/himself 'to a certain extent outside the reach of power; he [sic] upsets established law; he somehow anticipates the coming freedom' (Foucault, 1978: 6) from the oppression of the law. Within sport studies, for example, the resistant potential of women's sport has been examined through this framework: a female athlete who, despite numerous restrictions, financial and social, becomes a rugby player, an ice-hockey player, a boxer or a footballer and resists the oppressive power. She breaks the silent acceptance of male hegemony within sport, resists the ideological definition of acceptable femininity, upsets the established order by entering the realm of sport and by her example, anticipates the freedom women who participate in sport will experience. As we have demonstrated throughout this book, Foucault had several reservations about this conceptualisation of power that places the oppressive 'law' as an opposite to the 'oppressed,' yet disobedient citizen seeking liberation.

In Foucault's analysis, power is considered positively as a series of relations within which an individual interacts with others. Therefore, power is omnipresent: it is continuously produced in every human relationship. Consequently, Foucault proposed that power is not acquired, but is an interplay of nonegalitarian and mobile relations; power manifests inside relationships (rather than being imposed as an exterior force) and therefore, has a productive role. In sum, 'power is not an institution, and not a structure; neither is it a certain strength we are endowed with, it is the name that one attributes to a complex strategical situation in a particular society' (Foucault, 1978: 93). In this conceptualisation, major dominations are hegemonic effects that are sustained by confrontations within power relations; and power relations are both intentional and nonsubjective. When we approach sport from a Foucauldian perspective, power is no longer seen as something possessed by a few individuals or groups. A sporting individual is no longer assumed to be an obedient citizen who is governed by or resists this law-like power. Rather, sport comprises a transfer point for relations of power. From a Foucauldian point of view, sport in its present form is a result of different deployments of physical activity and competitive spirit upon different bodies in different periods of time. Sport as an institution has been shaped within relations of power, where individuals who participate, watch or produce sport interact with each other. This is a process of ceaseless struggles and confrontations that transform or strengthen the existing discursive construction of sport. This means that individuals are always operating within the power relations, some advancing strategically the objectives of the power relations, others resisting these objectives. Here we come to Foucault's insistence, also often cited within sport studies, that: 'Where there is power, there is resistance' (Foucault, 1978: 95).

Foucault reminded us that power manifests in discourses where it is joined together with knowledge. Discourses thus are socially constructed ways in which we 'know' about ourselves, our bodies or our practices. In his own work, Foucault (1970) interrogated how the 'human sciences' or medicine (1973) construct such ways of knowing. True to his notion of power as relational, Foucault emphasised that there are no dominating discourses that are externally imposed on individuals. He advised that 'we must not imagine a world of discourses divided between accepted discourses and excluded discourses, or between the dominant discourse and the dominated one; but as a multiplicity of discursive elements that can come into play in various strategies' (Foucault, 1978: 100). No discourse can, therefore, be judged as dominating or 'liberating' in advance and it is important to carefully trace the historical and societal circumstances for each discursive formation before labelling them as technologies of dominance. Discourses transmit and produce power, reinforce power, expose it and make it possible for an individual to advance or reverse power relations. Similarly, by analysing the discursive construction of sport, fitness or the physically active body, we can look at power positively as multiple, omnipresent, yet constantly changing relations between individuals. In Chapter 3, we examined, specifically, how we know about the 'fit' body through scientific discourse that merges a very specific understanding of health with a certain definition of fitness. It appeared that such discursive elements produced a body governed by the multi-faceted health apparatus. The chapter also provided an example of how to combine Foucault's archaeological and genealogical approaches to detect the discourses in health-related fitness texts.

While Foucault's own work was largely based on tracing the slow formation of discursive power relations through historical texts, it was also important for Foucault to identify the most immediate, the most local power relations that produce specific discourses and to map how these discourses were modified by power relations: how they were resisted, countered or strengthened by individual actions. Similarly, it is important for sport scholars to look for the localised power relations close to the experiences of the sporting people they study and then trace how discourses are shaped as a result of the actions of these individuals. This provides an investigation of how an individual operates within the power relations of sport to understand him/herself as a human being.

In Chapter 4 we mapped the localised power relations of a fitness club to demonstrate how its space allows for panoptic self-surveillance. We concluded that exercise practices tended to discipline individuals into docile bodies, but we also examined how individual exercisers operated such practices to (re)shape their fit bodies. In addition, in Chapters 5 and 6 we focused on the construction of gendered sporting identities through the experiences of men playing a traditionally 'masculine' sport, namely rugby union. These men participated in a discursive construction of gender through their sporting practices as they negotiated multiple discourses to understand themselves and sporting women as human beings. They joined the discursive field of gender relations by entering into 'the truth games' regarding the sporting bodies. These truth games dictated 'the specific techniques' that the male rugby players used to understand themselves (Foucault, 1988b: 18). Therefore, the gendered sporting identity was produced within an ever changing set of practices that were formed in the relationship between power, truth and the individual. A sporting identity, therefore, is not a discourse, but is created within discourses that shape sport, sporting practices and sporting bodies. In addition, no sporting identity can be assigned as 'resistant' or 'dominant' *per se*, but should be understood as formed within a complex set of discourses in a particular historical and cultural context. Foucault dedicated his later work to the formation of an individual's identity within such cultural constellations.

The latest dimension of Foucault's work – work that, sadly, was interrupted by his death – examined how individuals in power relations learned to recognise the discourses or knowledges of sexuality, how they acted upon this knowledge, and how they became to identify as human beings through this particular discourse. This led to Foucault's analysis of the technologies of the self: a slow formation of the self through practices of self upon the self. We engaged with the technologies of the self in the third section of this book. In the process of writing this section, we realised that while Foucault elaborated on how the technologies of self might be understood in today's context in his later interviews, he did not have a chance to formulate this concept in a more systematic manner. Consequently, a plethora of interpretations of this concept exists. In many of these readings 'resistance', rather than the creation of the self through consistent self-care practices, takes the centre stage. The technologies of the self in Ancient Greece, however, did not necessarily imply an attempt to 'free' an individual's identity. It must also be noted that Foucault understood the modern formation of the self (subjectivation) as a process of subjection tightly controlled by the scientific knowledge whereas the Ancient Greek (free male), unlike the modern individual, chose to build an identity free from the limitations of today's process of subjectivation. However, several writers have since elaborated on the idea of self-care practices as practices of freedom from the subjectivation where the individual is, on the one hand, subject to someone else by control and, on the other hand, tied to his or her own identity by self-knowledge derived from the 'human sciences' (Deleuze, 1988).

It is important to emphasise that subjectivation must not be confused with the law-like concept of power where agency, an individual's ability to resist power, is understood as a substance that one holds. As Foucault defined power and the self as relational – as forms that are constantly modifiable by strategic action by an individual – it is perhaps more accurate to talk about an individual using practices of freedom to modify discursive power relations by an ability to modify one's self. When we understand the subject as a form, resistance to its current identity requires deliberate strategic action by an individual. Therefore, Foucault emphasised the role of critical thought in any practice of freedom: an individual must consciously and critically interrogate his/her identity in order to 'liberate' it from the subjectivation of the discursive power relations. Because an individual is always a part of power relations, it is impossible to step outside these relations to create an identity unaffected by any discourse. Therefore, Deleuze (1988) suggested folding the discursive knowledge to create a more ethical self. Foucault argued that such ethical self-care necessitated a type of self-aesthetisisation practices: we should continually construct our identities as pieces of art, as creations in a constant process of development rather than think of them as fixed or given 'true' selves. He urged academics, not only to record examples of ethics of self care but to continually and consciously engage in such ethics:

> What can the ethics of an intellectual be ... if not this: to make oneself permanently capable of detaching oneself from oneself (which is the opposite of the attitude of conversion)? ... To be at once an academic and an intellectual is to try to manipulate a type of knowledge and analysis that is taught and received in the universities in such a way as to alter not only others' thoughts, but also one's own.
>
> (Foucault, 1988g: 263–264)

Although the role of an academic involves multiple practices, in this book we highlighted how academics in the field of sport can assume ethical practices of freedom through their research writing as well as through their teaching practices. It is equally important to academics, as to other 'specific intellectuals', to first and foremost disrupt unethical formations of power through critical thinking. This means continually questioning the limitations of current social theory and consequent tracing of spaces for freedom. The 'liberation' of thought, rather than attempts of conversion, should then make the transformation urgent enough for people to want to carry it out.

It is obvious that we, the authors, need to engage in technologies of the self through continual, critical questioning of how sport, exercise and physical activity are theorised. This involves also a critical approach to Foucault's theoretical formulations rather than the unconditional endorsement of his conceptual framework. Our aim in this book, however, has been to explain how Foucault's theory might inform sport research. In this sense, we concur with Alex McHoul (1997) who reflected on the process of writing his book *The Foucault Primer* and suggested that it was necessary to first write from a position of advocacy because a critique of Foucault without a full understanding of his theory was necessarily unconstructive. We hope that this book will solicit constructive comments concerning Foucault's contribution to sport research by providing a strong explanation of his work. This is the type of criticism that Foucault (1988h: 326) dreamed of taking 'scintillating leaps of imagination' and bringing ideals to life. Immersing ourselves in Foucault's work has, however, sensitised us to misinformed and often contradictory critiques of Foucault's work.

A typical critique of Foucault's work claims that because Foucault saw power as relational he somehow advocated total 'pluralism': power can be used by anybody at anytime, in any place (e.g. Evans and Davies, 2002). Other critics are concerned that Foucault's work lacks 'structure' as it is no longer possible to identify groups who clearly possess power to dominate others for their own benefit (e.g. Hartsock, 1996). In the absence of powerful groups, it is equally impossible to trace collective resistance by the powerless, oppressed and marginalised groups united by their desire for freedom (e.g. Deveaux, 1996). In a quite contradictory manner, some scholars assume that Foucault's work does not allow space for individuals to create change through resistance because of his understanding of power as deterministic: discursive power relations dominate so totally it is impossible to evoke agency. Foucault, therefore, has been argued to ignore the role of the individual in his theory. As we know Foucault's later work focused on how the individual came to understand his/herself within the discursive power relations disputing the argument of determinism. However, it resulted in increased criticism of neo-conservatism (e.g. Fraser, 1996; Habermas, 1986; McNay, 1994; Rochlitz, 1992; Taylor, 1986; see also Foucault, 1980h) as Foucault was accused to have returned, yet in a somewhat failed fashion, to humanistic Enlightenment. After a careful reading of Foucault's work, it is clear that he strongly rejected humanism and he continually and explicitly referred to his strong anti-humanist stance in several of his interviews. It is equally evident that Foucault's work does not oppose structures that result from power relations that are continually re-negotiated by individuals who exist within these asymmetrically organised structures. What Foucault rejected was the binary conceptualisation of the law-like power – which seems to cloud many of his critics' vision when they discuss Foucault's work – as too one-dimensional for understanding modern identity construction. We hope that engaging with Foucault in this book will help readers to problematise the limitations of the power-agency dualism to entertain the idea of the self as discursively constructed within constantly changing power relations. No doubt, however, there is space for additional interpretations of Foucault's theory and we look forward to reading such works.

Consequently, the need for interrogating sport as a potential technology of domination continues as power relations are perpetually renegotiated. For example, there is rich literature on sport governed by the neoliberal (state) apparatus emerging from the USA (e.g. Cole *et al.*, 2004; Giardina and Metz, 2005; King, 2003). Foucauldian inspired research on how sporting, exercising and coaching experiences are formed within such apparatus can provide further insights into the possibilities of transgressive sport and exercise politics. In addition, individuals with a larger margin for resistance within their operating power relations such as coaches, managers, owners, journalists, editors, government officials, event organisers, educators or researchers can be viewed as positive forces. It is important to analyse how these individuals might use their power ethically, within a minimum of domination, within the discursive power relations of sport and fitness. Alternatively, a Foucauldian critique can reveal a serious need for transformation in an organisation, field, industry or an event and we as ethical practitioners of academic knowledge should continue to search for ways to provide transgression in such situations. In this book, we have focused primarily on the discursive construction of the gendered identity in sport and fitness. More research is required into the discursive construction other types of 'modern' sporting identities such as 'raced', aged, disabled, sexual and national identities and how the limitations of these can be transgressed. A Foucauldian analysis might even demonstrate that such groupings of 'identities' is theoretically limiting and requires a critical reformulation.

In addition to new Foucauldian inspired readings of sport and exercise, we wish that Foucault's work has emphasised the role of an academic as an active social critic. Therefore, as we advocate in Chapter 10, academics should participate in the development of 'specific intellectuals' in coaching, physical education and fitness who can use the hypomnemata, for example, for continual ethical self care to transform their specific fields.

By writing this book, we aimed to present Foucault's framework of power relations, knowledge construction and the formation of the self in the context of sport and physical activity. This is an expansive task considering the breadth of Foucault's work and while we were naturally forced to make concessions regarding the content of this book, we hope we have inspired others to explore Foucault's ideas further. For us it has been a rewarding task that has illuminated alternative ways of understanding the physically active body. We hope, following Foucault (1988h: 326), to drag 'signs of existence' from their 'sleep' to destroy generalities and to interrogate our own truths. Only this way can we turn into active social critics who trace spaces for freedom within sport and physical activity.

Notes

1 An introduction to Michel Foucault: his work, life and effect

1 Although Foucault has typically been thought of as a 'philosopher' he was reluctant to accept this categorisation. This reluctance related to his critical view of contemporary philosophy and the work of Sartre and Merleau-Ponty. Foucault (1989a) argued that the texts of his compatriots provided totalising accounts of life and reality, as they made grand conclusions on 'what life, death, and sexuality were, if God existed or not, what liberty consisted of, what one had to do in political life, how to behave in regard to others, and so forth' (35). Although Foucault discussed similar themes within his work he tended to approach this subject matter from a different ontological and epistemological standpoint. Foucault, writing under the pseudonym Maurice Florence (1998) while re-editing the entry on 'Foucault' for an edition of the *Dictionnaire des philosophes*, stated that his 'first rule of method' (464) was to 'circumvent the anthropological universals ... in order to examine them as historical constructs' (464). In this manner, we suggest that Foucault was critical of being categorised as a 'philosopher' as he did not aim to provide universal truths on life, death, sexuality or God, but approached these topics as concepts developed by humans in specific eras and localities and, therefore, as constructs that were subject to change.

2 Jon Simons (1995) in support of Foucault's view, acknowledged that although there have been many political changes over the last one hundred years, such as the disintegration of the European colonial systems and the crumbling of the iron curtain, the end of twentieth century still looked similar to its middle and beginning:

> We are still tied to the identities around which ethnic, national and racial conflicts are fought. ... We are also bound in our political thinking to philosophies developed before the First World War, despite their failure to prevent the excesses of politics pursued around issues of identity.
>
> (Simons, 1995: 1)

The recent war and genocide in the Balkans or the on-going troubles in Afghanistan, Iraq and Palestine are apt examples of how the same identities and political philosophies that existed at the beginning of the twentieth century still shape political actions and violence. In response to such a recognition, Foucault argued:

> The conclusion would be that the political, ethical, social, philosophical problem of our days is not to try to liberate the individual from the state, and from the state's institutions, but to liberate us both from the state and from the type of individualization which is linked to the state. We have to promote new forms of subjectivity through refusal of this kind of individuality which has been imposed on us for several centuries.
>
> (Foucault, 1983a: 216)

Similarly, we suggest that the dominant ways that males and females or youth or the elderly have been known, lie at the heart of a range of problems in sport and exercise settings. Accordingly, the promotion of new forms of subjectivities, through refusal of existing forms, could be beneficial. This is not suggesting, of course, that such a political task is easily achieved.

3   Although we have drawn on some of James Miller's (1993) biography of Foucault, we have done so with careful reservation given the critiques of his controversial work (e.g. Cutting, 1994; Halperin, 1995). Cutting (1994: 23) stated that Miller overemphasised aspects of Foucault's life 'to the point of distortion' and, at best, his work is an 'exercise in speculation'. We add to this critique by suggesting that Miller's account of Foucault's life reveals, at times, his tentatively morbid and homophobic fascination with Foucault's sexual preferences and death. Indeed, Miller's stated premise for writing the book was related to his desire to examine the 'truths' surrounding a particularly harmful rumour concerned with Foucault's AIDS related death. In the end, Miller could not substantiate this particular rumour yet he had unwittingly contributed to its circulation.

4   James Scheurich and Kathryn McKenzie (2005) argued that Georges Canguilhem was Foucault's 'main intellectual mentor and teacher' (843) and a strong influence on French philosophers in general throughout the 1960s, yet his depth of influence is not widely noted.

5   Phenomenology was the second major influence at the time that Foucault was developing and undertaking his archaeological studies. The work of Husserl promoted the initial growth of phenomenology with his attempt to trace 'all meaning back to the meaning-giving activity of an autonomous, transcendental subject' (Dreyfus and Rabinow, 1983: xix). Husserl's work gave rise to the counter-existentialist movement as promoted by Merleau-Ponty and Jean-Paul Sartre, which argued against the dualistic belief that the subject exists transcendentally or outside of the ordinary causal order. Sartre, who was particularly influential in France after the war, argued that 'existence precedes essence'. This argument, according to Stokes (2004: 153), suggested 'that man first exists without purpose or definition, finds himself in the world and only then, as a re-action to experience, defines the meaning of his life'. Sartre further argued that, given there is no set purpose to life or inner essence to humanity, it is important for humans to realise that they are responsible for their actions. Humans, according to Sartre, are obliged to be free. Sartre's calls about freedom and responsibility, in the wake of Nazi occupation in German, gained widespread support. Yet Sartre's existential philosophy rested on the assumption of a knowing human subject. His existential philosophy was akin to humanism and Foucault rejected it.

Foucault, however, was influenced by the phenomenological work of Heidegger. Heidegger emphasised the importance of the historical cultural context in the formation of human subjects. He suggested that people were not always aware of the influence of this context and, accordingly, understandings of social life could not be simply related to meaning-giving or knowing subjects. In following this line of thought, Heidegger developed a method that rested on the assumption that social scientists can only offer interpretations of the interpretations of others. He adopted the name 'hermeneutics' for his research method.

6   Foucault (1980d: 118) was further concerned with how the 'concept of ideology refers ... to something of the order of a subject' or an inner self. Marxism assumes, for example, that the proletariat become alienated from their *true selves* due to their labouring requirements, but that their true selves will be restored after the predicted socialist revolution has occurred. The revolution, according to Marxism, will emancipate the workers. Foucault was *sceptical* of the notion that a 'real self' existed and that this 'self' lay dormant waiting for emancipation. Such ideas were in opposition to his argument that humans were constituted via the workings of discourses within specific social-historical contexts. Foucault was also concerned about the *effects of 'truth'* as related to the Marxist use of the concept of alienation. The idea that capitalism alienates workers from their real selves, for example, helps support the argument for socialist revolution. Yet, as Rabinow (1984: 4) reported, we suggest it is worth noting that 'in the last analysis, he [Foucault] doesn't take a stand on whether or not there is a human nature'. Foucault, in contrast, was more concerned with how particular concepts, such as the notions of a 'real self' or human nature, have been used, and the material consequences of this usage.

   The Marxist idea that there is a 'real self' was used by Jean-Marie Brohm (1981) to argue that sport was a product of bourgeois society and it represses inner drives and alienates participants from their real selves: 'Sport is the repressive cultural codification of movements. ... The representative of bourgeois values and the bourgeois social order. ... *Sport is alienating. It will disappear in a universal communist society*' (Brohm, 1981: 113, italics in original). From a Foucauldian perspective we suggest that the point of concern is not whether there really is a 'real self' but how Brohm used this concept, and the consequences of this usage. Brohm used this concept to challenge the dominance of capitalism and sport. The effects of this usage, if her argument had been sufficiently convincing, could have been considerable. In summary, a Foucauldian perspective is typically more concerned with the consequences associated with the usage of particular concepts, such as humanism, than whether these concepts are 'right' or 'wrong'.

   Foucault (1970: 262), in a more general critique, suggested that Marxism did not represent a radical epistemological break but was simply a product of the modernist *episteme*: 'Marxism exists in nineteenth century thought like a fish in water: that is, it is unable to breathe anywhere else'. Foucault predicted, with a degree of accuracy, that the legitimacy and longevity of Marxism was soon to wane.

7   Foucault's critical ethos developed in isolation from Critical Theory as developed in the Frankfurt School. Yet Foucault (1994), in modest fashion, acknowledged that such knowledge would have been beneficial:

> Now, obviously, if I had been familiar with the Frankfurt School, if I had been aware of it at the time, I would not have said a number of stupid things that I did say, and I would have avoided many of the detours I made while trying to pursue my own humble path – when, meanwhile, avenues had been opened up by the Frankfurt School.
>
> (Foucault, 1994: 440)

Foucault, however, commented on how the same problem, the workings of power, underpinned the two bodies of work and how he approached this problem in a similar manner to the critical theorists: 'It is a strange case of nonpenetration between two very similar types of thinking which is explained, perhaps, by that very similarity. Nothing hides the fact of a problem in common better than two similar ways of approaching it' (441).

8 Post-colonialism, as somewhat similar to post-structural feminism, has had a similarly tense but nevertheless productive relationship with Foucault. Edward Said (1991: 9), for example, was concerned that Foucault drew narrowly 'on his basically limited French evidence' to reach 'ostensibly universal conclusions'. Yet Said, in contrast to the traditional historians, was not particularly concerned about the ecological validity of Foucault's conclusions: he believed that they 'did not seriously mar the quality and power of his fundamental points' (9). Said's prime concern was that Foucault's work was Eurocentric. He lamented that Foucault's 'Eurocentrism was almost total, as if history took place only among a group of French and German thinkers' (10). Said (1994), nevertheless, recognised the value of Foucault's political tools and drew closely from his ideas to develop his theory of 'Orientalism'. Said, accordingly, and in a somewhat ironic manner used Foucault to help challenge the problems of colonialism and Eurocentrism.

2 Technologies of dominance: power, discourses and the disciplined bodies

1 Foucault's relentless use of masculine pronouns within his texts can be used as an example of how a particular *episteme* can shape but also obscure ways of knowing. Foucault's early writings, for example, occurred in an epistemological time period, prior to the second wave of feminism, that was pervaded by sexism. We, relatedly, suggest that he was likely to have been unaware of how his writing style reflected male dominance but also obscured the significance of females. Indeed, his androcentric writing style excluded any recognition of the influence of females in the history of ideas. Foucault (1970: xiv), nevertheless, acknowledged: 'it would hardly behove me, of all people, to claim that my discourse is independent of conditions and rules of which I am largely unaware, and which determine other work that is being done today'.

2 Although few researchers draw directly from Foucault's archaeological understandings of discourse, his concept of discourse has spawned a veritable industry with the likes of Norman Fairclough, Ian Parker and Margaret Wetherell appropriating his ideas.

3 Foucault's aim within the *Archaeology of Knowledge* to transgress humanist ways of knowing was not without risks. The prime risk was the charge of idealism: a charge that stemmed primarily from Marxist-humanists. This accusation suggested that Foucault's ideas were not concerned with a material reality, but were naively concerned with social imaginations. Foucault, however, was well aware of how his abstract theory acted to position him as an idealist. He suggested, as a partial explanation, that although his theory of discourse might be 'irritating' and 'unpleasant' (Foucault, 1972: 210) to some, it was 'written simply in order to overcome certain preliminary difficulties'. These difficulties referred specifically to his concerns with humanism, phenomenology and Marxism. Foucault's archaeological studies can, in this sense, be read as a reaction against the dominance of these influential social theories.

In his future writings Foucault (1980b) made it explicitly clear that his research was grounded in a material reality. He emphasised, for example, that:

'we should try to discover how it is that subjects are gradually, progressively, really and materially constituted through a multiplicity of organisms, forces, energies, materials, desires, thoughts etc.' (Foucault, 1980e: 97). And he urged, even more categorically: 'it is not enough to say that the subject is constituted in a symbolic system. It is not just in the play of symbols that the subject is constituted. It is constituted in real practices – historically analyzable practices' (Foucault, 1997c: 277).

3 Knowledge and truth: discursive construction of the fit and healthy body

1   For discussions of medicine as part of the political anatomy of disciplinary power see, for example, Robert Crawford's (1980) seminal article on the individualisation of health-care costs, David Armstrong's (1983) classic text on medical knowledge as discursive construction, Nicholas Fox's (1993) book on the medicalisation of health, Brian Turner's (1995) Foucauldian inspired text on the construction of medicine as a disciplinary power over bodies, and Deborah Lupton's (2003) more general discussion of the role of medicine as cultural power. In addition, an edited collection by Alan Petersen and Chris Waddell (1998) and another by Alan Petersen and Rachel Bunton (1997) address health and medicine from a Foucauldian perspective.

4 Exercise: disciplined into docile bodies

1   Johns and Johns (2000) examine a construction of 'docility–utility' in women's gymnastics.
2   First, the warm-up (up to 10 minutes) prepares the exerciser's body for the physical activity ahead and should include steps that prepare the cardiovascular system for the physical exertion of the class as well as easy stretching to mobilise the body. Second, there is the aerobic section (up to 40 minutes). This section is designed to improve cardiovascular fitness. Therefore, activities in this section should raise participants' heart rate to 80 per cent of their maximum (exceeding 80 per cent will utilise the anaerobic energy production system that does not engage the cardiovascular system). This section can be further divided into three sections: the first section is designed as a progressively more intense section toward the second, the higher intensity part. Both consist of a choreographed series of steps that are designed to move the participants across the stage. The choreography breaks down bodily movement

> into its elements; the position of the body, limbs, articulations is defined; to each movement are assigned a direction, an aptitude, a duration; the order of succession is prescribed. Time penetrates the body and with it all the meticulous controls of power.
>
> (Foucault, 1991a: 152)

This section should also include a gradual cooling down that acts as a transition to the next section. The toning section (up to 10 minutes) is designed to improve muscle strength and endurance. Unlike the aerobics segment, toning movements target specific muscle groups and are mostly performed lying down on the floor. Usually, only one or two muscle groups are exercised at a time, to ensure that the participants focus on the correct group. Therefore, the body parts are isolated with each exercise. The exercise session finishes with a cool down.

This section is designed to transition the body from exercise back to everyday movement. It is also the ideal segment to improve flexibility through stretching exercises.

3   For more detailed information on the development of the fit body ideal, see Markula (1993).

4   There are several studies of women bodybuilders' perceptions of their activity. From a Foucauldian perspective see, for example, Balsamo (1994), Castelnuovo and Guthrie (1998), Haber (1996), Roussell and Griffett (2000) and Wesely (2001).

5   Other studies, yet not from a Foucauldian perspective, that examine women's and men's perceptions of the exercising body are Haravon (1995), Loland (2000) and McDermott (2000).

5 Sport and the discursive construction of gendered bodies

1   In Foucault's later writings he started to use the term 'truth' either interchangeably or in replacement of 'discourse'. In summarising his ideas concerned with power, for example, he suggested that:

> 'Truth' is to be understood as a system of ordered procedures for the production, regulation, distribution, circulation and operation of statements. 'Truth' is linked in a circular relation with systems of power which produce and sustain it, and to effects of power which it induces and which extend it. A 'regime' of truth.
>
> (Foucault, 1980d: 133)

7 The technologies of the self

1   A therapeutic approach known as narrative therapy offers one 'liberational' reading based on Foucault's work. Narrative therapists do not employ Foucault's terms technologies of the self or practices of freedom per se, but narrative therapy might be of special interest to the readers of this book because it can inform ethical practice of sport psychology. We have, therefore, chosen to introduce it as one way to detach an athlete's identity from the scientifically defined unified self.

Narrative therapy derives from Foucault's work to emphasise the role of language to construct our thinking. For example, 'problems' that athletes might experience, such as burn-out, need to be acknowledged as constructed in language by previous discussions among athletes, coaches or the media. From a narrative therapy perspective such problems become patterns of thought privileged by the dominant discourses that limit the range of solutions to the 'problem'. As the 'problem' becomes part of the problem, the linguistic content needs then to be problematised. Jim Denison explained further:

> [D]escribing someone as burnt out, for example, implies a deficit in the individual's management of self. It sets in place a set of assumptions which guide us to know how to go on and fix him. Starting with a different linguistic frame to describe burnout, such as, 'external pressure', may lead to a new set of thoughts about the nature of burnout, locating it in the discursive interactions that take place around training perhaps, which in turn may influence us to go on and correct it a different way.
>
> (2006: 6, italics in original)

As a first step to revealing the linguistic construction of many of our 'problems', the narrative therapist pays detailed attention to how the 'problem' is described by the individual and to the discourse into which that way of describing it fits. Next, a richer description of the 'problem' takes place to locate it closer within the culturally available stories in the person's local context. After 'externalising' the problem from the individual by locating it into the discursive and local cultural contexts, the next task is to look for alternative, under-used or unnoticed local knowledge that may already lie in the individual's existing repertoire and can be used to solve the 'problem'. Through these steps a new self-story can be fashioned, a story that provides more options to dealing with 'problems' than offered by the story structured within the dominant discourse. More detailed information regarding narrative therapy can be found in Gerald Monk, John Winslade, Kathy Crocket and David Epston's (1997) volume *Narrative Therapy in Practice: The Archaeology of Hope.*

8 Aesthetic self-stylisation: mindful fitness as practice of freedom

1   Monroe (1998) regarded the following components as additional characteristics of mindful fitness:

> a mental component:
>   noncompetitive, non judgemental, process oriented
> proprioceptive awareness:
>   low level muscular activity, mental focus on muscle and movement
>   sense
> features breath centring:
>   breath the primary centring activity
> focuses on anatomical alignment or proper physical form:
>   particular movement patterns
>   spinal alignment
> is energy centric:
>   flow of one's intrinsic energy or vital life force (chi or prana).

2   The most common English translation for the term yoga is 'union' referring to the union of the individual self with the Universal Self (Strauss, 2005). The yoga practice today originates from a text by Patanjali titled Yoga Sutras (dated tentatively between 200BC and 200AD). This text details an eight-stage programme to guide toward the union of the self and the Universal. This yoga system begins with guidelines for moral living and then proceeds to advice on physical practice and breathing techniques and finally provides guidelines on reaching different states of mental attention through meditation. This classical yoga is called Raja yoga. However, as the popularity of yoga has increased the understanding of its practice has also proliferated. The most common western practices of yoga now include only the physical exercise, the hatha. Hatha yoga consists of several poses, asanas, that are performed to discipline the body and mind through physical postures. These asanas can then be performed in different order or in different emphasis or style. Thus, several variations of yoga now exist. Many of these

are associated with a particular teacher such as Bikram Choudhury, B.K.S. Iyengar, or Swamis Vishnudevananda, Vivekananda and Sivananda. Others are more based on a particular style of executing the asanas such as astanga or kundalini (Hollingshead, 2002; Strauss, 2005). While these differ in terms of style and execution of the movements, all yoga consists of separate physical postures (asanas) that are carefully executed with precision, slowness, concentration, proper breathing, and relaxation to increase general body control.

3   Similar to yoga, Tai Chi consists of precisely defined movements, but instead of being executed separately, they flow together in round patterns of resistance against and compliance to force. In Tai Chi, the entire continuous movement pattern is performed standing up (certain yoga asanas take place on the floor) and initiated from the body's centre. Therefore, movements (or power) cannot be forced or 'muscled' but should be executed with 'ease' supported by a relaxed mind.

4   Pilates is a movement form created by Joseph Pilates in the USA in the late 1920s (Gallagher and Kryzanowska, 1999). Originally, he titled his exercise programme as 'Contrology: The science and art of coordinated body-mind-spirit development through natural movements under strict control of the will' (Gallagher and Kryzanowska, 1999: 11).

5   There is substantial contemporary literature on yoga, Pilates and Tai Chi that, alongside the other 'new age' or alternative therapy literature, is increasingly popular. However, scholarly literature is somewhat scarce. Strauss's (2005) ethnographic analysis of yoga is one of the few academic studies regarding yoga. The Pilates text referenced in this chapter is written by Romana Kryzanowska, a student of Pilates and Sean Gallagher, a controversial figure within the Pilates community as he attempted to 'trademark' the Pilates exercise form entirely to his studio in New York City. He, however, failed in his attempt. The information concerning Tai Chi was obtained through personal information from a practitioner who has been engaged with Tai Chi for 25 years.

9 The ethics of self-care: the academic self as a work of art

1   Foucault often used the term 'intellectual' when he discussed his own work or the work of other academics. However, intellectual clearly has other meanings in the French context. As a term, Foucault claimed, it is somewhat overused often to a point of annoyance. He explained:

> The word *intellectual* strikes me as odd. Personally, I've never met any intellectuals. I've met people who write novels, others who treat the sick. People who work in economics and others who write electronic music. I've met people who teach, people who paint, and people of whom I have never really understood what they do. But intellectual, never.
>
> On the other hand, I've met a lot of people who talk about 'the intellectual.' And listening to them, I've got some idea of what such an animal could be. It's not difficult – he's quite personified. He's guilty about pretty well everything: about speaking out and about keeping silent, about doing nothing and about getting involved in everything. ... In short, the intellectual is raw material for a verdict, a sentence, a condemnation, an exclusion.
>
> (Foucault, 1988h: 324, italics in original)

Despite such a critique, Foucault continued to refer to intellectuals in several of his interviews. In this book, we use the term intellectual to refer mainly to academics while they clearly form only a group of intellectuals in Foucault's sense of the term.

2   Pierre Hadot (1992) provided a critique of Foucault's reading of the practice of writing hypomnemata in Ancient Greece. Foucault defined the purpose of these spiritual notebooks as to collect already existing thoughts of others, to detach one's soul from the concerns of the future to contemplate the past. Hadot agreed that both Stoics and Epicureans promoted an attitude which consisted of liberating oneself both from a concern about the future and from the weight of the past in order to be able to concentrate on the present moment. They wrote down previous dogmatic thoughts, however, because 'by writing, by noting these things down, it is not alien thought that one is making one's own; rather, one is using formulations which one considers to be well made in order to make present, to bring alive, that which is already present within the reason of the writer' (Hadot, 1992: 229).

Foucault assumed that this exercise, as entirely eclectic, would imply an element of personal choice, which would thus explain the notion of the 'constitution of self'. As Foucault explained:

> Writing as a personal experience made through the self and for the self is an art of disparate truth or, more precisely, a considered way of combining the traditional authority of that which has already been said with the uniqueness of the truth which is affirmed in it, and the particular nature of the circumstances which determine its usage.
>
> (in Hadot, 1992: 229)

Foucault interpreted that by writing down such disparate thoughts, the individual could forge his/her spiritual identity. According to Hadot, this is inaccurate because

> First ... these thoughts are not disparate, but chosen for their coherence. Secondly – and most importantly – the point was not to forge a spiritual identity by writing but to free oneself from one's individuality, to raise oneself to universality. It is therefore inaccurate to talk of 'writing about the self'; not only is it not oneself that one is writing about, but also the writing does not constitute the self: as in other spiritual exercises, it changes the level of the self; it universalises it.
>
> (Hadot, 1992: 229)

Hadot, therefore, found Foucault's interpretation of practices of self too 'individual' and without addressing the relation to 'universal reason'. Despite these precautions, Hadot agreed with Foucault that such practices can offer a model for today's practice of ethical self-care.

References

Albert, E. (1999) 'Dealing with Danger: the Normalization of Risk in Cycling', *International Review for the Sociology of Sport*, 34 (2): 157–171.

American College of Sport Medicine (1995) *ACSM's Guidelines for Exercise Testing and Prescription* (5th edn), Baltimore, MD: Lippincott.

American College of Sport Medicine (2000) *ACSM's Guidelines for Exercise Testing and Prescription* (6th edn), Baltimore, MD: Lippincott.

Andrews, D.L. (1993) 'Desperately Seeking Michel: Foucault's Genealogy, the Body, and Critical Sport Sociology', *Sociology of Sport Journal*, 10: 148–167.

Andrews, D. (2000) 'Posting Up: French Post-Structuralism and the Critical Analysis of Contemporary Sporting Cultures', in J. Coakley and E. Dunning (eds) *Handbook of Sports Studies*, London: Sage.

Andrews, D. and Loy, J. (1993) 'British Cultural Studies and Sport: Past Encounters and Future Possibilities', *Quest*, 45: 225–276.

Armstrong, D. (1983) *Political Anatomy of the Body: Medical Knowledge in Britain in the Twentieth Century*, Cambridge: Cambridge University Press.

Ashton-Shaeffer, C., Gibson, H.J., Autry, C.E. and Hanson, C.S. (2001) 'Meaning of Sport to Adults with Physical Disabilities: A Disability Sport Camp Experience', *Sociology of Sport Journal*, 18: 95–114.

Aycock, A. (1992) 'The Confession of the Flesh: Disciplinary Gaze in Casual Bodybuilding', *Play and Culture*, 5: 338–357.

Balsamo, A. (1994) 'Feminist Bodybuilding', in S. Birrell and C.L. Cole (eds) *Women, Sport and Culture*, Champaign, IL: Human Kinetics.

Bartky, S. (1988) 'Foucault, Femininity, and the Modernization of Patriarchal Power', in I. Diamond and L. Quinby (eds) *Feminism and Foucault: Reflections On Resistance*, Boston, MA: Northeastern University Press.

Baudrillard, J. (1987) *Forget Foucault*, New York: Semiotext(e).

Beisser, A.R. (1967) *The Madness in Sports*, New York: Appleton-Century-Crofts.

Bird, L. (2005, June) 'Slash Your No. 1 Health Risk – Today', *Zest*, 40–45.

Blair, S.N., Brill, P.A. and Barlow, C.E. (1994) 'Physical Activity and Disease Prevention', in H.A. Quinney, L. Gauvin and A.E.T. Wall (eds) *Toward Active Living*, Champaign, IL: Human Kinetics.

Bolin, A. (1992) 'Vandalized Vanity: Feminine Physiques Betrayed and Portrayed', in F. Mascia-Lees and P. Sharpe (eds) *Tattoo, Torture, Adornment and Disfigurement: The Denaturalisation of the Body in Culture and Text*, Albany, NY: State University of New York Press.

Bordo, S. (1993) *Unbearable Weight: Feminism, Western Culture, and the Body*, Berkeley and Los Angeles, CA: University of California Press.

Bouchard, C., Shephard, R.J., Stephens, T.S., Sutton, J.R. and Mcpherson, B.D. (1990) *Exercise, Fitness, and Health: A Consensus of Current Knowledge*, Champaign, IL: Human Kinetics.

Bové, P. (1988) 'Foreword: the Foucault Phenomenon: the Problematics of Style', in G. Deleuze, *Foucault*, Minneapolis, MN: University of Minnesota Press.

Brohm, J. (1981) 'Theses Toward A Political Sociology of Sport', in M. Hart and S. Birrell (eds) *Sport in the Sociocultural Process*, Dubuque, IA: Wm. C. Brown Company.

Bruner, E. (1996) 'My Life in An Ashram', *Qualitative Inquiry*, 2: 300–319.

Bryson, L. (1990) 'Challenges to Male Hegemony', in M.A. Messner and D.F. Sabo (eds) *Sport, Men, and the Gender Order: Critical Feminist Perspectives*, Champaign, IL: Human Kinetics.

Burrows, L. (2004) 'Understanding and Investigating Cultural Perspectives in Physical Education', in J. Wright., D. Macdonald and L. Burrows (eds) *Critical Inquiry and Problem Solving in Physical Education*, London: Routledge.

Burstyn, V. (1999) *The Rites of Men: Manhood, Politics, and the Culture of Sport*, Toronto: University of Toronto Press.

Butler, J. (1993) *Bodies that Matter: On the Discursive Limits of 'Sex'*, New York: Routledge.

Cahn, S. (1994) *Coming On Strong: Gender and Sexuality in Twentieth-Century Women's Sport*, New York: Free Press.

Carrigan, T., Connell, R. and Lee, J. (1985) 'Hard and Heavy: Toward A New Sociology of Masculinity', *Theory and Society*, 14: 551–603.

Castelnuovo, S. and Guthrie, S.R. (1998) *Feminism and the Female Body: Liberating the Amazon Within*, Boulder, CO: Lynne Renner.

Caudwell, J. (1999) 'Women's Football in the United Kingdom: Theorising Gender and Unpacking the Butch Lesbian Image', *Journal of Sport and Social Issues*, 23 (4): 390–402.

Caudwell, J. (2002) 'Women's Experiences of Sexuality within Football Contexts: A Particular and Located Footballing Epistemology', *Football Studies*, 5 (1): 24–45.

Chandler, T.J.L. (1996) 'The Structuring of Manliness and the Development of Rugby Football at the Public Schools and Oxbridge, 1830–1880', in J. Nauright and T. Chandler (eds) *Making Men: Rugby and Masculine Identity*, London: Frank Cass & Co.

Chapman, G.E. (1997) 'Making Weight: Lightweight Rowing, Technologies of Power, and Technologies of the Self', *Sociology of Sport Journal*, 14: 205–223.

Coakley, J. and White, A. (1992) 'Making Decisions: Gender and Sport Participation Among British Adolescents', *Sociology of Sport Journal*, 9, 1: 20–35.

Cole, C.L. (1993) 'Resisting the Canon: Feminist Cultural Studies, Sport, and Technologies of the Body', *Journal of Sport and Social Issues*, 17 (2): 77–97.

Cole, C.L. (1994) 'Resisting the Canon: Feminist Cultural Studies, Sport, and Technologies of the Body', in S. Birrell and C. Cole (eds) *Women, Sport, and Culture*, Champaign, IL: Human Kinetics.

Cole, C.L. (1996) 'American Jordan: P.L.A.Y., Consensus, and Punishment', *Sociology of Sport Journal*, 13: 366–397.

Cole, C.L. (1998) 'Addiction, Exercise, and Cyborgs: Technologies of Deviant Bodies', in G. Rail (ed.) *Sport in Postmodern Times*, Albany, NY: State University of New York Press.

Cole, C.L., Giardina, M.D. and Andrews, D.L. (2004) 'Michel Foucault: Studies of Power and Sport', in R. Giulianotti (ed.) *Sport and Modern Social Theorists*, London: Palgrave Macmillan.

Cole, C.L. and Hribar, A. (1995) 'Celebrity Feminism: *Nike Style* Post-Fordism, Transcence, and Consumer Power' *Sociology of Sport Journal*, 12: 347–369.

Collins, T. (1998) *Rugby's Great Split: Class, Culture and the Origins of Rugby League Football*, London: Frank Cass Publishers.

Connell, R.W. (1987) *Gender and Power*, Cambridge: Polity Press.

Connell, R.W. (1990) 'Iron Man', in M.A. Messner and D.F. Sabo (eds) *Sport, Men and the Gender Order: Critical Feminist Perspectives*, Champaign, IL: Human Kinetics.

Connell, R.W. (1995) *Masculinities*, St Leonards, NSW: Allen & Unwin.

Connell, R.W. (2001) 'Introduction and Overview', *Feminism and Psychology*, 11 (1): 5–9.

Connell, R.W. (2002) 'Masculinities and Globalisation', in H. Worth, A. Paris and L. Allen (eds) *The Life of Brian: Masculinities, Sexualities and Health in New Zealand*, Dunedin, NZ: University of Otago Press.

Cooper, K.H. (1968) *Aerobics*, New York: Simon & Schuster.

Cooper, K.H. (1970) *New Aerobics*, Philadelphia, PA: J.B. Lippincott.

Corbin, C.B. and Lindsey, R. (1994) *Concepts of Physical Fitness with Laboratories*, (8th edn), Madison, WI: Brown & Benchmark.

Cox, B. and Thompson, S. (2000) 'Multiple Bodies: Sportswomen, Soccer and Sexuality', *International Review for the Sociology of Sport*, 35 (1): 5–20.

Crawford, R. (1980) 'Healthism and the Medicalization of Everyday Life' *International Journal of Health Services*, 10: 365–388.

Crosset, T. (1990) 'Masculinity, Sexuality, and the Development of Early Modern Sport', in M.A. Messner and D.F. Sabo (eds) *Sport, Men and the Gender Order: Critical Feminist Perspectives*, Champaign, IL: Human Kinetics.

Curry, T.J. (1993) 'A Little Pain Never Hurt Anyone: Athletic Career Socialization and the Normalization of Sports Injury', *Symbolic Interaction*, 16 (3): 273–290.

Curry, T.J. (1998) 'Beyond the Locker Room: Campus Bars and College athletes', *Sociology of Sport Journal*, 15 (2): 205–215.

Cutting, G. (1994) 'Introduction to Michel Foucault: A User's Manual', in G. Cutting (ed.) *The Cambridge Companion to Foucault*, Cambridge: Cambridge University Press.

Danahar, G., Schirato, T. and Webb, J. (2000) *Understanding Foucault*, St Leonards, NSW: Allen & Unwin.

Davies, D. (1998) 'Health and the Discourse of Weight Control', in A. Petersen and C. Waddell (eds) *Health Matters: A Sociology of Illness, Prevention and Care*, St Leonards, NSW: Allen & Unwin.

Davis, K. and Davis, P. (2005, April) 'Mind–Body Millennium', *IDEA Fitness Journal*, 11.

De Garis, L. (2000) '"Be A Buddy to Your Buddy": Male Identity, Aggression, and Intimacy in a Boxing Gym', in J. Mckay, M. Messner and D. Sabo (eds) *Masculinities, Gender Relations, and Sport*, Thousand Oaks, CA: Sage.

Deleuze, G. (1988) *Foucault*, London: Athlone Press.

Denison, J. (2006) 'Understanding Problematic Sporting Stories: Narrative Therapy and Applied Sport Psychology', *Junctures*, 5 (1): 99–105.

Deveaux, M. (1996) 'Feminism and Empowerment: A Critical Reading of Foucault', in S. Hekman (ed.) *Feminist Interpretations of Michel Foucault*, University Park, PA: Pennsylvania State University Press.

Diamond, I. and Quinby, L. (eds) (1988) *Feminism and Foucault: Reflections of Resistance*, Boston, MA: North Easton University Press.

Donaldson, M. (1993) 'What Is Hegemonic Masculinity?' *Theory and Society*, 22 (5): 643–657.

Dreyfus, H.L. and Rabinow, P. (1983) *Michel Foucault: Beyond Structuralism and Hermeneutics* (2nd edn), Chicago, IL: University of Chicago Press.

Duncan, M.C. (1994) 'The Politics of Women's Body Images and Practices: Foucault, the Panopticon and Shape Magazine', *Journal of Sport and Social Issues*, 18: 48–65.

Duncan, M.C. and Hasbrook, C.A. (1988) 'Denial of Power in Televised Women's Sport', *Sociology of Sport Journal*, 5: 1–21.

Dunning, E. and Sheard, K. (1979) *Barbarians, Gentlemen and Players: A Sociological Study of the Development of Rugby Football*, Oxford: Martin Robertson.

Duquin, M.E. (1994) 'The Body Snatchers and Dr Frankenstein Revisited: Social Construction and Deconstruction of Bodies and Sport', *Journal of Sport and Social Issues*, 18 (3): 268–281.

Dworkin, S. (2003) 'A Woman's Place is in the ... Cardiovascular Room?? Gender Relations, the Body, and the Gym', in A. Bolin and J. Granskog (eds) *Athletic Intruders: Ethnographic Research On Women, Culture, and Exercise*, Albany, NY: State University of New York Press.

Dworkin, S. and Wachs, F.L. (1998) 'Disciplining the Body: HIV-Positive Male Athletes, Media Surveillance, and Policing of Sexuality' *Sociology of Sport Journal*, 15: 1–20.

Dyer, K.F. (1982) *Challenging the Men: the Social Biology of Female Sporting Achievement*. St Lucia, Australia: University of Queensland Press.

Eckermann, L. (1997) 'Foucault, Embodiment, and Gendered Subjectivities: The Case of Voluntary Self-Starvation', in A. Petersen and R. Bunton (eds) *Foucault, Health and Medicine*, London: Routledge.

Eribon, D. (1991) *Michel Foucault*, Cambridge, MA: Harvard University Press.

Eskes, T.B., Duncan, M.C. and Miller, E.M. (1998) 'The Discourse of Empowerment: Foucault, Marcuse and Women's Fitness Texts', *Journal of Sport and Social Issues*, 22 (3): 317–344.

Evans, J. and Davies, B. (2002) 'Theoretical Background', in A. Laker (ed.) *The Sociology of Sport and Physical Education*, London: RoutledgeFalmer.

Featherstone, M. (1991) 'The Body in Consumer Culture', in M. Featherstone, M. Hepworth and B.S. Turner (eds) *The Body: Social Process and Cultural Theory*, London: Sage.

Felshin, J. (1974) 'The Triple Option for Women in Sport', *Quest*, Monograph XXI: 36–40.

Fernandez-Balboa, J.M. (1997a) 'Introduction: the Human Movement Profession:

From Modernism to Postmodernism, in J.M. Fernandez-Balboa (ed.) *Critical Postmodernism in Human Movement, Physical Education, and Sport*, Albany, NY: State University of New York Press.

Fernandez-Balboa, J.M. (1997b), 'Physical Education Teacher Preparation in the Postmodern Era: Toward A Critical Pedagogy', in J.M. Fernandez-Balboa (ed.) *Critical Postmodernism in Human Movement, Physical Education, and Sport*, Albany, NY: State University of New York Press.

Fitzclarence, L. and Hickey, C. (2001) 'Real Men Don't Eat Quiche: Old Narratives in New Times', *Men and Masculinities*, 4 (2): 118–139.

Florence, M. (1998) 'Foucault', in J.D. Faubion (ed.) *Michel Foucault Aesthetics: Essential Works of Foucault 1954–1984, Volume 2*, London: Penguin Books.

Fonda, J. (1981) *Jane Fonda's Workout Book*, New York: Simon & Schuster.

Foucault, M. (1965) *Madness and Civilisation: A History of Insanity in the Age of Reason*, New York: Pantheon Books.

Foucault, M. (1970) *The Order of Things: An Archaeology of the Human Sciences*, London: Tavistock.

Foucault, M. (1972) *The Archaeology of Knowledge and Discourse on Language*, New York: Pantheon Books.

Foucault, M. (1973) *The Birth of the Clinic: An Archaeology of Medical Perception*, London: Tavistock.

Foucault, M. (ed.) (1975) *'I, Pierre Rivière, Having Slaughtered My Mother, My Sister, and My Brother: A Case of Parricide in the 19th Century'*, New York: Pantheon.

Foucault, M. (1977a) 'Intellectuals and Power' in D.F. Bouchard (ed.) *Language, Counter-Memory, Practice: Selected Essays and Interview by Michel Foucault*, Ithaca, NY: Cornell University Press.

Foucault, M. (1977b) 'Revolutionary Action: "Until Now"', in D.F. Bouchard (ed.) *Language, Counter-Memory, Practice: Selected Essays and Interview by Michel Foucault*, Ithaca, NY: Cornell University Press.

Foucault, M. (1977c) 'Nietzsche, Genealogy, History', in D.F. Bouchard (ed.) *Michel Foucault: Language, Counter-Memory, Practice: Selected Essays and Interviews*, Ithaca, NY: Cornell University Press.

Foucault, M. (1978) *The History of Sexuality, Volume 1: An Introduction*, London: Penguin Books.

Foucault, M. (1980a) 'The Politics of Health in the Eighteenth Century', in C. Gordon (ed.) *Power/Knowledge: Selected Interviews and Other Writings 1972–1977*, Harlow, England: Harvester.

Foucault, M. (1980b) 'The Eye of Power', in C. Gordon (ed.) *Power/Knowledge: Selected Interviews and Other Writings 1972–1977*, Harlow, England: Harvester.

Foucault, M. (1980c) 'Body/Power', in C. Gordon (ed.) *Power/Knowledge: Selected Interviews and Other Writings 1972–1977*, Harlow, England: Harvester.

Foucault, M. (1980d) 'Truth and Power', in C. Gordon (ed.) *Power/Knowledge: Selected Interviews and Other Writings 1972–1977*, Harlow, England: Harvester.

Foucault, M. (1980e) 'Two Lectures', in C. Gordon (ed.) *Power/Knowledge: Selected Interviews and Other Writings 1972–1977*, Harlow, England: Harvester.

Foucault, M. (1980e) 'Prison Talk', in C. Gordon (ed.) *Power/Knowledge: Selected Interviews and Other Writings 1972–1977*, Harlow, England: Harvester.

Foucault, M. (1980f) 'Power and Strategies', in C. Gordon (ed.) *Power/Knowledge: Selected Interviews and Other Writings 1972–1977*, Harlow, England: Harvester.

Foucault, M. (1980h) 'The Confession of the Flesh', in C. Gordon (ed.) *Power/Knowledge: Selected Interviews and Other Writings 1972–1977*, Harlow, England: Harvester.

Foucault, M. (1980i) 'Questions On Geography', in C. Gordon (ed.) *Power/Knowledge: Selected Interviews and Other Writings 1972–1977*, Harlow, England: Harvester.

Foucault, M. (1983a) 'The Subject and Power', in H.L. Dreyfus and P. Rabinow (eds) *Michel Foucault: Beyond Structuralism and Hermeneutics*, 2nd edn, Chicago, IL: University of Chicago Press.

Foucault, M. (1983b) 'On the Genealogy of Ethics: An Overview of Work in Progress', H.L. Dreyfus and P. Rabinow (eds) *Michel Foucault: Beyond Structuralism and Hermeneutics*, 2nd edn, Chicago, IL: University of Chicago Press.

Foucault, M. (1984a) 'What Is Enlightenment?', in P. Rabinow (ed.) *Foucault Reader*, New York: Pantheon Books.

Foucault, M. (1984b) 'Nietzsche, Genealogy, History', in P. Rabinow (ed.) *Foucault Reader*, New York: Pantheon Books.

Foucault, M. (1985) *The History of Sexuality Volume 2: The Use of Pleasure*, London: Penguin Books.

Foucault, M. (1986) *The History of Sexuality, Volume 3: The Care of the Self*, New York: Pantheon.

Foucault, M. (1987) 'The Ethic of Care for the Self as a Practice of Freedom', in J. Bernauer and D. Rasmussen (eds) *The Final Foucault*, Cambridge, MA: MIT Press.

Foucault, M. (1988a) 'Truth, Power, Self', in L.H. Martin, H. Gutman and P.H. Hutton (eds) *Technologies of the Self: A Seminar with Michel Foucault*, Amherst, MA: University of Massachusetts Press.

Foucault, M. (1988b) 'Technologies of the Self', in L.H. Martin, H. Gutman and P.H. Hutton (eds) *Technologies of the Self: A Seminar with Michel Foucault*, Amherst, MA: University of Massachusetts Press.

Foucault, M. (1988c) 'The Minimalist Self', in L.D. Kritzman (ed.) *Michel Foucault Politics, Philosophy, Culture: Interviews and Other Writing 1977–1984*, London: Routledge.

Foucault, M. (1988d) 'On Power', in L.D. Kritzman (ed.) *Michel Foucault Politics, Philosophy, Culture: Interviews and Other Writing 1977–1984*, London: Routledge.

Foucault, M. (1988e) ' Power and Sex', in L.D. Kritzman (ed.) *Michel Foucault Politics, Philosophy, Culture: Interviews and Other Writing 1977–1984*, London: Routledge.

Foucault, M. (1988f) 'Practicing Criticism', in L.D. Kritzman (ed.) *Michel Foucault Politics, Philosophy, Culture: Interviews and Other Writing 1977–1984*, London: Routledge.

Foucault, M. (1988g) 'The Concern for Truth', in L.D. Kritzman (ed.) *Michel Foucault Politics, Philosophy, Culture: Interviews and Other Writing 1977–1984*, London: Routledge.

Foucault, M. (1988h) 'The Masked Philosopher', in L.D. Kritzman (ed.) *Michel Foucault Politics, Philosophy, Culture: Interviews and Other Writing 1977–1984*, London: Routledge.

Foucault, M. (1988i) 'An Aesthetics of Existence', in L.D. Kritzman (ed.) *Michel Foucault Politics, Philosophy, Culture: Interviews and Other Writing 1977–1984*, London: Routledge.

Foucault, M. (1989a) 'Foucault Responds to Sartre', in S. Lotringer (ed.) *Foucault Live: Interviews, 1966–84*, New York: Semiotext(e).

Foucault, M. (1989b) 'An Aesthetics of Existence', in S. Lotringer (ed.) *Foucault Live: Interviews, 1966–84*, New York: Semiotext(e).

Foucault, M. (1989c) 'The Concern for Truth', in S. Lotringer (ed.) *Foucault Live: Interviews, 1966–84*, New York: Semiotext(e).

Foucault, M. (1991a) *Discipline and Punish: The Birth of the Prison*, London: Penguin Books.

Foucault, M. (1991b) *'Remarks On Marx: Conversations with Duccio Trombadori'*, New York: Semiotext(e).

Foucault, M. (1991c) 'Governmentality', in G. Burchell, C. Gordon and P. Miller (eds) *The Foucault Effect: Studies in Governmentality with Two Lectures by and an Interview with Michel Foucault*, London: Harvester.

Foucault, M. (1994) 'Structuralism and Poststructuralism', in J.D. Faubion (ed.) *Michel Foucault Aesthetics: Essential Works of Foucault 1954–1984, Volume 2*, New York: Penguin Books.

Foucault, M. (1997a) 'Michel Foucault: An Interview by Stephen Riggins', in P. Rabinow (ed.) *Michel Foucault: Ethics, Subjectivity and Truth, Volume One*, London: Penguin Books.

Foucault, M. (1997b) 'Sexual Choice, Sexual Act', in P. Rabinow (ed.) *Michel Foucault: Ethics, Subjectivity and Truth, Volume One*, London: Penguin Books.

Foucault, M. (1997c) 'The Social Triumph of the Sexual Will', in P. Rabinow (ed.) *Michel Foucault: Ethics, Subjectivity and Truth, Volume One*, London: Penguin Books.

Foucault, M. (1997d) 'Sex, Power, and the Politics of Identity', in P. Rabinow (ed.) *Michel Foucault: Ethics, Subjectivity and Truth, Volume One*, London: Penguin Books.

Foucault, M. (1997e) 'Preface to the *History of Sexuality, Volume Two*', in P. Rabinow (ed.) *Michel Foucault: Ethics, Subjectivity and Truth, Volume One*, London: Penguin Books.

Foucault, M. (1997f) 'Sexuality and Solitude', in P. Rabinow (ed.) *Michel Foucault: Ethics, Subjectivity and Truth, Volume One*, London: Penguin Books.

Foucault, M. (1997g) 'On the Genealogy of Ethics: An Overview of Work in Progress', in P. Rabinow (ed.) *Michel Foucault: Ethics, Subjectivity and Truth, Volume 1*, London: Penguin Books.

Foucault, M. (2000) 'Against Replacement Penalties', in J.D. Faubion (ed.) *Michel Foucault: Power: Essential Works of Foucault 1954–1984, Volume 3*, London: Penguin.

Fox, N. (1993) *Postmodernism, Sociology and Health*, Buckingham, England: Open University Press.

Fraser, N. (1996) 'Michel Foucault: A "Young Conservative"', in S. Hekman (ed.) *Feminist Interpretations of Michel Foucault*, University Park, PA: Pennsylvania State University Press.

Gallagher, S.P. and Kryzanowska, R. (1999) *The Pilates Method of Body Conditioning*, Philadelphia, PA: Bainbridgebooks.

Gard, M. and Meyen, R. (2000) 'Boys, Bodies, Pleasure and Pain: Interrogating Contact Sports in Schools', *Sport, Education and Society*, 5 (1): 19–34.

Giardina, M.D. and Metz, J.L. (2005) 'All-American Girls? Corporatizing National Identity and Cultural Citizenship with/in the USA', in M.L. Silk, D.L. Andrews and C.L. Cole (eds) *Sport and Corporate Nationalism*, New York: Berg.

Giroux, H.A. (1994) 'Doing Cultural Studies: Youth and the Challenge of Pedagogy', *Harvard Educational Review*, 64, 3: 278–309.

Giulianotti, R. (2005) *Sport: A Critical Sociology*, Cambridge: Polity Press.

Gordon, C. (1991) 'Government Rationality: An Introduction', in G. Burchell, C. Gordon and P. Miller (eds) *The Foucault Effect: Studies in Governmentality with Two Lectures by and an Interview with Michel Foucault*, London: Harvester

Gordon, C. (2000) 'Introduction', in J.D. Faubion (ed.) *Michel Foucault: Power: Essential Works of Foucault 1954–1984, Volume 3*, London: Allen Lane, Penguin.

Gramsci, A. (1971) *Selections From Prison Notebooks*, London: Lawrence & Wishart.

Gruneau, R.S. (1976) 'Class or Mass: Notes on the Democratisation of Canadian Amateur Sport', in R.S. Gruneau and J.G. Albinson (eds) *Canadian Sport: Sociological Perspectives*, Toronto: Addison-Wesley.

Gruneau, R. (1993) 'Modernization or Hegemony: Two Views on Sport and Social Development', in J. Harvey and H. Cantelon (eds) *Not Just A Game: Essays in Canadian Sport Sociology*, Ottawa: University of Ottawa Press.

Guthrie, S.R. and Castelnuovo, S. (2001) 'Disability Management Among Women with Physical Impairments: the Contribution of Physical Activity', *Sociology of Sport Journal*, 18: 5–10.

Guttman, A. (1978) *From Ritual to Record: the Nature of Modern Sports*, New York: Columbia University Press.

Haber, H.F. (1996) 'Foucault Pumped: Body Politics and the Muscled Women', in S.J. Hekman (ed.) *Feminist Interpretations of Michel Foucault*, University Park, PA: Penn State University Press.

Habermas, J. (1982) 'The Entwinement of Myth and Enlightenment: Re-Reading Dialectic of Enlightenment', *New German Critique*, 22.

Habermas, J. (1986) 'Taking Aim at the Heart of the Present', in D. Couzens Hoy (ed.) *Foucault: A Critical Reader*, Oxford: Basil Blackwell.

Hadot, P. (1992) 'Reflections On the Notion of "the Cultivation of the Self"', in T.J. Armstrong (ed.) *Michel Foucault, Philosopher: Essays Translated From French and German*, Harlow, England: Harvester Wheatsheaf.

Halas, J. and Hanson, L.L. (2001) 'Pathologizing Billy: Enabling and Constraining the Body of the Condemned', *Sociology of Sport Journal*, 18: 115–126.

Hall, M.A. (1982) 'Towards A Feminist Analysis of Gender Equality in Sport', in N. Theberge and P. Donnelly (eds) *Sport and the Sociological Imagination*, Fort Worth, TX: Texas Christian University Press.

Halperin, D. (1995) *Saint Foucault: Towards A Gay Hagiography*, New York: Oxford University Press.

Hamilton, P. (2002) 'Editor's Foreword', in B Smart (ed.) *Michel Foucault: Revised Edition*, London: Routledge.

Haravon, L. (1995) 'Exercises in Empowerment: Toward a Feminist Aerobic Pedagogy', *Women in Sport and Physical Activity Journal*, 4: 23–44.

Marshall, J. (1997) 'Personal Autonomy as an Aim of Education: A Foucauldian Critique', in C. O'Farrell (ed.) *Foucault: the Legacy*, Brisbane: QUT Press.

Martin, P.Y. (1998) 'Why Can't a Man Be More Like a Woman? Reflections on Connell's Masculinities', *Gender and Society*, 12 (4): 472–472.

Messner, M.A. (1992) *Power at Play: Sports and the Problem of Masculinity*, Boston, MA: Beacon Press.

Messner, M.A. (2002) *Taking the Field: Women, Men and Sports*, Minneapolis, MN: University of Minnesota Press.

Messner, M.A. and Sabo, D.F. (eds) (1990) *Sport, Men, and the Gender Order: Critical Feminist Perspectives*, Champaign, IL: Human Kinetics.

Messner, M.A. and Sabo, D. (1994) *Sex, Violence and Power in Sports*, Freedom, CA: Crossing.

Miller, J. (1993) *The Passion of Michel Foucault*, New York: Anchor Books.

Miller, T. (1998) 'Scouting for Boys: Sport Looks at Men', in D. Rowe and G. Lawrence (eds) *Tourism, Leisure, Sport: Critical Perspectives*, Rydalmere, NSW: Hodder Education.

Mills, S. (2003) *Michel Foucault*, London: Routledge.

Monk, G., Winslade, J., Crockett, K. and Epston, D. (1997) *Narrative Therapy in Practice: The Archaeology of Hope*, San Francisco, CA: Jossey-Bass.

Monroe, M. (1994) 'Seeing Our Clients in a Whole New Way', *IDEA Today*, June–July: 35–42.

Monroe, M. (1998) 'Mind–Body Fitness Goes Mainstream', *IDEA Health and Fitness Source*, June–July: 34–44.

Morford, W.R. and McIntosh, M.J. (1993) 'Sport and Victorian Gentleman', in A. Ingham and J. Loy (eds) *Sport in Social Development: Traditions, Transitions and Transformations*, Champaign, IL: Human Kinetics.

Morris, M. (1988) 'The Pirate's Fiancée: Feminists and Philosophers, or Maybe Tonight It'll Happen', in I. Diamond and L. Quinby (eds) *Feminism and Foucault: Reflection on Resistance*, Boston, MA: Northeastern University Press.

Mrozek, D.J. (1989) 'Sport in American Life: From National Health to Personal Fulfilment, 1980–1940' in K. Grover (ed.) *Fitness in American Culture: Images of Health, Sport, and the Body, 1930–1940*, Amherst, MA and Rochester, NY: University of Massachusetts Press and Margaret Woodbury Strong Museum.

Nauright, J.R. and Chandler, T.J.L. (eds) (1996) *Making Men: Rugby and Masculine Identity*, London: Frank Cass & Co.

Nelson, M.B. (1994) *The Stronger Women Get, the More Men Love Football: Sexism and the American Culture of Sports*, New York: Harcourt Brace & Company.

Newton, T. (1998) 'Theorizing Subjectivity in Organizations: The Failure of Foucauldian Studies?' *Organization Studies*, 19 (3), 415–447.

Nietzsche, F. (1990) *The Birth of Tragedy and the Genealogy of Morals*, New York: Doubleday.

O'Leary, T. (2002) *Foucault and the Art of Ethics*, London: Continuum.

Olssen, M. (1999) *Michel Foucault: Materialism and Education*, Westport, CT: Bergin & Garvey.

Paffenberger, R.S., Hyde, R.T., Wing, A.L., Lee, I-M. and Kambert, J.B. (1994) 'An Active and Fit Way-of-Life Influencing Health and Longevity', in H.A. Quinney, L. Gauvin and A.E.T. Wall (eds) *Toward Active Living*, Champaign, IL: Human Kinetics.

Haravon Collins, L. (2002) 'Working Out Contradictions: Feminism and Aerobics', *Journal of Sport and Social Issues*, 26: 85–109.

Hardman, A.E. and Stensel, D.J. (2003) *Physical Activity and Health: the Evidence Explained*, London: Routledge.

Hargreaves, J. (ed.) (1982) *Sport, Culture and Ideology*, London: Routledge & Kegan Paul.

Hargreaves, J. (1986) *Sport, Power and Culture: A Social and Historical Analysis of Popular Sports in Britain*, Cambridge: Polity Press.

Hart, M.M. (1981) 'On Being Female in Sport', in M. Hart and S. Birrell (eds) *Sport in the Sociocultural Process*, Dubuque, IA: Wm. C. Brown Company.

Hartsock, N.C.M. (1996) 'Postmodernism and Political Change: Issues for Feminist Theory', in S. Hekman (ed.) *Feminist Interpretations of Michel Foucault*, University Park, PA: Pennsylvania State University Press.

Harvey, J. and Sparks, R. (1991) 'The Politics of the Body in the Context of Modernity' *Quest*, 43: 164–189.

Haskell, W.L. (1994) 'Physical/Physiological/Biological Outcomes of Physical Activity', in H.A. Quinney, L. Gauvin and A.E.T. Wall (eds) *Toward Active Living*, Champaign, IL: Human Kinetics.

Health and Fitness (2005) July.

Health and Fitness (2005) October.

Heikkala, J. (1993) 'Discipline and Excel: Techniques of the Self and Body and the Logic of Competing', *Sociology of Sport Journal*, 10: 397–412.

Hekman, S.L. (1996) Editor's Introduction, in S. Hekman (ed.) *Feminist Interpretations of Michel Foucault*, University Park, PA: Pennsylvania State University Press.

Heyward, V.H. (2002) *Advanced Fitness Assessment and Exercise Prescription*, (4th edn), Champaign: IL: Human Kinetics.

Hickey, C., Fitzclarence, L. and Matthews R. (eds) (1998) *Where the Boys Are: Masculinity, Sport and Education*, Geelong: Deakin Centre for Education and Change.

Hollingshead, S. (2002) 'Yoga for Sports Performance', *IDEA Health and Fitness Source*, April: 35–42.

Holstein, J.A. and Gubrium, J.F. (1995) 'The Active Interview', *Qualitative Research Methods Series*, Vol. 37, Thousand Oaks, CA: Sage.

Holt, R. (1989) *Sport and the British: A Modern History*, Oxford: Clarendon Press.

Howe, P.D. (2003), 'Kicking Stereotypes into Touch: An Ethnographic Account of Women's Rugby', in A. Bolin and J. Granskog (eds) *Athletic Intruders: Ethnographic Research On Women, Culture, and Exercise*, Albany, NY: New York State University Press.

Howley, E. and Franks, B.D. (2003) *Health Fitness Instructor's Handbook*, Champaign, IL: Human Kinetics.

Humberstone, B. (2002) 'Femininity, Masculinity and Difference: What's Wrong with A Sarong?', in A. Laker (ed.) *The Sociology of Sport and Physical Education*, London: Routledge.

Hunt, J. (1995) 'Divers' Accounts of Normal Risk', *Symbolic Interaction*, 18 (4): 439–462.

Johns, D.P. and Johns, J.S. (2000) 'Surveillance, Subjectivism and Technologies of Power: An Analysis of the Discursive Practice of High-Performance Sport', *International Review for the Sociology of Sport*, 35: 219–234.

Kanapol, B. (1998) 'Confession as Strength: A Necessary Condition for Critical Pedagogy, *Educational Foundations*, 12, 2: 63–76.

Kenyon, G.C. (1968) 'Sociological Considerations' *Journal of Health, Physical Education and Recreation*, 39: 31–33.

King, S.J. (2003) 'Doing Good by Running Well'. in J.Z. Bratich, J. Packer and C. McCarthy (eds) *Foucault, Cultural Studies, Governmentality*, New York: Simon & Schuster.

Kirk, D. (1998) *Schooling Bodies: School Practice and Public Discourse 1880–1950*, London: Leicester University Press.

Kirk, D. (2004a) 'Towards a Critical History of the Body, Identity and Health: Corporeal Power and School Practice', in J. Evans, B. Davies and J. Wright (eds) *Body Knowledge and Control: Studies in the Sociology of Physical Education and Health*, London: Routledge.

Kirk, D. (2004b) 'New Practices, New Subjects and Critical Inquiry: Possibility and Progress', in J. Wright., D. Macdonald and L. Burrows (eds) *Critical Inquiry and Problem Solving in Physical Education*, London: Routledge.

Klein, A.M. (1993) *Little Big Men: Bodybuilding Subculture and Gender Construction*, Albany, NY: State University of New York Press.

Kvale, S. (1996) *Interviews: An Introduction to Qualitative Research Interviewing*, Thousand Oaks, CA: Sage.

La Forge, R. (1994) 'The Science of Mind–Body Fitness', *IDEA Today*, June–July: 57–65.

La Forge, R. (1998) 'Research Case for Mindful Exercise Grows', *IDEA Health and Fitness Source*, July–August: 40.

Laidlaw, C. (1999) 'Sport and National Identity: Race Relations, Business, Professionalism', in B. Patterson (ed.) *Sport Society and Culture in New Zealand*, Palmerston North, NZ: Dunmore Press.

Lenskyj, H.J. (1986) *Out of Bounds: Women, Sport and Sexuality*, Toronto: Women's Press.

Lenskyj, H.J. (1994) 'Sexuality and Femininity in Sport Contexts: Issues and Alternatives', *Journal of Sport and Social Issues*, 18: 356–376.

Light, R. and Kirk, D. (2000) 'High School Rugby, the Body and the Reproduction of Hegemonic Masculinity', *Sport, Education and Society*, 5 (2): 163–176.

Lloyd, M. (1996) 'A Feminist Mapping of Foucauldian Politics', in S. Hekman (ed.) *Feminist Interpretations of Michel Foucault*, University Park, PA: Pennsylvania State University Press.

Loland Waaler, N. (2000) 'The Art of Concealment in a Culture of Display: Aerobicizing Women's and Men's Experience and Use of their Own Bodies', *Sociology of Sport Journal*, 17: 111–129.

Loy, J. (1968) 'The Nature of Sport: A Definitional Effort' *Quest*, Monograph X: 1–15.

Loy, J. (1995) 'The Dark Side of Agon: Fratriarchies, Performative Masculinities, Sport Involvement, and the Phenomenon of Gang Rape', in K. Bette and A. Rutten (eds) *International Sociology of Sport: Contemporary Issues*, Stuttgart: Verlag SN.

Loy, J. and McElvogue, J.F. (1970)'Racial Segregation in American Sport', *International Review of Sport Sociology*, 5: 5–23.

Loy, J., Andrews, D. and Rinehart, R. (1993) 'The Body in Culture and Sport', *Sport Science Review*, 2 (1): 69–91.

Lupton, D. (2003) *Medicine As Culture* (2nd edn), London: Sage.

Lynch, R. (1993) 'The Cultural Repositioning of Rugby League and ANZALS Leisure Research Series*, 1: 105–119.

MacDonald, D. (2002) 'Critical Pedagogy: What It Might Look Like and W It Matter?', in A. Laker (ed.) *The Sociology of Sport and Physical Ed. London: Routledge.

Macey, D. (1994) *The Lives of Michel Foucault*, London: Vintage.

McDermott, L. (2000) 'A Qualitative Assessment of the Significance of Perception to Women's Physical Activity Experiences: Revising Discussio Physicalities', *Sociology of Sport Journal*, 17: 331–363.

McGregor, J. (1994) 'Media Sport', in L. Trenberth and C. Collins (eds) *Sp Management in New Zealand: An Introduction*, Palmerston North, NZ: Du more Press.

McHoul, A. (1997) 'Condensing Foucault', in C. O'Farrell (ed.) *Foucault: Th Legacy*, Brisbane, Australia: QUT Publications.

McIntosh, P.C. (1963) *Sports in Society*, London: C.A. Watts.

McKay, J. (1997) *Managing Gender: Affirmative Action and Organizational Power in Australia, Canadian, and New Zealand Sport*, Albany: State University of New York Press.

McKay, J., Messner, M. and Sabo, D. (2000) 'Studying Sport, Men, and Masculinities from Feminist Standpoints', in J. Mckay, M. Messner and D. Sabo (eds) *Masculinities, Gender Relations, and Sport*, Thousand Oaks, CA: Sage.

McNay, L. (1994) *Foucault: A Critical Introduction*, Cambridge: Polity Press.

McRobbie, A. (1997) 'The Es and the Anti-Es: New Questions for Feminism and Cultural Studies', in M. Ferguson and P. Golding (eds) *Cultural Studies in Questions*, London: Sage.

Maguire, J. and Mansfield, L. (1998) '"No Body's Perfect": Women, Aerobics, and the Body Beautiful', *Sociology of Sport Journal*, 15: 109–137.

Malson, H. (1998) *The Thin Woman: Feminism, Post-Structuralism and the Social Psychology of Anorexia Nervosa*, London: Routledge.

Markula, P. (1993) *Total-Body-Tone-Up: Paradox and Women's Realities in Aerobics*, Ph.D. Dissertation, University of Illinois at Urbana-Champaign.

Markula, P. (1995) 'Firm But Shapely, Fit But Sexy, Strong But Thin: the Postmodern Aerobicizing Female Bodies', *Sociology of Sport Journal*, 12: 424–453.

Markula, P. (2000) '"Gotta Do the Marathon": Women's Running as a Truth-Game', *Aethlon*, xviii, 1: 89–106.

Markula, P. (2001) 'Beyond the Perfect Body: Women's Body Image Distortion in Fitness Magazine Discourse', *Journal of Sport and Social Issues*, 25: 158–179.

Markula, P. (2003a) 'Postmodern Aerobics: Contradiction and Resistance', in A. Bolin and J. Granskog (eds) *Athletic Intruders: Ethnographic Research on Women, Culture, and Exercise*, Albany, NY: State University of New York Press.

Markula, P. (2003b) 'The Technologies of the Self: Sport, Feminism, and Foucault', *Sociology of Sport Journal*, 20: 87–107.

Markula, P. (2004) '"Tuning into One's Self": Foucault's Technologies of the Self and Mindful Fitness', *Sociology of Sport Journal*, 21: 302–321.

Marshall, J. (1996) *Michel Foucault: Personal Autonomy and Education*, Dordrecht: Kluwer.

Patton, M. (1990) *Qualitative Evaluation and Research Methods* (2nd edn), Newbury Park, CA: Sage.

Peters, M. (1996) 'Habermas, Poststructuralism and the Question of Postmodernity', in M. Peters, W. Hope, J. Marshall and S. Webster (eds) *Critical Theory, Poststructuralism and the Social Context*, Palmerston North, NZ: Dunmore Press.

Peterson, A. and Bunton, R. (eds) (1997) *Foucault, Health and Medicine*, London: Routledge.

Peterson, A. and Waddell, C. (eds) (1988) *Health Matters: A Sociology of Illness, Prevention and Care*, St Leonards, NSW: Allen & Unwin.

Polkinghorne, D.E. (1988) *Narrative Knowing and the Human Sciences*, New York: State University of New York Press.

Pollock, M.L., Feigenbaum, M.S. and Brechue, W.F. (1995) 'Exercise Prescription for Physical Fitness', *Quest*, 47: 320–337.

Pringle, R. (2001) 'Competing Discourses: Narratives of a Fragmented Self, Manliness and Rugby Union', *International Review for the Sociology of Sport*, 36 (4): 425–439.

Pringle, R. (2002) 'Living the Contradictions: A Foucauldian Examination of my Youthful Rugby Experiences', in H. Worth, A. Paris, and L. Allen (eds) *Life of Brian: Masculinities, Sexualities and Health in New Zealand*, Dunedin, NZ: University of Otago Press.

Pringle, R. (2003) 'Doing the Damage? An Examination of Masculinities and Men's Rugby Experiences of Pain, Fear and Pleasure', Unpublished Doctoral Dissertation, University of Waikato, Hamilton, New Zealand.

Pringle, R. (2005) 'Masculinities, Sport, and Power: A Critical Comparison of Gramscian and Foucauldian Inspired Theoretical Tools', *Journal of Sport and Social Issues*, 29 (3): 256–278.

Pringle, R. and Markula, P. (2005) 'No Pain Is Sane After All: A Foucauldian Analysis of Masculinities and Men's Rugby Experiences', *Sociology of Sport Journal*, 22 (4): 472–497.

Probyn, E. (1993) *Sexing the Self: Gendered Positions in Cultural Studies*, London: Routledge.

Pronger, B. (1995) 'Rendering the Body: The Implicit Lessons of Gross Anatomy', *Quest*, 47 (4): 427–446.

Rabinow, P. (1984) 'Introduction', in P. Rabinow (ed.) *The Foucault Reader*, New York: Pantheon Books.

Rabinow, P. (1997) 'Introduction', in P. Rabinow (ed.) *Michel Foucault: Ethics, Subjectivity and Truth, Volume One*, London: Penguin Books.

Rail, G. (1998) 'Introduction', in G. Rail (ed.) *Sport and Postmodern Times*, Albany, NY: State University of New York Press.

Rail, G. and Harvey, J. (1995) 'Body at Work: Michel Foucault and the Sociology of Sport', *Sociology of Sport Journal*, 12: 164–179.

Richards, T. (1999) 'New Zealanders' Attitudes to Sport as Illustrated by Debate over Rugby Contacts with South Africa', in B. Patterson (ed.) *Sport, Society and Culture in New Zealand*, Palmerston North, NZ: Dunmore Press.

Richardson, L. (1997) *Fields of Play: Constructing an Academic Life*, New Brunswick, NJ: Rutgers Press.

Rinehart, R. (1998) 'Born-Again Sport: Ethics in Biographical Research', in G.

Rail (ed.) *Sport and Postmodern Times*, Albany, NY: State University of New York Press.

Rochlitz, R. (1992) 'The Aesthetics of Existence: Post-Conventional Morality and the Theory of Power in Michel Foucault', in T.J. Armstrong (ed.) *Michel Foucault, Philosopher: Essays Translated From French and German*, Harlow, England: Harvester Wheatsheaf.

Roderick, M., Waddington, I. and Parker, G. (2000) 'Playing Hurt: Managing Injuries in English Professional Football', *International Review for the Sociology of Sport*, 35 (2): 165–180.

Roussel, P. and Griffett, J. (2000) 'The Path Chosen By Female Bodybuilders: A Tentative Interpretation', *Sociology of Sport Journal*, 17: 130–150.

Rowe, D. (1995) 'Big Defence: Sport and Hegemonic Masculinity', in A. Tomlinson (ed.) *Gender, Sport and Leisure: Continuities and Challenges*, University of Brighton: Chelsea School Research Centre.

Rowe, D. and McKay, J. (1998) 'Sport: Still A Man's Game', *Journal of Interdisciplinary Gender Studies*, 3 (2): 113–128.

Ryan, P. (2004) 'IDEA Fitness Trends Report', *IDEA Fitness Journal*, July–August: 122–127.

Ryan, P. (2005) 'Programs and Equipment that are Leading the Industry', *IDEA Fitness Journal*, July–August: 91–93.

Sabo, D. (1986) 'Pigskin, Patriarchy and Pain', *Changing Men: Issues in Gender, Sex and Politics*, 16 (Summer): 24–25.

Sabo, D. (1998) 'Masculinities and Men's Health: Moving Toward Post-Superman Era Prevention', in M. Kimmel and M. Messner (eds) *Men's Lives* (4th edn), Needham Heights, MA: Allyn & Bacon.

Sabo D. and Gordon, D. (eds) (1995) *Men's Health and Illness: Gender, Power, and the Body*, Newbury Park, CA: Sage.

Sabo, D.F. and Panepinto, J. (1990) 'Football Ritual and the Social Reproduction of Masculinity', in M.A. Messner and D.F. Sabo (eds) *Sport, Men, and the Gender Order: Critical Feminist Perspectives*, Champaign, IL: Human Kinetics.

Sabo, D. and Runfola, R. (eds) (1980) *Jock: Sports and Male Identity*, Englewood Cliffs, NJ: Prentice-Hall.

Sabo, D., Gray, P.M. and Moore, L. (2000) 'Domestic Violence and Televised Athletic Events', in J. Mckay, M. Messner and D. Sabo (eds) *Masculinities, Gender Relations, and Sport*, Thousand Oaks, CA: Sage.

Said, E. (1991) 'Michel Foucault, 1926–1984', in J. Arac (ed.) *After Foucault: Humanist Knowledge, Postmodern Challenges*, New Brunswick, NJ: Rutgers University Press.

Said, E. (1994) *Orientalism*, New York: Vintage Books.

Sapora, A.V. and Mitchell, E.D. (1961) *The Theory of Play and Recreation*, New York: Ronald.

Sawicki, J. (1991) *Disciplining Foucault: Feminism, Power, and the Body*, New York: Routledge.

Schacht, S.P. (1996) 'Misogyny on and off the "Pitch": The Gendered World of Male Rugby Players', *Gender and Society*, 10 (5): 550–565.

Scheurich, J.J. and McKenzie, K.B. (2005) 'Foucault's Methodologies: Archaeology and Genealogy', in N.K. Denzin and Y.S. Lincoln (eds) *The Sage Handbook of Qualitative Research* (3rd edn), Thousand Oaks, CA: Sage.

Sharkey, B.J. (2002) *Fitness and Health* (5th edn), Champaign, IL: Human Kinetics.

Sheard, K. and Dunning, E. (1973) 'The Rugby Football Club as a Type of Male Preserve: Some Sociological Notes', *International Review of Sport Sociology*, 5 (3): 5–24.

Shephard, R.J. (1995) 'Physical Activity, Fitness, and Health: the Current Consensus', *Quest*, 47: 288–303.

Sheridan, A. (1980) *Michel Foucault: The Will to Truth*, London: Tavistock.

Shogan, D. (1999) *The Making of High Performance Athletes: Discipline, Diversity, and Ethics*, Toronto: University of Toronto Press.

Shogan, D. and Ford, M. (2000) 'A New Sport Ethics: Taking König Seriously' *International Review for the Sociology of Sport*, 35: 49–58.

Simons, J. (1995) *Foucault and the Political*, London: Routledge.

Smart, B. (1986) 'The Politics of Truth and the Problem of Hegemony' in D.C. Hoy (ed.) *Foucault: A Critical Reader*, Oxford: Basil Blackwell.

Smart, B. (2002) *Michel Foucault: Revised Edition*, London: Routledge.

Smith, D. (1999) 'The Civilising Process and the History of Sexuality: Comparing Norbert Elias and Michel Foucault', *Theory and Society*, 28: 79–100.

Smith Maguire, J. (2002) 'Michel Foucault: Sport, Power, Technologies and Governmentality', in J. Maguire and K. Young (eds) *Theory, Sport and Society*, London: Elsevier.

SPARC (2005) 'Push Play Fact Summary', available online at <http://www.ausport.gov.au/fulltext/1999/nz/summary.pdf> (accessed 16 September 2004).

Spargo, T. (1999) '*Foucault and Queer Theory*', Cambridge: Icon Books.

Sparkes, A. and Smith, B. (1999) 'Disrupted Selves and Narrative Reconstructions', in A. Sparkes and M. Silvennoinen (eds) *Talking Bodies: Men's Narratives of the Body and Sport*, Jyvaskyla: Sophi.

Speer, S.A. (2001) 'Reconsidering the Concept of Hegemonic Masculinity: Discursive Psychology, Conversational Analysis and Participants' Orientations', *Feminism and Psychology*, 11 (1): 107–135.

Spitzack, C. (1990) *Confession Excess: Women and the Politics of Body Reduction*, Albany, NY: State University of New York Press.

Spitzack, D. (1993) 'The Spectacle of Anorexia Nervosa', *Text and Performance Quarterly*, 12: 1–20.

Star, L. (1999a) 'New Masculinities Theory: Poststructuralism and Beyond', in R. Law, H. Campbell and J. Dolan (eds) *Masculinities in Aotearoa/New Zealand*, Palmerston North: Dunmore Press.

Star, L. (1999b) '"Blacks Are Back": Ethnicity, Male Bodies, Exhibitionary Order', in R. Law, H. Campbell and J. Dolan (eds) *Masculinities in Aotearoa/New Zealand*, Palmerston North, NZ: Dunmore Press.

Stokes, P. (2004) *Philosophy: 100 Essential Thinkers*, Leicester: Arcturus.

Stone, G.P. (1955) 'American Sports: Play and Display, *Chicago Review*, IX: 83–100.

Stothart, B. (1994) 'The Physical Culture Connection', *Journal of Physical Education New Zealand*, 27 (4): 24–27.

Strauss, S (2005) *Positioning Yoga: Balancing Acts Across Cultures*, New York: Berg.

Taylor, C. (1986) 'Foucault on Freedom and Truth', in D.C. Hoy (ed.) *Foucault: A Critical Reader*, Oxford: Basil Blackwell.

Theberge, N. (1991) 'Reflections on the Body in the Sociology of Sport', *Quest*, 43: 148–167.

Thompson, S. (1988) 'Challenging the Hegemony: New Zealand's Women's Opposition to Rugby and the Reproduction of Capitalist Patriarchy', *International Review for the Sociology of Sport*, 23 (2): 205–223.

Tomlinson, A. (1998) 'Power: Domination, Negotiation, and Resistance in Sports Cultures', *Journal of Sport and Social Issues*, 22 (3): 235–240.

Trahan, J. (2005) 'Pilates Plus', *Health and Fitness*, October: 84–88.

Trujillo, N. (1995) 'Machines, Missiles, and Men: Images of the Male Body on ABC's Monday Night Football', *Sociology of Sport Journal*, 12: 403–423.

Turner, B.S. (1995) *Medical Power and Social Knowledge*, (2nd edn), London: Sage.

US Department of Health and Human Services (2002) 'Physical Activity Fundamental to Preventing Disease', available online at <http//aspe.hhs.gov/health/resports/physicalactivity> (accessed 20 June 2002).

Wesely, J.K. (2001) 'Negotiating Gender: Bodybuilding and the Natural/Unnatural Continuum', *Sociology of Sport Journal*, 18: 162–180.

Wetherell, M. and Edley, N. (1999) 'Negotiating Hegemonic Masculinity: Imaginary Positions and Psycho-Discursive Practices', *Feminism and Psychology*, 9 (3): 335–356.

White, P.G. and Gillett, J. (1994) 'Reading the Muscular Body: A Critical Decoding of Advertisements in *Flex* Magazine', *Sociology of Sport Journal*, 11: 18–39.

Whitson, D. (1989) 'Discourses of Critique in Sport Sociology: A Response to Deem and Sparks', *Sociology of Sport Journal*, 6: 60–65.

Whitson, D. (1990) 'Sport in the Social Construction of Masculinity', in M.A. Messner and D.F. Sabo (eds) *Sport, Men, and the Gender Order: Critical Feminist Perspectives*, Champaign, IL: Human Kinetics.

Whitson, D. and MacIntosh, D. (1990) 'The Scientization of Physical Education: Discourses of Performance', *Quest*, 42 (1): 40–51.

Willis, P. (1982) 'Women in Sport and Ideology', in J. Hargreaves (ed.) *Sport, Culture and Ideology*, London: Routledge & Kegan Paul.

Wright, J. (2004) 'Post-Structural Methodologies: the Body, Schooling and Health', in J. Wright., D. Macdonald and L. Burrows (eds) *Critical Inquiry and Problem Solving in Physical Education*, London: Routledge.

Young, K. and White, P. (1995) 'Sport, Physical Danger, and Injury: the Experiences of Elite Women Athletes', *Journal of Sport and Social Issues*, 19 (1): 45–61.

Young, K., White, P. and McTeer, W. (1994) 'Body Talk: Male Athletes Reflect on Sport, injury, and Pain', *Sociology of Sport Journal*, 11: 175–194.

Index